In honour of Catholic University Chaplaincies working in the Archdiocese of Sydney

Then the one who had received the five talents came forward, bringing five more talents, saying, "Master, you handed over to me five talents; see, I have made five more talents."
His master said to him, "Well done, good and trustworthy servant; you have been trustworthy in a few things, I will put you in charge of many things; enter into the joy of your master."
(Mt 25:20-21)

Contents

Foreword: *James Franklin* — 1
Preface: *Robert M. Haddad* — 3

1. Growing Up Catholic - *David Collits* — 5
2. Which Catholicism? - *Zachary Vermeer* — 17
3. Christ and the Mass - *Robert M. Haddad* — 27
4. The Bible and the Church - *Daniel Miller* — 51
5. The Way of Salvation - *Thomas Waugh* — 69
6. It's Just Grace - *Glenn Bolas* — 97
7. Mary - *Kiran Newman* — 127
8. It Is Finished - *Thomas Kwok* — 169

Postscript: *Robert M. Haddad* — 183
Appendix: The New Catholicism - *David Schutz* — 187
Further Reading — 197

Answering the Anti-Catholic Challenge

A response to Ray Galea's
"Nothing in my hand I bring"

Edited by Robert M. Haddad
Foreword by James Franklin

Modotti Press
AN IMPRINT OF CONNOR COURT PUBLISHING

Published in 2012 Modotti Press (An imprint of Connor Court Publishing Pty Ltd)

Copyright as a collection © Robert M. Haddad 2012.
Copyright of the individual chapters remains with the authors.

All rights reserved. No part of this book may be reproduced or transmitted in any form or by any means, electronic or mechanical, including photocopying, recording or by any information storage and retrieval system, without prior permission in writing from the publisher.

Modotti Press
Connor Court Publishing Pty Ltd, PO Box 7257, Redland Bay QLD 4165
sales@connorcourt.com
www.connorcourt.com

ISBN: 9781921421563 (pbk.)

Nihil Obstat: Fr John Flader DCL

Imprimatur: + Cardinal George Pell
        Archbishop of Sydney

Date: 16 July, 2010

The *Nihil Obstat* and *Imprimatur* are a declaration that a book or pamphlet is considered to be free from doctrinal or moral error. It is not necessarily implied that those who have granted them agree with the contents, opinions or statements expressed.

Front cover design: Ian James

Foreword

In 2002, the Anglican Archbishop of Sydney, Peter Jensen set a target of 10 per cent of Sydneysiders to become "Bible-believing" Christians within ten years.

"By Bible-believing", the Archbishop said, "I mean the Bible taking precedence over Church tradition, human reason and Christian experience."[1] For the Catholic, the fundamental flaw in the Evangelical version of Christianity is its expectation that there will be conflict between the Bible and Christian tradition, reason and experience. That is a profoundly unbiblical attitude. The Bible does not advocate bibliolatry, but records the story of a Church and its reflection on its own beginnings. Jesus, according to the Bible itself, does not advocate commitment to texts, but instead promises to be with his community of disciples "to the end of the age" (Matt. 28:20).

There is always a temptation, especially to young minds with an urge to purity, to translate shock at the failings of institutions and people into a return to an alleged doctrinal purity. Young Catholics unsure of their faith can find attractive the appeal of an apparent return to the unadorned scriptures. So there is a recurring need to explain in straightforward terms the Catholic story of the continuity of Catholic faith with scriptural tradition. The work in your hands lays out that story with clarity and force. It deserves attentive reading by all who deal with the challenge of Evangelicalism.

- **Professor James Franklin**[2] **(UNSW)**
February 2010

---

1 *The Sydney Morning Herald,* 14 October, 2002.
2 James Franklin is the author of *Corrupting the Youth: A History of Philosophy in Australia, Catholic Values and Australian Realities* (Connor Court) and *Life to the Full* (Connor Court).

Preface

World Youth Day 2008 was an exciting time for Catholics in Australia, particularly Sydney. It was an opportunity to re-vitalise the faith of many young Catholics and to introduce the Gospel of Jesus Christ to many others who had not previously been bothered to give it any serious consideration. It proved to be a life-changing event for many.

However, not everyone was excited by the imminent visit of Pope Benedict XVI. Some, although not all, of the secular humanist persuasion were not convinced that Australia would benefit from the Papal presence. Some of our Protestant brothers and sisters, particularly those of the Evangelical tradition, were uncertain as to whether the event could properly be termed "Christian" and seized upon the opportunity to introduce young Catholics to "Biblical Christianity", or rather, Christianity as understood within the Calvinist Tradition. Additionally, websites, CDs, talks, book/lets were employed to warn all and sundry about the 'errors' of "Roman" Catholics. One such book was *Nothing in my hand I bring* by Ray Galea.

Ray Galea is a former-Catholic who is currently a senior minister at St Albans Multicultural Bible Ministry at Rooty Hill in western Sydney. Galea was requested to write the book for printing and distribution by Matthias Media in the lead up to World Youth Day. Galea responded with a 114-page book with the stated aim of "Understanding the differences between Roman Catholic and Protestant beliefs."

Answering the Anti-Catholic Challenge (*AACC*) is that response. Each chapter responds to a specific chapter in Galea's book and provides well-grounded and point-by-point rejoinders to the charges made by him against Catholicism. I believe that *AACC* is fair-minded, rigorous and accurate in its dealing with the issues in question. All the authors are young people. All either reverts or converts to Catholicism. All with a love for God, Jesus Christ and his Church. All who would give their hearts, minds and souls for Jesus Christ. Nothing more needs to be said.

- **Robert M. Haddad**
February 2012

1
Growing Up Catholic

David Collits[1]

Introduction

Ray Galea's *Nothing In My Hand I Bring* begins with a chapter entitled, *"Growing up Catholic."* In this chapter he provides a personal sketch of his early Maltese Catholic upbringing, his university days, his search for truth, and his eventual renunciation of the Catholicism in which he had been raised. Galea also relates his experiences with particular Catholics and how they practised their faith, experiences he implies contributed to his eventual move away from the Catholic Church. While not seeking to question the veracity of Galea's personal experiences, it is my purpose to highlight certain claims made by him concerning Catholicism *per se* and to bring some balance thereto.

Growing up Catholic

Galea was born and raised in what he describes as a "devout Maltese Australian Roman Catholic home" (p. 11). His early memories of Catholicism are "mostly positive", noting that his family attended Mass three times a week and prayed the Rosary together every night (even while his dad slept on his lounge chair). He expresses appreciation for the discipline of regular Mass attendance, the "God-talk" of his faithful mother (p. 12), a sincere parish priest, and nuns who were mostly kind. In his own words, "It was truly a loving Catholic home and a caring Catholic community" (p. 15). There is even praise for the *Gloria*, a prayer said or sung in Catholic liturgy throughout most of the year, as a prayer that "doesn't get any better than that!" (p. 14).

---

1 David Collits is a lawyer working in Sydney and is currently undertaking a research Masters. In his thesis he will be exploring Pope Benedict's thought on law.

However, these experiences were insufficient to maintain Galea's Catholic faith in later life. Like many other teenage people then and now (and not just Catholics I might add), Galea wanted a relationship with God on his own terms, that is, a God who would agree everything he did (p. 16). This resulted in Galea becoming what some in the Catholic Church would call a "nominal Catholic", that is, a Catholic in name only. Galea then proceeds to tell us how, upon being challenged by a university friend named Anne, he began his search for truth, his decision to read the "primary documents" (the Bible) to examine the claims of Christ for himself, and his eventual decision to become a Christian and renounce Catholicism (pp. 16-20).

Catholics and Christ

In giving his account of his personal journey towards "the truth of the Lord Jesus", however, Galea makes a number of observations/comments about Catholics and Catholicism that are overly generalised and stereotypical. According to Galea, Catholics are "more about belonging than believing" (p. 15), are mostly "not at all devout" (p. 15) and are "suspicious of people who made too much of Jesus" (p. 16). He goes on to state that he himself was "much more comfortable with Mary" (p. 16), and had "no personal sense of Jesus' ... centrality for the Christian life" (p. 16).

Though Galea's descriptions of Catholics may genuinely reflect his own experiences, they do not accord with the experience of this writer or Catholic teaching. For example, Pope Benedict XVI in his *Jesus of Nazareth* makes this statement: "Intimate friendship with Jesus [is that] on which everything depends" (xii). The same Pope in his first encyclical stressed that all Catholic dogma, ideas and knowledge stem from the encounter with the person of Christ (*Deus Caritas Est*, n. 1). The current Archbishop of Philadelphia, Charles Chaput, states that "At its root, Christianity is an experience: a life-changing, *personal* experience of the risen Jesus Christ."[2] The *Catechism of the Catholic Church* (CCC) has an entire Part (Part III) entitled *"Life in Christ." Good* Catholics certainly do not believe a personal relationship with Christ to be unimportant, the profession of which causes

---

2 'New Life in Christ: What it Looks Like, What it Demands', First Things Blog (see http://www.firstthings.com/), 11 May 2009, emphasis added).

embarrassment. Furthermore, Galea himself would admit that there are likewise hoards of Protestants, especially Anglicans (over 95% according to the consistent findings of National Church Life Surveys from 1991-2006), who are only 'cultural Christians', who belong more than believe, who are certainly not devout, who never speak of friendship with Jesus in personal terms, or bow down to his complete authority.

Just one example of a central Catholic teaching and practice should be enough to dispel any doubts as to whether or not a personal relationship with Christ is important to good Catholics. The Catholic Church formally teaches that, in the Eucharist, Christ is truly present Body, Blood, Soul and Divinity (a belief, by the way, that is evident in the writings of the Church Fathers as early as St Ignatius of Antioch AD 107; cf. Chapter 3 of this book). It is difficult to conceive of a more intimate way of having a personal relationship with Christ than receiving him in the form of Holy Communion. As one eminent Catholic spiritual writer, Abbot Marmion, notes, the "Eucharist is specifically the sacrament of union [with Christ]"; when we receive Christ, "we unite ourselves to Life itself."[3] In this union with Christ, we are "sharers in his Body and Blood … [and] form a single body [the Church]" (CCC 1331). In the depths of a faithful Catholic's Eucharistic Communion with Christ there is a real, intimate union with him. He, with the Father, comes and rests with us, and abides with us (Jn 14:23). We are *his* home. He makes his home with us by giving us his Body and Blood. We are his friends and not his servants (cf. Jn 15:15).

Contrary to Galea's subjective experience, a personal relationship with Christ is meant to be at the very heart of Catholic life and practice. This relationship with Christ both recognises his exalted status (cf. Galea at p. 16) and is a deeply and personally felt friendship. Any Catholic who says he is not a friend of Christ and has no relationship with him is not living an authentic Catholic life. This is how I have found my own experience of Catholic life; likewise, my many Catholic friends. I love Jesus and speak with him everyday, and certainly when I receive him in Holy Communion.

Other Particular Issues

Ray Galea makes many more comments with respect to Catholics and

---

3 *Christ, The Life of the Soul*, Sands & Co., London and Edinburgh, 1925, p. 239.

Catholicism, too many to respond to in the limited space allotted to me. Nevertheless, there are some stand-out remarks that deserve a specific response.

i) The first relates to Galea's claim that since the Nicene Creed clarified the Trinity and the divinity of Christ 'I've since realised that I could have been a Catholic in the fourth century" (p. 14).

Like Galea, Catholics certainly do believe and argue that the Trinity is "revealed in the Bible." We also believe that the Nicene Creed "clarified" this teaching. Without realising it, however, you might think Galea in this passage is trying to have his cake and eat it. In his Chapter 4, *The Bible and the Church,* Galea argues rigorously that the Bible is both "sufficient" and "clear" and that we do not need interpretation "by the experts in Rome" (p. 58). If the Bible is as sufficient and clear as Galea claims then why was the Council of Nicea needed to clarify teaching on the Trinity in the first place? Why does Galea quote this Council with respect, a Council that claims to have authority outside of the Bible, a Council that was attended by 318 Bishops who all said the Mass and acknowledged the authority of the Bishop of Rome (Pope Sylvester) through his two representatives, Vitus and Vincent, priests of Rome?

I find even more surprising Galea's claim that he "could have been a Catholic in the fourth century." If that were so, then Galea would have had to reconcile his 16th century Anglican/Calvinist beliefs with the following:

On the Eucharist:

> St Ephrem of Edessa, Homilies 4, 4 (ante AD 373)
> *And extending His hand, He gave them the Bread which His right hand had made holy: 'Take all of you eat of this, which my word has made holy. Do not now regard as bread that which I have given you; but take, eat this Bread, and do not scatter the crumbs; for what I have called My Body, that it is indeed. One particle from its crumbs is able to sanctify thousands and thousands, and is sufficient to afford life to those who eat of it. Take, eat, entertaining no doubt of faith, because this is My Body, and whoever eats it in belief eats in it Fire and Spirit.*

On the Mass:

> St Ambrose of Milan, Commentaries on Twelve of David's Psalms 38, 25 (Inter AD 381-397)

We saw the Prince of Priests coming to us, we saw and heard Him offering His Blood for us. We follow, inasmuch as we are able, being priests; and we offer the sacrifice on behalf of the people. And even if we are of but little merit, still, in the sacrifice, we are honourable. For even if Christ is not now seen as the one who offers the sacrifice, nevertheless it is He Himself that is offered in sacrifice here on earth when the Body of Christ is offered. Indeed, to offer Himself He is made visible to us, He whose word makes holy the sacrifice that is offered.

On Purgatory:

St Gregory of Nyssa, Sermon on the Dead (AD 383)
After his departure out of the body, he gains knowledge of the difference between virtue and vice, and finds that he is not able to partake of divinity until he has been purged of the filthy contagion in his soul by the purifying fire.

On the Perpetual Virginity of Mary:

St Jerome, Against Helvidius 17 & 18 (c. AD 383)
I now ask to which class you consider the Lord's brethren in the Gospel must be assigned. They are brethren by nature, you say. But Scripture does not say so; it calls them neither sons of Mary, nor of Joseph. Shall we say they are brethren by race? ... The only alternative is to adopt the previous explanation and understand them to be called brethren in virtue of the bond of kindred, not of love and sympathy, nor by prerogative of race, nor yet by nature ... It is clear that our Lord's brethren bore the name in the same way that Joseph was called his father.

On Tradition:

St Augustine of Hippo, Letter to Januarius 54, 1, 1 (c. AD 400)
But in regard to those observances which we carefully attend and which the whole world keeps, and which derive not from Scripture but from Tradition, we are given to understand that they are recommended and ordained to be kept, either by the Apostles themselves or by plenary councils, the authority of which is quite vital in the Church.

The above are just a small sample of quotes concerning a limited number of subjects. As can be seen, this smattering of early Christian commentary teaches intrinsically *Catholic* truths; truths that were Catholic then as well as now. If Galea did live in the fourth century he would not have much doctrinal agreement with the most famous Fathers, Doctors and Saints of the early Church.

    ii) The second relates to Galea's fond memories of his Catholic upbringing, through which he received both a "foundation" and "deep convictions on a number of ethical matters, such as the protection of the unborn" (p. 14).

One's upbringing is always a personal matter and, apart from what Galea tells us in his book, we obviously do not know the manner and form of Galea's upbringing. As a general comment though, in sympathy for Galea, it seems that he did receive a fairly good Catholic upbringing in his tender years but we do not know whether he received a solid catechetical formation as he grew older. If not, sad to say, he was denied his baptismal right, a common problem in the Church today and one good Catholics struggle to repair. Nevertheless, Galea at least received "deep convictions on a number of ethical matters" as just quoted.

However, it should be pointed out to Galea that these "deep convictions" have their basis in authoritative Church interpretation rather than in simple clear Bible teaching. There are many "ethical matters" of concern today, including abortion, embryonic stem cell research, surrogacy, same-sex relationships, masturbation, just to name a few. Of these, only some are directly addressed in Scripture, leaving room for debate and disagreement among Christians of all denominations. Other issues are of little or no concern at all for certain Protestants, including artificial contraception, in-vitro fertilisation, divorce and re-marriage. This confusion is due wholly and solely to private interpretation of Scripture. On the other hand, Catholics have certainty on all these issues due to the clear and consistent teaching of the Magisterium (Popes and Bishops of the world united to him) built up over twenty centuries. This certainty goes both to the truth of teachings themselves and the fact that they will never change. On the other hand, the Anglican Church is notorious for breaking with almost two millennia of tradition when it sanctioned the use of artificial contraception at the Lambeth Conference in 1930. Not just Galea, but all Christians have a debt to the Catholic Church for its rock-solid ethical teachings.

    iii) The third relates to how Galea while still a Catholic felt drawn to examine "the claims of Christ" through a study of "the primary documents" and how this led him to spend six months "reading and talking to priests and ministers" to find out more about the differences between Catholics and Protestants and how their teachings compared "with the teaching of Jesus and the apostles" (pp. 17-19).

Galea's search for truth was undoubtedly a genuine one. However, did Galea receive a good grounding in Catholic apologetics and scriptural exegesis? Was he introduced to the Church Fathers or to the lives of the great Saints? There are many Catholics who have received all these blessings and they are wonderful Christians as a result. These Catholics usually do not study the claims of Christ for themselves as they take his claims as a given. Nevertheless, there is a rich treasure-house of Catholic writings in defence of the uniqueness of Christ spanning nearly two millennia that are easily accessible for those who wish to investigate.

Going to the Bible is a great place to start to learn about Christ but is each and every Bible really a "primary document"? Which Bible did Galea read? Presumably an English language one. That being the case, just how reliable was the translation he used? This is an important question. The Tyndale Bible, for example, had originally 2,000 mistranslations when it first appeared in the early 16th century.[4] As we will see in Chapter 4, private interpretation of the Bible is one of the most unreliable ways of reaching certain truth, as Calvin and Melanchton privately admitted to each other. Strictly speaking, the "primary sources" are the original manuscripts written by the Apostles and Evangelists. They no longer exist. The next best things are the 24,000 codices, manuscripts, and minuscules dating back between the early second and fourth centuries.

Spending the next six months "talking to priests and ministers to find out the differences between Catholics and Protestants" is a highly commendable exercise. Nonetheless, sadly not all Catholic priests are trained apologists and/or have all the answers. Simply because a particular priest or number of priests "do not have answers" does not mean that no answers are available. The Catholic Church has comprehensive and Biblically based answers for theological controversies of every type. One

---
4 The Right Rev. Henry G. Graham, *Where We Got the Bible: Our Debt to the Catholic Church*, TAN Books & Publishers, 1911, Ch. 8, para. iii.

of her major publications of the twentieth century, the *Catechism of the Catholic Church*, is a wonderful resource, replete with references to the Bible and great Christian thinkers. It provides the enquiring mind with rich answers to many questions. Furthermore, when Galea was searching for answers did the Protestant ministers he spoke to really represent Catholicism accurately, or did they engage in demolishing straw-men caricatures?

Did Galea ask the Protestant ministers he met to explain why there were so many differences in belief and practice between the various tens of thousands of different Protestant denominations, not to mention the irreconcilable differences within Anglicanism itself? What certainty does Galea have that Evangelicalism is the correct form of Protestantism? When the term "Protestant" is used, does one expect anyone to really believe that those who oppose Catholicism form one monolithic body united in faith and practice? Indeed, this fragmentary nature of Protestantism directly contradicts Christ's prayer that we Christians may be one (Jn 17:21, CCC #820). The Catholic Church, although a "broad church", is nevertheless, by definition, united with the Vicar of Christ, the successor to St Peter and is, as such, one. One may ask the question, *Which Catholicism?*; but more urgent questions for someone seeking truth and who is considering the claims of Protestantism should be *Which Protestantism?; Which Anglicanism?*

> iv) The fourth relates to Galea's 'discovery' "that every 'distinctive' teaching of Roman Catholicism seemed to undermine the person and work of the Lord Jesus" (p. 20).

One has to wonder whether Galea "discovered that every 'distinctive' teaching of Roman Catholicism seemed to undermine the person and work of the Lord Jesus" through his own private reading of Scripture or via the influence of Evangelical Anglican ministers who 'unpacked' Catholicism for him. Sure, as noted above he mentions that he spoke "to priests" (p. 19) but were they really well versed in the art of apologetics? Which, if any, Catholic books did Galea read during his six-month search for truth? Nowhere does Galea mention by name any Catholic apologetical works that explain Catholic teaching *vis à vis* Scripture. I have read Catholic works that present overwhelming Scriptural defences for Catholic beliefs.

These works are legion and increasing almost by the day. A simple Google search would put you in touch with the works of converts to Catholicism such as Scott Hahn, Dave Armstrong, Robert Sungenis, Stephen K. Ray, Tim Staples and James Akin, as well as local Australian authors such as Fr Peter Joseph and Robert Haddad. Robert Haddad is one example of someone who was heavily influenced by Baptists and Evangelicals at High School and University only to commit much of his life defending the Catholic Faith after reading old-time classics such as *Faith of Our Fathers* (Card. Gibbons) and *The Question Box* (Fr Conway).

This is not the place to provide a detailed defence of the 'distinctive' Catholic teachings that Galea in his search for truth found objectionable; that will be the task of those writing in response to his other chapters. Nevertheless, the following is a very brief outline showing that the most controversial Catholic teachings do have clear support in the Scriptures:

The necessity of faith and works co-operating for salvation:
if I have all faith, so as to remove mountains, but have not love, I am nothing (1 Cor. 13:2).

For in Christ Jesus neither circumcision nor uncircumcision is of any avail, but faith working through love (Gal. 5:6).

So faith by itself, if it has no works, is dead (Js 2:17).

Baptism as a sacrament that saves:
Baptism, which corresponds to this, now saves you ... (1 Pet. 3:21).

The universal jurisdiction of St Peter over the entire Church:
Simon, Simon, behold, Satan demanded to have you, that he might sift you like wheat, but I have prayed for you that your faith may not fail; and when you have turned again, strengthen your brethren (Lk 22:31-32).

'Simon, son of John, do you love me more than these?' He said to him, 'Yes, Lord; you know that I love you.' He said to him, 'Feed my lambs'" (Jn 21:15).

The authority of the Church:
if I am delayed, you may know how one ought to behave in the household of God, which is the church of the living God, the pillar and bulwark of the truth (1 Tim. 3:15).

Apostolic succession:
This is why I left you in Crete, that you might amend what was defective, and appoint elders in every town as I directed you ... (Tit. 1:5).

Mary as Mother of God:
And why has this happened to me, that the mother of my Lord comes to me? (Lk 1:43).

The Eucharist as the Body and Blood of Christ:
The cup of blessing which we bless, is it not a participation in the blood of Christ? The bread which we break, is it not a participation in the body of Christ? (1 Cor. 10:16).

Purgatory as a place of temporary punishment and cleansing:
If any man's work is burned up, he will suffer loss, though he himself will be saved, but only as through fire (1 Cor. 3:15).

The forgiveness of sins through the ministry of men:
And when he had said this, he breathed on them, and said to them, 'Receive the Holy Spirit. If you forgive the sins of any, they are forgiven; if you retain the sins of any, they are retained' (Jn 20:22-23).

Far from undermining the person and work of Jesus Christ, these texts (and many others not quoted) go to prove that Christ invites us collectively and individually to co-operate and work with him to achieve our own personal salvation and that of others. Without this co-operation salvation is not possible.

Conclusion

At the end of Chapter 1 Galea states:

> ... my prayer is that you will seek the truth about Jesus, and that when you find it—as God promises that you will if you honestly seek—you will grasp it and hold it tight. For as hard as the search can be, and as painful as the consequences may sometimes be, when you find the truth, as Jesus said, it sets you free (pp. 21-22).

My Catholic upbringing was not merely a cultural one; through my family and friends and works of the Church I know and live (though imperfectly) Catholicism in its fullness. Through my reading, prayer and liturgical life, and most deeply held intuitions about God and man, I know that the Catholic Faith is the fullness of Christianity and the Catholic Church the true Church of Christ founded on St Peter nearly 2,000 years ago. I have the truth about Jesus in the Catholic Church and intend to hold onto it tightly. This is not due to any merits of my own, but solely due to the grace and goodness of God.

As a Catholic, I rejoice in having God as my Father, Jesus as my Lord and Saviour, Mary as my spiritual mother, the angels and saints as my spiritual brothers and friends. I also have peace of mind through a divine teaching authority that gives certainty with respect to the meaning of Scripture and authoritative teaching concerning new developments and controversies. I thank God for giving me an intellect and will to co-operate with his grace and the seven sacraments as fountains from which the infinite merits of Christ's Cross flow. The list goes on and on ... the writings of the Church Fathers, the profound teachings of the Doctors, the heroic examples of the great Saints who more perfectly imitated Christ. In the midst of all these— the Eucharist as the source and summit of the Christian life!

In contrast, what does Protestantism offer? No continuous history before the 16th century; no valid succession to the Apostles; no connection with the Fathers of the Church; no Church Councils to definitively resolve disputes; no unity of ecclesiastical government; no certainty of doctrine; no consistency of belief; no uniformity in worship; no fixed number of sacraments; no presence of Christ in the Eucharist; no verifiable miracles; no tradition to safeguard against novelties; no official traditions of heroic celibacy or poverty, etc., etc. Instead, we are offered private interpretation of Scripture that has led to untold confusion and contradiction and a plethora of self-proclaimed prophets giving rise to tens of thousands of different denominations agreeing on little more than their anti-Catholic tenets.

I, along with the other contributors to this book, invite Ray Galea to reopen his search for truth. It does not exist entirely in Evangelicalism or in any other successor to Luther, Calvin, Cranmer, etc., but, as we will discover, in the Church that Christ founded on St Peter and his successors.

2

Which Catholicism?

Zachary Vermeer[1]

The English writer G.K. Chesterton once made an interesting observation about the Christian Faith: that it has been criticised from diametrically opposite perspectives. To Machiavelli, Christianity was an effeminate religion, whose message of peace and love, even of one's enemies, was completely unrealistic and unsuitable for tough, practical-minded rulers and soldiers. To modern liberals, Christianity is a harsh and dogmatic religion, intolerant of other creeds and cultures, the source of wars and persecutions throughout history. Chesterton's response was that something that attracted such divergent hatred was either extraordinarily good or extraordinarily bad, but there was no doubt that it was extraordinary.

A similar puzzle is presented when we consider two different Protestant criticisms of the Catholic Church. On the one hand, Protestants have long portrayed Catholicism as the enemy of free thought, a massive monument to groupthink, and a monstrous dictatorship in which the slavish laity have no choice but to follow the every whim of the Pope. This view sees Protestantism as the triumph of independent thought and the rights of the private conscience: Protestantism as the forebear of liberalism. However, the problem for Protestants who make this argument is that these weapons are just as easily turned against the basic doctrines that all Christians share rather than the specifically Catholic 'additions' they reject. The bulk of people in formerly Christian societies, including many people who still call themselves Christians, have appealed to their own understanding and their own consciences to reject Christian sexual morality, Christian teaching about the uniqueness of Christ as the one Saviour for humanity, even the central Christian doctrine of Christ's divinity. The criticism of

---

[1] Zachary Vermeer studied Arts and Law at the University of Sydney and subsequently earned a Master's degree in law at Oxford University. He has worked as a lecturer in law at the University of Notre Dame, Australia.

the authority of the Church opens a dangerous door to the rejection of all outside authority, including that of the Bible and of God himself, in a world where mass culture teaches that "it's all about me" and that no one has the right to criticise whatever I happen to think or want.

So, in recent years a different critique of Catholicism has been aired: Catholicism is not too authoritarian, but not authoritarian enough. Catholicism's image as a faith with clear teachings that unite all its followers is argued to be false advertising. There seem to be all kinds of brands of Catholicism nowadays: "Traditional Catholicism", "Charismatic Catholicism", "John Paul II Catholicism", "Liberal Catholicism", and "liberation theology" to name just a few. There is also the fact that nowadays many Catholics, at least in the Western world, do not agree with some of the official teachings of the Church, and do not think that prevents them being good Catholics. Does this mean that Catholicism is no better than Protestantism in providing clarity of faith—that in the end, you must make up your own mind from your own reading of the Bible? To answer this, we need to first think about human nature, and what it indicates about God's plan for the Church.

There are two tendencies in human nature that are always pulling apart. On the one side, we are communal beings. We all live in the same world, against the background of the one objective physical reality; the actions of each of us affect other people. Moreover, we need to live in relationships with other human beings, or our human potentiality will be stunted. No aspect of human life, least of all faith, is a merely personal experience; it always is influenced by, and influences in turn, other people, and without the support of a community, no inner revelation has a lasting impact. That is why God has chosen to save us, not by a purely internal, individual experience, but by making us part of the Church. Christ died to make us part of his Body, that is, the Church; we are saved by being joined to Christ and, in Christ, to other people who share the same faith and are filled with the same divine love. The Church, to be a body, must be united by one life, one faith, one love, otherwise it is not a body, but a collection of amputated limbs and organs; otherwise the community is imperfect.

Yet, at the same time, people are inescapably different, and each individual whom God creates is unique. Just consider what a wide variety of human personality types exist: the gulf that separates the extrovert from the introvert, the 'doer' from the intellectual, the optimist from the pessimist. To these natural differences add the effects of context: differences in culture, differences in education and upbringing, differences in life experience. All these things separate human beings from each other, to the point that mutual comprehension becomes almost impossible. Everyone asks himself sometimes: how can other people enjoy things that I find so boring, and fail to enjoy what thrills me so much? Yet God wills this variety: just as he looked on the myriads of different creatures he had created "and saw that they were good", so the great diversity among human beings allows his infinite glory to be displayed in many different ways. That is why the image of the Body is so appropriate for the Church: although all united by one common life, every part of the body is unique and different, which is all to the good: a body that was all pancreases would not be a body at all.

So the Church is a Body, united by "one Lord, one faith, one Baptism" (Eph. 4:5), but with a great variety of different expressions of that faith, reflecting the variety of the people within it. A budding theologian of the 20th century will have a different experience of the Faith from a peasant girl of the 12th century, who will have a different experience from the converted Roman soldier of the 2nd: but they are united in the one Body. They know different amounts of theology, their experience of life is different, but they are part of this one living organic community founded by Christ two millennia ago and held together at every moment by his love.

However, since we live in a fallen world, the equilibrium between unity and diversity is not easy to keep. Legitimate diversity is always in danger of mutating into a breach of the unity of the Faith. Unity around the basics of the Faith must be preserved, and a visible governing authority is necessary to do that, just as in any earthly political community. If I were a member of the Australian Republican Movement, for example, and I started arguing in every possible ARM forum that Australia is a "crowned republic" already and no constitutional change in required, the executive of the ARM has the right to tell me that I am wrong about the meaning of republicanism, and even to expel me. If it could not do this, the organisation could be destroyed from the inside. Now, it is Catholic teaching that God has established such a supreme authority for his Church: the bishops as successors to the Apostles, chosen by Christ himself, led by St Peter, to whom Christ gave the special threefold command to "feed my sheep" (Jn 21) with right doctrine. Protestants argue that God has not done this because it was not necessary: the Bible provides anyone with the criterion to distinguish between legitimate diversity of viewpoint and dangerous innovations that will destroy unity. Although the Bible does indeed play this role, to rely on it by itself is naive. Human beings are diverse enough that the diversity of their personalities and cultures will colour their interpretations of Scripture, and many will see their own preferences reflected back at them from the sacred page. (As the German aphorist Georg Lichtenberg observed: "A book is a mirror: if an ape looks into it an apostle is hardly likely to look out"). History supports this contention. Since the Reformation, there have been myriads of different Protestant groups, each interpreting Scripture somewhat differently, every decade more and more splits, more and more denominations. Most Protestants acknowledge this, but argue that their key doctrines, faith alone and Scripture alone, etc., are self-evident from Scripture; yet neither of them is heard of for 1,500 years after the founding of Christianity and attempts to find support for them in any of the great theologians or bishops of the first three-quarters of Christian history, Eastern or Western, have proved unsuccessful. Furthermore, the latter doctrine of *sola scriptura* is self-contradictory simply by virtue of the fact that the canon of the Bible is not specified anywhere from Genesis to Revelation—we only know what the canon is thanks to the tradition and teaching of the Catholic Church. Moreover, Scripture itself warns that it is liable to be misunderstood. St Peter, the first bishop of Rome and Pope, states in his second letter:

> ... our most dear brother Paul also, according to the wisdom given him, as written to you, as indeed he did in his epistles, speaking in them of these things. In these epistles there are certain things difficult to understand, which the unlearned and the unstable distort, just as they do the rest of the Scriptures also, to their own destruction (2 Pet. 3:15-16).

Thus, Scripture itself tells us that the Bible alone is not sufficient to either maintain unity in the face of human diversity or prevent misunderstanding in interpretation. There must be a parallel living authority to uphold true doctrine and interpretation in the face of every new challenge, to restrain the pressures of the centrifugal force of diversity that continually threaten to break up Christianity into a thousand different viewpoints, and to prevent Christianity going the way of the world every time the world changes. So it is that Christ has established the office of the Pope who, either alone or in union with the other bishops of the world and under the guidance and protection of the Holy Spirit, is the authoritative teacher of all Christians.

Has this authority to teach and govern in order to preserve the Church's unity always been exercised perfectly? No, not necessarily. Although we believe that when teaching solemnly on faith and morals the Holy Spirit protects the Pope and the Bishops from error, in their day-to-day prudential decisions they can make mistakes. St Thomas Aquinas, who for centuries has been considered the greatest of Catholic theologians, was at first condemned by the Archbishop of Paris. On the other hand, some argue that the hierarchy today should discipline more directly contemporary liberal priests who undermine central Christian doctrines. However, despite all this we have faith that, through God's providence, true doctrine in faith and morals will always be maintained. Not so with Protestantism and its insistence on private interpretation of Scripture. Ninety years ago all Christian denominations taught that artificial contraception was wrong; now only the Catholic Church does. The Catholic Church has remained the same, has maintained its unity with its past self despite the seismic shift in the surrounding culture; all the other churches are caught in flux. They are not the same as they were then; who is to say what they will teach in another 90 years?

There remains one powerful objection. It is all very well to talk about the tradition of the Church and the teaching of the Pope and bishops as providing the criterion of what is authentic Christian teaching: on paper that appears satisfactory, but in the real world, one might argue, it is not. In the real world the majority of Catholics are hazy on the exact teachings of the Church. In the West especially they do not live their lives very differently from liberal secular people; in some parts of the developing world, popular Catholicism is mixed up with pre-Christian pagan practices. Catholicism, for most Catholics, seems to be more about being part of a culture than belief in fixed doctrines. For Protestants, this seems conclusive evidence that, whatever fancy apologetic arguments can be devised for it, Catholicism as a reality is deeply flawed.

I would argue that the shock and horror at this reality, though justified, is a little adolescent. Any belief, once it has been held by a broad group of people for one or two generations, starts to embed itself in everyday life as culture: shared memories, traditions, rituals, ways of speaking and thinking, which all visibly unite members of the group with each other, with their ancestors who shared the same beliefs but are no more, and, it is hoped, with their future descendants. Now, there is a danger, one that serious Catholics also recognise, of that culture becoming more important than the belief that gave birth to it. Culture in such a case becomes a dead shell that continues independent of real faith. Certainly, some Catholic cultures have shown this problem. It is wrong, however, to say that it is a uniquely Catholic one. There is no better example of this development than the Church of England. By the nineteenth century at least, being Anglican for many people had much less to do with being Christian than being English. The hymns, the beautiful service, the King James Bible, the cathedrals, were loved not because they were Christian, because they brought the soul closer to a God in whom many no longer really believed, but because they were English, because they created a bond with one's English ancestors, because they symbolised English values of orderly beauty, politeness, and tolerance. (Of course, as this sense of Englishness has declined in our multicultural times, the whole *raison d'être* of the Anglican Church has vanished, and it is collapsing before our very eyes, as the cultural glue is no longer strong enough to hold together the incompatible theologies within it). The same could be said of all the state Protestant churches of Europe. Even in modern America, the most devout of all Protestant countries, there is a strain of Evangelicalism in which the flag, army, and Founding Fathers are seemingly just as sacred as anything Christian, and in which being Evangelical is the logical corollary to being American.

A religious faith is always going to be linked with a certain culture if it is to endure long. A religion that was completely cultureless, which was just a series of intellectual propositions, could never appeal to the vast majority of humanity. The fact that many Catholics cannot give a particularly good explanation of Catholic doctrine is regrettable, but it is not surprising: I would suggest the same applies for Buddhists, Hindus, and even many Evangelicals. A religion must be incarnated in everyday life if it is to endure; it cannot be merely a matter of knowledge. The danger of the culture becoming more important than the faith is real; but faith can be equally undermined, in the long run, if it lacks a rich, independent culture that permeates everyday life. Certainly, the beauty of Catholic culture, from Mozart Requiems down to Irish wakes, has been the first step for many towards Christian belief, and has kept many firm in the midst of the temptations of doubt.

There are more churchgoing Catholics who hold liberal views than churchgoing Evangelical Protestants who do so. Why? Both Catholics and Protestants have been badly affected by the deluge of secularism that has ratcheted up several notches in the last forty years; many on both sides have been lured away by the liberal siren call. Yet Catholics are more likely to stay churchgoers, or at least tick Catholic on the census form, even when they no longer believe in many Catholic doctrines, than Protestants in the same situation. In part this is due to the specific historical context in Australia and other Anglo-Saxon countries: Catholics have traditionally been an embattled minority here, and a minority identity is more psychologically ingrained than one shared by the majority, since it has needed to be more tenaciously defended; thus it is less easily given up. In part it is due to the fact that attendance at Mass has always been emphasised by the Catholic Church to a far greater extent than church attendance has been emphasised by Protestants; so even as they become less Catholic, the habits of generations still carry many Catholics to Sunday Mass. Also, in part, it has something to do with the beauty of Catholicism, an attraction which is difficult ever to completely overcome: the unbelievable consolation of knowing Christ's real presence within you at Communion; that infinitely beautiful image of true love, love which is never free from suffering, the crucifix; the stories and statues of the saints, so touching, so beautiful, making Christ known in a million different ways in every clime and age.

Such cultural Catholicism, divorced from full Catholic belief, is not ideal; yet it is not worthless. A small congregation or group can be made up of zealots who follow all the rules and know every jot and tittle of doctrine; after a generation or two the group will get too big, the broader world and its temptations will reassert its influence, the original fervour will cool somewhat, and the zealous minority will have to break off yet again to form yet another purified denomination. In Catholicism there is a similar phenomenon; in every age there are some groups, once on fire, now in decline, and new movements that arise in their place. Nevertheless, the magnificence of the Catholic Church is that, as its name implies ('catholic' equals 'universal'), it provides a home for all humanity, in all cultures and ages, the half-hearted sinners as well as the passionate saints. Catholicism seeks to make the former into the latter. Its doctrine is clear, it does not buckle under the pressure of majority opinion, and it remains the same, obdurate and magnificent. Yet she is also grateful to God that the lukewarm keep one ear open to her message.

In a real sense, Galea diverts attention from one of Protestantism's most obvious failings—its splintering into tens of thousands of separate sectarian groups with no uniformity in government, discipline and doctrine, a fact that obviously contradicts the will of Christ as exhibited in his priestly prayer "that they (his followers) may all be one" (Jn 17). To nullify Catholic attempts to exploit such an embarrassment, Galea on page 24 purports to argue that Catholicism and Protestantism are nowadays "quite similar" as "both contain a wide spectrum of beliefs and attitudes, among both clergy and laity."

Is what Galea says here correct? By no means. As Galea himself states on page 28, "… it's important to understand and engage with *the official and authoritative teaching of the Roman Catholic Church* (emphasis added), which is normative and binding on all Catholics." In this statement Galea acknowledges that there is a single and official Catholicism. Then why raise the question of *"Which Catholicism?"* Why bother mention forms of Catholicism that are really not official Catholicism but rather products of twentieth century dissent and protest? Dissenting forms of Catholicism exist because, despite everything Christ has done to establish a single Church that teaches a single doctrine, people are still inherently free to accept or reject it. That has been the case since the time of Judas and will sadly continue until the end of time. Sixteenth century Protestantism is just one example of the abuse of human freedom over the centuries.

The real obligation on Galea is to counter Catholicism by putting forward *the official and authoritative teaching of the Protestant Church*. This he cannot do because there is no such thing as either "the Protestant Church" or a single Protestant body of doctrine. The best he can do is claim on page 29 that the original European Protestants were united under the four slogans of "Christ alone, the Bible alone, faith alone and grace alone." This sounds nice and neat, but let us examine some of the nitty gritty. Do all Protestants who believe in Christ alone believe in the Trinity and the divinity of Christ? No. Do all Protestants who believe in the Bible alone possess the same translation or interpret it the same as regards, for example, the number of sacraments, the style of Church government, women in ministry, divorce and remarriage, sexual ethics, etc? No. Do all Protestants who believe in faith alone share the same beliefs about the necessity and effect of baptism, whether justification and sanctification are one and the same thing, whether justification is infused or imputed, whether initial justification predestines to final justification, the meritorious value of good works done in faith, how Abraham was justified, etc? No. Do all Protestants who believe in grace alone share the same beliefs about whether the will is free or not, whether grace is resistible or irresistible, whether one can lose his/her salvation after initial justification? No.

What is commonly called "Protestantism" has proved unable to safeguard unity, a problem observable at its origins in the disputes between Luther and Zwingli, and which has got only worse over the centuries. Nor should anyone pretend that the scale of divisions among Catholics even remotely approaches the number of irreversible divisions within Protestantism. An examination also requires all and sundry to face up to the unscriptural, a-historical, man-made tradition of *sola scriptura* and its accompanying rejection of the visible and living teaching authority founded by Christ upon St Peter and the Apostles (which continues today in the Pope and the bishops of the world) and Apostolic Tradition.

What should concern Galea and the readers of his book before attacking Catholicism is to seek answers to the following three questions: "Why the divisions within Protestantism?" "Which Protestantism?" "Which Anglicanism?" Only when one is ready and willing to admit that division and contradiction are contrary to the will of Christ rather than from Christ will they be in an adequate position to examine and critique the claims and teachings of the One, Holy, Catholic and Apostolic Church founded by Christ and centred today in Rome.

3

Christ and the Mass

Robert M. Haddad[1]

Introduction

The Catholic Church teaches that in every Mass the bread and wine, by the words of consecration pronounced by the priest, become the Body, Blood, Soul and Divinity of Jesus Christ, while still retaining the appearances of bread and wine. The Church calls the presence of the Body and Blood, etc., of Christ under the forms of bread and wine the 'Real Presence.' The process by which this change is effected is described as 'transubstantiation.'

The Catholic teaching on the Mass is often either largely misunderstood or grossly misrepresented by non-Catholics. It is, therefore, essential to outline exactly what the Catholic Church actually teaches. Vatican II succinctly outlined the Church's teaching on the Mass as follows:

> At the Last Supper, on the night he was betrayed, our Saviour instituted the Eucharistic Sacrifice of his Body and Blood. He did this in order to perpetuate the sacrifice of the Cross throughout the centuries until he should come again, and so to entrust to his beloved spouse, the Church, a memorial of his death and resurrection: a sacrament of love, a sign of unity, a bond of charity, a paschal banquet in which Christ is consumed, the mind is filled with grace, and a pledge of future glory is given to us.[2]

Ray Galea is one non-Catholic who has many objections to Catholic teaching on the Priesthood, Real Presence and the Sacrifice of the Mass. He outlines his problems in his book under three headings (p. 32):

1. The role of the human priest in the place of Christ.
2. The turning of bread and wine into Christ.

---

[1] Robert M. Haddad is a part-time apologist who has worked in education since 1989. A former Convener of the University of Sydney Catholic Chaplaincy, Robert is currently the Director of the Confraternity of Christian Doctrine for the Archdiocese of Sydney.
[2] Vatican Council II, *Sacrosanctum Concilium*, 1963, #47.

3. The renewing of Christ's sacrifice for the forgiveness of sins.

It is the purpose of this chapter to respond to Galea by providing a correct presentation of Catholic teaching concerning the Mass and the priesthood, an outline of the Biblical foundations for belief in the Real Presence and the Sacrifice of the Mass, Patristic evidence of the Apostolic origins and ancient belief in the Real Presence and the Mass, an understanding of the historical development of doctrine concerning the term 'transubstantiation', and a treatment of various miscellaneous issues raised throughout Galea's chapter.

Catholic teaching concerning the Mass and the priesthood
The Mass as a Sacrifice

If in the Mass the Body and Blood of Christ become present on the altar, why do we need the Mass itself? Why could not the priest just consecrate the bread and wine in an office somewhere and bring along Holy Communion to hand out? The answer is that the Mass is about much more than just providing Holy Communion to the people. This is what Galea tries to explain when he discusses the Sacrifice of the Mass. Immediately, though, he commits a serious error—serious not just in its content but also in how avoidable it is. He writes (p. 44): "But the Mass is not a remembrance, nor even an act of 'thanksgiving' (which is what the word 'Eucharist' means)." Had Galea consulted the *Catechism of the Catholic Church*, he would have found an explanation of what the Mass is, and the many names by which it is known. One of these is "the *memorial* of the Lord's Passion and Resurrection" (#1330). It is also called 'Eucharist', "because it is an action of thanksgiving to God" (#1328). How Galea, purporting to present the true Catholic teaching, can have written that the Mass is neither a remembrance nor an act of thanksgiving is mystifying. He is correct, however, in what he goes on to say: "It's a sacrifice." The *Catechism* explains that the Eucharist is also called the "Holy Sacrifice", "because it makes present the one sacrifice of Christ the Saviour and includes the Church's offering. The terms *holy sacrifice of the Mass, sacrifice of praise, spiritual sacrifice, pure and holy sacrifice* are also used, since it completes and surpasses all the sacrifices of the Old Covenant" (#1330).

So in what sense is the Mass a sacrifice, and what sort of sacrifice is it? The Church teaches that when Christ took the elements of bread and wine and spoke of these as his Body and Blood which would be "given up", he was identifying the Last Supper with the sacrifice that he was to make the following day on Calvary. In commanding his disciples to "do this in memory of me", Christ also made clear that this was a sacrifice that he wanted his disciples to continue. In the Mass, the consecration of the bread and wine take place separately, with the words of consecration first pronounced over the bread and then over the wine. This double, ritual consecration symbolises the actual separation of Christ's Body and Blood on the cross. In the unbloody sacrifice of the Mass, the bloody sacrifice of Calvary is re-presented, "its memory perpetuated until the end of the world" (Council of Trent, [1562], Session XXII, Ch. 1).

Why a sacrifice?

Galea essentially has two main objections to the notion of the Mass as a sacrifice (he does not object to the Biblical readings and prayers, however, that comprise the rest of the Mass). First, he points out that the New Testament is clear that Christ died only once for our sins, at a particular space and time in human history. He comments, "it is very hard to see how something can be continually renewed if it was finally and definitively finished in space and time" (p. 45). Secondly, the Letter to the Hebrews presents, says Galea, "a stunning image of a job completed. And once that sacrifice has been made, there can be no other" (p. 46). In other words, Christ's sacrifice was so perfect that there is no need for further sacrifices like that of the Mass.

The Catholic Church also believes that Christ only died once for sin and cannot die again in accordance with Romans 6:9-20: "We know that Christ, being raised from the dead, will never die again; death no longer has dominion over him. The death he died, he died to sin, once for all; but the life he lives, he lives to God." Christ does not "die again" in the Mass; neither is he "re-sacrificed." At the same time, it is no contradiction to say that in the Mass Christ's once and for all death on Mt Calvary is sacramentally made present (or re-presented), so that all generations until the end of time may be present at and spiritually benefit from that very same death. How is this possible? It is possible because in heaven Mt Calvary is eternally present before God through the ministrations of

Christ in the heavenly temple. Scripture tells us that Christ is not merely praying or interceding on our behalf at the right-hand of the Father; he is also perpetually offering his once-and-for-all sacrifice as the eternal High Priest. Note the following:

1. Hebrews 6:20: Christ is a "priest forever" in the line of Melchizedeck;
2. Hebrews 8:2: Christ is ministering in the "true tabernacle";
3. Hebrews 12:24: "Jesus is our spokesman with his blood, which has better things to say than Abel's had";
4. Revelation 5:6: "Amid the four figures and the elders, a Lamb standing upright, yet slain (as I thought) in sacrifice."

Galea's picture of Jesus at the right-hand of the Father is one who has "sat down" after his ascension and simply "continues to act as a mediator on our behalf" (pp. 46-47). This is only part of the picture. On the other hand, Hebrews-Revelation combine to present a bigger picture of Christ as a living eternal priest appearing slain in sacrifice and yet ministering with his blood before the Father. The words 'priest', 'ministering', 'blood', 'slain', 'sacrifice' portray a Christ currently offering a sacrifice to the Father. Christ as priest can now be offering only one sacrifice to the Father and no other, namely his sacrifice on Mt Calvary. Mt Calvary thus transcends space and time—it has become a supra-temporal reality. It is this reality that is made present before Christians in a sacramental and unbloody manner through the Mass. Thus, rather than ignoring Christ's bodily ascension into heaven as claimed by Galea (p. 43), the Mass simultaneously makes present Mt Calvary and what Christ is currently doing in heaven.

St Augustine describes the Mass as a "daily sign" of Christ's sacrifice "in the sacrifice of the Church" (*City of God*, Bk 10:20). This is why when Galea asks, "Does God need a weekly reminder of Christ's once-for-all death? Or are we the ones who need the reminder?" (p. 47), we may answer that it is indeed us who need the reminder (and the Church offers this reminder every day on altars around the world, not just on Sundays). As St Irenaeus in the late second century explained:

> The oblation of the Church, therefore, which the Lord gave instructions to be offered throughout all the world, is accounted with God a pure sacrifice, and is acceptable to him; not that he

stands in need of a sacrifice from us, but that he who offers is himself glorified in what he does offer, if his gift be accepted (*Against Heresies* Bk 4:18).

What of Galea's second objection that the perfect sacrifice has already been made by Christ, at a given time and place in history, and there is therefore no need for further sacrifices? As the Church holds that the sacrifice of the Mass is the same sacrifice as Mt Calvary, this objection does not carry any weight. If it were a new sacrifice, Galea would have a point. As it is the same sacrifice, the sacrifice of the Mass cannot add anything to the sacrifice on Calvary, nor does it in some way imply that the sacrifice on Calvary was inadequate. Mt Calvary is a past event, but the distribution of its spiritual fruits to Christ's faithful is a continuous process, in which the Mass plays a central role.

The Priesthood

Now that we have considered the place of sacrifice in the Church, we are better placed to consider the priesthood, since it is almost a universal definition of a priest that he is one who offers sacrifice. The priesthood is intimately linked to the sacrifice of the Mass, and accordingly the Church teaches that the priesthood was instituted at the Last Supper. The other side to the priesthood, the forgiveness of sins, was bestowed upon the disciples on Easter Sunday, when Jesus appeared to them and said: "Receive the Holy Spirit. If you forgive the sins of any, they are forgiven; if you retain the sins of any, they are retained" (Jn 20:22).

Galea's main objection to the Catholic priesthood is that "the New Testament knows nothing of the idea" (p. 35). He points out that Church leaders and ministers are never called 'priests' in the New Testament. They are called 'shepherds', 'elders' or 'overseers' (p. 35).

Is this correct? In response, it is good to start with a quote from the English priest and convert from Anglicanism, Ronald Knox, who said:

> In arguing, never disguise from yourself the strength of the other man's case. The Reformers, when they claimed that there was no warrant in Scripture for regarding the Christian ministry as a sacrificial priesthood, were choosing quite a good wicket to play on.[3]

---

3 Mon. Ronald Knox, *The Hidden Stream*, London: Burns and Oates, 1952, p. 185.

Knox goes on to explain that the official title of a Catholic priest is still 'presbyter.' This is the Greek word that is translated as 'elder' in the New Testament. Except in reference to Christ, the early Christians avoided the word 'priest' (in Greek *hiereus*) because it was the word that people were accustomed to using when referring to the Jewish priests in the Temple. It would have been confusing if all of a sudden it were applied to a different group of people.

However, the following verse of St Paul is significant:

> *But on some points I have written to you very boldly by way of reminder, because of the grace given me by God to be a minister (Leitourgon) of Christ Jesus to the Gentiles in the priestly service (hierorgounta) of the gospel of God, so that the offering of the Gentiles may be acceptable, sanctified by the Holy Spirit* (Rom. 15:16).

Leitourgon is the Greek parent from which is derived the modern word liturgy, understood as public religious worship or service. Protestants claim that *Leitourgon* here only refers to the public service of preaching the word of God. However, such an argument runs into difficulty in the light of Hebrews 8:1-2 which uses the same word to describe the very priesthood of Christ: "Now the point in what we are saying is this: we have such a high priest, one who is seated at the right hand of the throne of the Majesty in heaven, a minister (*Leitourgos*) in the sanctuary and the true tent which is set up not by man but by the Lord." Furthermore, the term *hierorgounta* (from *hiereus* meaning priest) used to describe St Paul's Gospel work implies a work that is more than simple preaching, for the office of priest, as understood by the Jews, always involved the carrying out of material sacrifices.

Galea also argues from Hebrews chapters 7 to 10 that as Christ is the fulfilment of the Old Testament priesthood Christians do not need human priests any more; Christ has filled that role completely and perfectly forever (p. 34). That being the case, Catholic priests are a created class inserted "between us and Christ" and their existence somehow insinuates that there is "something unfinished or inadequate about Christ's priesthood" (p. 35). Galea's analysis of Hebrews presents a nice, neat and simple picture, but it does not sit well with the rest of the New Testament, which clearly provides evidence that specific men, by a ritual imposition of hands and by prayer, were set apart from all other Christians to perform certain 'tasks':

Select from among yourselves seven men of good standing, full of the Spirit and of wisdom, whom we may appoint to this task ... They had these men stand before the apostles, who prayed and laid their hands on them (Acts 6:3-6).

While they were worshiping the Lord and fasting, the Holy Spirit said, Set apart for me Barnabas and Saul for the work to which I have called them. Then after fasting and praying they laid their hands on them and sent them off. So, being sent out by the Holy Spirit, they went down to Seleucia; and from there they sailed to Cyprus ... (Acts 13:2-4).

And after they had appointed elders for them in each church, with prayer and fasting they entrusted them to the Lord in whom they had come to believe ... (Acts 14:23).

I remind you to rekindle the gift of God that is within you through the laying on of my hands ... (2 Tim. 1:6).

I left you behind in Crete for this reason, so that you should put in order what remained to be done, and should appoint elders in every town, as I directed you (Tit. 1:5).

One of the principal tasks of these ordained men was to perform the liturgical action commanded by Christ at the Last Supper, "Do this in remembrance of me":

They devoted themselves to the apostles' teaching and fellowship, to the breaking of bread and the prayers (Acts 2:42).

Day by day, as they spent much time together in the temple, they broke bread at home and ate their food with glad and generous hearts (Acts 2:46).

However, the 'breaking of the bread' shows only one side of the priesthood. The other side is the power of forgiving sin. That Christ solemnly bestowed the power and authority on the Apostles to remit and retain sins is evident from John 20:21-23:

As the Father has sent me, so I send you ... Receive the Holy Spirit. If you forgive the sins of any, they are forgiven them; if you retain the sins of any, they are retained.

In this verse we see that Christ bestowed upon his Apostles the following: (i) mission (*"As the Father has sent me, so I send you..."*); (ii) power (*"Receive the Holy Spirit"*), and (iii) discretion whether or not to exercise this power (*"If you forgive...; if you retain"*). This verse cannot be explained away by claiming that the Apostles were simply authorised to go out and preach "repentance and forgiveness of sins ... to all nations" (Lk 24:47). If such were the case, verse 23 would serve absolutely no purpose.

Furthermore, we see a ministerial priesthood also operating in the administration of other sacraments. In Acts 8:14-17 we read that Sts Peter and John went to the Samaritans and "laid their hands on them and they received the Holy Spirit." Since time immemorial the ordinary minister of Confirmation has been only a Bishop (or at least one ordained to the priesthood as in the Eastern Rites), who places his hand on the candidate and anoints the forehead with Holy Oil mixed with balsam while saying the words "Be sealed with the Gift of the Holy Spirit."

Finally, St James advises his readers to call upon the elders (presbyters) of the Church in times of life-threatening illness: "Is any among you sick? Let him call for the elders of the church, and let them pray over him, anointing him with oil in the name of the Lord; and the prayer of faith will save the sick man, and the Lord will raise him up; and if he has committed sins, he will be forgiven" (Js. 5:14-15).

Galea also objects to the idea that Catholic priests can have a "share" in Christ's priesthood as they are "normal, sinful human beings" (pp. 34-35) while Christ is the sinless "one mediator" between God and man (1 Tim. 2:5-6). By virtue of their sinfulness, the sacrifices purportedly offered by Catholic priests can never be effective or acceptable in the eyes of God. It is certainly true that only Christ as the spotless Lamb could offer to the Father a sacrifice that was perfect and infinitely pleasing to God. It does not follow, however, that Christ could not bestow upon "normal, sinful human beings" a participation in his own priesthood in order to visibly apply the fruits of his redemptive work to successive generations until the end of the world. How do we know that Christ gave such participation? The proof lies in 1 Cor. 11:24-25 and John 20:21-23, which clearly show that Christ himself, for the sake of all Christians, gave to his disciples both the power and authority to do what he did, namely, repeat the Last Supper and forgive sins. Ultimately, however, Christ offers the sacrifice of the Mass; the priest merely acts in his stead as a secondary, instrumental agent.

Without perhaps realising it, Galea himself admits that sinful humans can be priests and offer pleasing sacrifices to God. This he does when he discusses the idea of the 'priesthood of all believers', through which all Christians can come before God and "*offer him 'sacrifices'*—such as offering our very bodies and all that we do" (p. 36). Why does Galea not conclude here, as he does for the Catholic priesthood, that the sacrifices of ordinary sinful Christians are 'ineffective' and downgrade the work of Christ? Why should any spiritual sacrifices from human beings be necessary now that Christ has made the one perfect sacrifice? Why does Galea not say here, as he says of the Catholic priesthood, "You don't need human priests any more; Christ has filled that role completely and perfectly forever"? (p. 34). And what ever happened to faith alone? If a human priesthood is no longer needed on the ground that Christ is the one mediator, then it is necessary to reject all forms of human priesthood, including the priesthood of all believers.

Galea says that the idea of the priesthood of all believers was condemned by the Council of Trent (p. 36). Galea gets his Conciliar history terribly wrong. What the Council of Trent condemned was the notion of any equivalence between the common priesthood and the ministerial priesthood. It was the belief that there is only one kind of priesthood— the common priesthood—that was rightly condemned by the Council of Trent (Session 23, ch. 4).

Contrary to Galea's assertions, the Catholic Church recognises both kinds of priesthood—the ministerial priesthood and the common priesthood of all believers. Galea acknowledges this in an endnote tucked away near the back of his book (p. 116, note 7). In explaining the Church's teachings, he should have quoted directly from the *Catechism*, where it is explained that the ministerial priesthood and the common priesthood are each a participation in the one priesthood of Christ. The question is then posed—what is the essential difference between the two? The answer:

> While the common priesthood of the faithful is exercised by the unfolding of baptismal grace–a life of faith, hope, and charity, a life according to the Spirit–, the ministerial priesthood is at the service of the common priesthood. It is directed at the unfolding of the baptismal grace of all Christians. The ministerial priesthood is a *means* by which Christ unceasingly builds up and leads his Church. For this reason it is transmitted by its own sacrament, the sacrament

of Holy Orders.[4]

The Catholic understanding of priesthood, then, is that there is one High Priest, Jesus Christ, as well as his ministerial priesthood and a common priesthood. This three-layered structure of the priesthood was pre-figured in the Israel of the Old Testament, where there was a high priest as well as a ministerial priesthood, the Levites, who were one of the twelve tribes of Israel. In addition, however, the entire people of Israel were "a kingdom of priests and a holy nation" (Ex. 19:6). The Catholic Church then sees the Old Testament priesthood, in its entirety, as fulfilled in the priesthood exercised by Christ and instituted by him.

A final point about the 'mediatorship' of priests. It is true that there is a sense in which Catholic priests do stand between God and us. This is not, though, in the manner of a roadblock but of a bridge, by which we attain union with Christ in the Eucharist, and are restored to God's friendship through the forgiveness of our sins. In both these instances God acts through his priests. Nevertheless, at all times we can still approach God directly through our own prayers, without the aid of any priest.

The Biblical foundations for belief in the Real Presence and the Sacrifice of the Mass

The above notwithstanding, Galea explains the doctrine of transubstantiation quite accurately—namely, when the bread and wine change into the Body and Blood of Christ the characteristics of the bread and wine (their taste, texture, and so on) remain the same. It is their substance (what the bread and wine actually *are*) that changes. After the priest pronounces the words of consecration, then, what looks, tastes, smells and feels like bread and wine are now the Body, Blood, Soul and Divinity of Christ. However, since the change is not perceptible to the senses it is very difficult to argue from reason alone whether this change *does or does not* occur. On the other hand, it is possible to debate on a philosophical level whether the change *can or cannot* occur, but Galea does not attempt to provide a philosophical refutation of the doctrine. He only asserts that it is "illogical", "fanciful" (p. 39) and a "bizarre doctrine" (p. 47), but offers no arguments from logic or elsewhere in philosophy. Galea's arguments are confined to Scripture

---

4 CCC #1547.

and history.

The Catholic Church has always taught the doctrine of the Real Presence so firmly because its foundation is so clear in Scripture. Galea acknowledges that there are some Scripture passages that seem to point to some kind of Real Presence of Christ in the Eucharist (p. 41). There are the accounts of the Last Supper, where Christ explicitly says "this is my body … this is my blood" (Mt 26:26). There is also Christ's teaching in John 6, where he repeatedly refers to the flesh and blood that he will give to be eaten and drunk by his followers. Then there is St Paul in 1 Corinthians 11:25, who quotes Jesus as saying, "This cup is the new covenant in my blood."

There is, though, considerably more to the scriptural basis for the Real Presence than what Galea presents. Chapter 6 of St John's Gospel, for example, is the account of a lengthy teaching that far exceeds the two verses quoted by Galea. It is unnecessary to analyse all 46 verses of the 'Promissory Discourse' in John 6. Let us just look at a number of verses not quoted by Galea. In verse 51 Jesus says, "The bread which I shall give for the life of the world is my flesh." The next verse is critical: "The Jews then disputed amongst themselves, saying, "How can this man give us his flesh to eat?" Despite what Galea claims (p. 41), we see here that the Jews understood Jesus to be speaking literally. Jesus did not correct them. He persisted with his teaching, firstly with verses 53 and 54 as quoted by Galea, and then with those that follow: "For my flesh is food indeed, and my blood is drink indeed. He who eats my flesh and drinks my blood abides in me and I in him." Jesus even used the phrase "he who eats me" (v. 57). Faced with this unusual teaching, how did his listeners respond? "Many of his disciples, when they heard it said, 'This is a hard saying; who can listen to it?'" (v. 60). The fact that Jesus said nothing to correct the literal understanding of his audience is significant. Not only had he corrected misinterpretations previously (as with Nicodemus, who misunderstood Jesus to be speaking literally of the need to be "born again" [Jn 3:3-8], and the disciples, who misunderstood him to be speaking literally of Lazarus having "fallen asleep" [Jn 11:11-15]), but we are even told, "After this many of his disciples drew back and no longer went about with him" (v. 66).

Galea also quotes St Paul in 1 Corinthians 11:25, who in turn quotes Christ at the Last Supper as having said, "This cup is the new covenant in my blood." But St Paul said a lot more than that on this topic in the very same letter. Earlier on, he had asked, "The cup of blessing which we bless, is it not a participation in the blood of Christ? The bread which we break, is it not a participation in the body of Christ?" (1 Cor. 10:16). Also, in the verse that follows that quoted by Galea, St Paul said: "Whoever, therefore, eats the bread or drinks the cup of the Lord in an unworthy manner will be guilty of profaning the body and blood of the Lord" (1 Cor. 11:27). This is extremely strong language to be using of someone's actions if they had merely eaten and drunk unworthily *symbols* of the Body and Blood of Christ. St Paul's dire words only make sense if the offender is eating and drinking unworthily the actual and true Body and Blood of Christ.

What about Our Lord's words at the Last Supper? Galea argues that it is "fairly obvious" (p. 42) that when Jesus said the words "this is my body ... this is my blood", he was using figurative language, just as he also called himself "the vine", "the door", "the light", and other expressions. The words "body" and "blood", though, can hardly be regarded in the same way. Why? Because none of the terms "vine", "door", or "light" have any of the 'preparatory background' that the terms "body" and "blood" do. A year before the Last Supper Jesus pledges (Jn 6:27) to give to his disciples a special bread from heaven attached with a promise that whoever eats of it will abide in him and one day be "raised up." In the same discourse Jesus identifies this heavenly bread directly with his flesh (v. 51). This identification causes his audience to ask, "How can this man give us his flesh to eat?" (v. 52). In response, Jesus only reinforces the literal understanding held by the audience. All this precedes the Last Supper in which he delivers on the promise made in John 6:27. Therefore, unlike the words "vine", "door" and "light" there is every reason for the Church to understand the words "body" and "blood" in a literal rather than metaphorical sense.

In support of his figurative interpretation, however, Galea cites "the great" St Augustine of Hippo who "was in no doubt", commenting of Jesus' instruction to "eat his flesh" in John 6 as follows: "It is a figure, therefore, teaching us that we partake of the benefits of the Lord's passion and that we must sweetly and profitably treasure up in our memories that his flesh was crucified and wounded for us" (*On Christian Doctrine*, Bk 3). There is no denying that St Augustine said this, and it does not cause us any concern that he did. Symbols can co-exist with realities. The Church explicitly teaches that, as well as the Real Presence, there are symbolic elements to the Eucharist, for example that the separate consecrations of the bread and wine signify the separation of Christ's Blood from his Body on the Cross. The follow-up question is, can we conclude from Galea's quotation that St Augustine did not believe in the Real Presence? From his other writings it is clear that we cannot. In St Augustine's *Sermon 272*, for example, we read: "What you see is the bread and the chalice; that is what your own eyes report to you. But what your faith obliges you to accept is that the bread is the Body of Christ and the chalice the Blood of Christ." St Augustine's views, therefore, are considerably more nuanced than Galea makes out. He saw both symbol and reality, where Galea sees only a symbol. The same can be said of other Church Fathers whom we will quote in the next section of this chapter.

In discussing the Eucharist and Scripture, we have only briefly looked at the New Testament. We have not yet considered the Old Testament. For a fuller scriptural treatment of the Eucharist, we could discuss the significance of 'types' of the Eucharist prefigured in the rites and history of the Hebrew/Jewish peoples, such as found in chapter 12 of Exodus, in which we read of the institution of the Passover, where the participants ate the flesh of the lamb, whose bones were not to be broken, and whose blood was shed to save God's people from death. We could also discuss Exodus 16, in which we read of the manna from heaven, which God would send to give his people strength for the journey into the Promised Land. Jesus himself linked the manna from heaven to himself as the bread of life (Jn 6:48-51), which is given as food for our journey towards eternal life. We should, however, give some detailed discussion to certain prophecies in the Old Testament that undoubtedly relate to the Eucharist.

The Old Testament predicted that the Messiah would offer a true sacrifice to God in the form of bread and wine, that Jewish sacrifices would one day be brought to an end, and that in their stead the Gentiles would in every place offer a daily and pleasing sacrifice to God's Name. In Genesis 14 we read that Melchizedek, the king of Salem and priest, offered sacrifice under the form of bread and wine:

> *After his return from the defeat of Chedorlaomer and the kings who were with him, the king of Sodom went out to meet him at the Valley of Shaveh (that is, the King's Valley). And Melchizedek king of Salem brought out bread and wine; he was priest of God Most High. And he*

> blessed him and said, Blessed be Abram by God Most High, maker of heaven and earth; and blessed be God Most High, who has delivered your enemies into your hand! And Abram gave him a tenth of everything (vv. 17-20).

Psalm 110 [109] foretold that the Messiah would be a Priest "after the order of Melchizedek":

> The Lord says to my lord: Sit at my right hand, till I make your enemies your footstool ... The Lord has sworn and will not change his mind, You are a priest for ever after the order of Melchizedek (vv. 1 and 4).

The author of the Letter to the Hebrews clearly identifies Christ to be this priest:

> For it is evident that our Lord was descended from Judah, and in connection with that tribe Moses said nothing about priests. This becomes even more evident when another priest arises in the likeness of Melchizedek, who has become a priest, not according to a legal requirement concerning bodily descent but by the power of an indestructible life. For it is witnessed of him, Thou art a priest forever, after the order of Melchizedek (7:14-17).

"After the order of Melchizedek" means 'in the manner of Melchizedek.' Melchizedek brought forth bread and wine and sacrificed them by offering them to Abraham to eat. Christ is a priest after this manner by offering his Body and Blood under the veil of bread and wine for us to eat.

The Book of Daniel chapter 9 speaks of the end of the Jewish priesthood and its sacrifices:

> After the sixty-two weeks, an anointed one shall be cut off and shall have nothing, and the troops of the prince who is to come shall destroy the city and the sanctuary. Its end shall come with a flood, and to the end there shall be war. Desolations are decreed. He shall make a strong covenant with many for one week, and for half of the week he shall make sacrifice and offering cease; and in their place shall be an abomination that desolates, until the decreed end is poured out upon the desolator (vv. 26-27).

The Jewish priesthood would be replaced by a Christian one drawn from "all the nations", according to the Prophet Isaiah:

> And they shall bring all your brethren from all the nations as an offering to the Lord, upon horses, and in chariots, and in litters, and upon mules, and upon dromedaries, to my holy mountain Jerusalem, says the Lord,

just as the Israelites bring their cereal offering in a clean vessel to the house of the Lord. And some of them also I will take for priests and for Levites, says the Lord (Is. 66:20-21).

Also, Jewish sacrifices would be replaced by Gentile ones as predicted by the Prophet Malachi:

I have no pleasure in you, says the Lord of hosts, and I will not accept an offering from your hands. For from the rising of the sun to its setting my name is great among the nations, and in every place incense is offered to my name, and a pure offering; for my name is great among the nations, says the Lord of hosts (Mal. 1:10-11).

Christian sacrifices will be performed on an altar from which Jews will not be allowed to eat:

We have an altar from which those who serve the tent have no right to eat (Heb. 13:10).

Where is the prophecy of Malachi fulfilled today? James Cardinal Gibbons answers as follows:

We may divide the inhabitants of the world into five different classes of people, professing different forms of religion—Pagans, Jews, Mohammedans, Protestants and Catholics. Among which of these shall we find the [pure offering] of which the prophet speaks? Not among the Pagan nations; for they worship false gods, and consequently cannot have any sacrifice pleasing to the Almighty. Not among the Jews; for they have ceased to sacrifice altogether, and the words of the prophet apply not to the Jews, but to the Gentiles. Not among the Mohammedans; for they also reject sacrifices. Not among any of the Protestants sects; for they all distinctly repudiate sacrifices. Therefore, it is only in the Catholic Church that is fulfilled this glorious prophecy; for whithersoever you go, you will find the [pure offering] offered on Catholic altars. If you travel from America to Europe, to Oceania, to Africa, or Asia, you will see our altars erected, and our Priests daily fulfilling the words of the prophets by offering the clean oblation of the Body and Blood of Christ.[5]

Protestants, on the contrary, can only argue that the offering of the nations prophesied by Malachi is merely metaphorical—with no particular

---
5 Card. Gibbons, *The Faith of Our Fathers*, TAN Books and Publishers, Inc., 1980 Ed., p. 254.

support from the text itself. The context of Malachi, however, clearly refers to an actual, physical offering. The Mass is clearly the only offering that fulfils this prophecy.

Patristic evidence for the Apostolic origins of belief in the Real Presence

Around AD 107, St Ignatius, the third Bishop of Antioch and disciple of St John the Evangelist, wrote critically of certain people who:

> ... abstain from the Eucharist and from prayer, because they do not confess that the Eucharist is the flesh of our Saviour Jesus Christ, flesh which suffered for our sins and which the Father, in his goodness, raised up again. They who deny the gift of God are perishing in their disputes. (*Letter to the Smyrnaeans* 7)

This quotation is an important one for many reasons, not least because after reading Galea one is left with the impression that the Catholic belief in the Real Presence of Christ in the Eucharist and the Sacrifice of the Mass are non-Biblical beliefs that only arose during the Middle Ages. The writings of St Ignatius, however, as well as the following extracts from other early Church Fathers, clearly evidence the existence in the first four Christian centuries of a widespread belief that during the Mass the bread and wine mysteriously change into the real Body and Blood of Jesus:

> St Justin Martyr, First Apology 66 (c. AD 155)
> *For not as common bread nor common drink do we receive these; but since Jesus Christ our Saviour was made incarnate by the word of God and had both flesh and blood for our salvation, so too, as we have been taught, the food which has been made into the Eucharist by the Eucharistic prayer set down by him, and by the change of which our blood and flesh is nourished is both the flesh and the blood of that incarnate Jesus ... The Apostles, in the Memoirs which they produced, which are called Gospels, have thus passed on that which was enjoined upon them: that Jesus took bread and, having given thanks, said, 'Do this in remembrance of me; this is my body.' And in like manner, taking the cup, and having given thanks, he said, 'This is my blood.' And he imparted this to them only.*

> St Irenaeus of Lyons, Against Heresies 4, 33, 2 (c. AD 180)
> *If the Lord were from other than the Father, how could he rightly take*

bread, which is of the same creation as our own, and confess it to be his Body, and affirm that the mixture in the cup is his Blood?

Origen, Homilies on Exodus 13, 3 (post AD 244)
You who are wont to assist in the Divine Mysteries, know how, when you receive the Body of the Lord you take reverent care, lest any particle of it should fall to the ground and a portion of the consecrated gift escape you. You consider it a crime—and rightly so—if any particle thereof fall down through negligence.

Origen, Against Celsus 8, 33 (c. AD 248)
We give thanks to the Creator of all, and, along with thanksgiving and prayer for the blessings we have received, we also eat the bread presented to us; and this bread becomes by prayer a sacred Body, which sanctifies those who sincerely partake of it.

St Cyril of Jerusalem, Catechetical Lectures 22, 9 (c. AD 350)
That the seeming bread is not bread, though sensible to taste, but the Body of Christ; and that the seeming wine is not wine, though the taste will have it so, but the Blood of Christ.

St Ephrem of Edessa, Homilies 4, 4 (ante AD 373)
And extending his hand, he gave them the bread which his right hand had made holy: 'Take all of you eat of this, which my word has made holy. Do not now regard as bread that which I have given you; but take, eat this bread, and do not scatter the crumbs; for what I have called my Body, that it is indeed. One particle from its crumbs is able to sanctify thousands and thousands, and is sufficient to afford life to those who eat of it. Take, eat, entertaining no doubt of faith, because this is my Body, and whoever eats it in belief eats in it fire and spirit.

St Augustine of Hippo, Explanation of the Psalms 33, 1 (Inter AD 392-418)
'And he was carried in his own hands.' But, brethren, how is it possible for a man to do this? Who can understand it? Who is it that is carried in his own hands? A man can be carried in the hands of another; but no one can be carried in his own hands. How this should be understood literally of David, we cannot discover; but we can discover how it is meant of Christ. For Christ was carried in his own hands, when, referring to his own Body, he said: 'This is my body' for he carried that Body in his hands.

St Augustine of Hippo, *Explanation of the Psalms* 98, 9 (Inter AD 392-418)
He took flesh from the flesh of Mary. He walked here in the same flesh, and gave us the same flesh to be eaten unto salvation. But no one eats that flesh unless first he adores it ... and not only do we not sin by adoring, we do sin by not adoring.

Patristic evidence for the Apostolic origins of belief in the Holy Sacrifice of the Mass

Regarding the Mass, Galea does not make any specific historical arguments. Perhaps he does not think the history of the sacrifice worth mentioning, given that he omits with ellipsis points the words "according to the apostolic tradition" from the following pronounced by the Council of Trent:

> Therefore, the Mass may properly be offered *according to apostolic tradition* for the sins, punishments, satisfaction, and other necessities of the faithful on earth, as well as for those who have died in Christ and are not yet wholly cleansed.[6]

Does Galea believe that the Mass was offered in and immediately after apostolic times? Probably not, especially as he claims that any notion of a human Christian priesthood did not exist before the "fifth and sixth centuries" (p. 36). On the other hand, it is indeed the belief of the Church that the Mass is offered according to the tradition of the Apostles and their successors the bishops, and for good reason. In the *Didache*, dated to either the late first or early second century AD, we read:

> *Assemble on the Lord's day, and break bread and offer the Eucharist. But first make confession of your faults, so that your sacrifice may be a pure one ... For this is the offering of which the Lord has said, 'Everywhere and always bring me a sacrifice that is undefiled, for I am a great king, says the Lord and my name is the wonder of nations'* (14:1).

Other quotes that can be adduced from the first and second centuries include:

St Clement of Rome, Letter to the Corinthians 44, 4 (c. AD 98)
Our sin will not be small if we eject from the episcopate those who

---
6 Council of Trent, Session 22, Ch. 2.

blamelessly and holily have offered its Sacrifices. Blessed are those presbyters who have already finished their course, and who have obtained a fruitful and perfect release.

St Ignatius of Antioch, Letter to the Philadelphians 4, 1 (c. AD 110)
Take care, then, to use one Eucharist, so that whatever you do, you do according to God: for there is one flesh of Our Lord Jesus Christ, and one cup in the union of his Blood; one altar, as there is one bishop with the presbytery and my fellow servants, the deacons.

St Irenaeus of Lyons, Against Heresies 4, 17, 5 (c. AD 180)
He took that created thing, bread, and gave thanks and said, This is my Body. And the cup likewise, which is part of that creation to which we belong, he confessed to be his Blood, and taught the new oblation of the new covenant, which the Church, receiving from the Apostles, offers to God throughout the world ... concerning which Malachi, among the twelve prophets thus spoke beforehand: From the rising of the sun to the going down, my name is glorified among the gentiles, and in every place incense is offered to my name and a pure sacrifice ... indicating in the plainest manner that in every place sacrifice shall be offered to him, and at that a pure one.

Further examples from the second and third centuries can be given, but it may be more worthwhile to go straight to the fifth century and consider what St Augustine had to say on this topic, since both Galea and the Catholic Church hold him in a mutual high regard. St Augustine saw the sacrifice of the Mass as "the highest and true sacrifice" (*City of God*, Bk 10:20), one that commemorates the sacrifice of Christ on Calvary and one that can be offered on behalf of the dead:

Before the coming of Christ, the flesh and blood of this sacrifice were foreshadowed in the animals slain; in the passion of Christ the types were fulfilled by the true sacrifice; after the ascension of Christ, this sacrifice is commemorated in the sacrament (*Reply to Faustus the Manichean* Bk 6:5).

For the whole Church observes this practice which was handed down by the Fathers that it prays for those who have died in the communion of the Body and Blood of Christ, when they are commemorated in their own place in the Sacrifice itself; and the Sacrifice is offered also in memory of them, on their behalf (*Sermons* 172:2).

Also, St Augustine's own mother, in one of the most beautiful passages contained in the *Confessions* (Bk 9:2), instructed her son to always remember her at the Lord's altar: *"This one request I make of you, that, wherever you be, you remember me at the Lord's altar."* Yes, the great St Augustine (and St Monica) both believed in the Holy Sacrifice, as the Catholic Church had before him and has ever since.

Does it matter that these Fathers and Saints from so long ago held the Catholic Church's view on the Eucharist and the Mass? Yes, it matters greatly. They testify to a continuous tradition over twenty centuries verifying that when Christ said "this is my body ... this is my blood" he meant these words to be understood literally. If Galea is right about the Church being in error about the Eucharist, then the Church got things seriously wrong from the very beginning.

The opinions of two Protestant Church historians should also be noted here. Firstly, Philip Schaff in his book *History of the Christian Church*, gives an overview of the Patristic Eucharistic theology:

> The doctrine of the sacrament of the Eucharist was not a subject of theological controversy and ecclesiastical action till the time of Paschasius Radbert, in the ninth century ... In general, this period, ... was already very strongly inclined toward the doctrine of transubstantiation, and toward the Greek and Roman sacrifice of the mass, which are inseparable in so far as a real sacrifice requires the real presence of the victim.[7]

Secondly, J.N.D. Kelly, in his *Early Christian Doctrines*, states:

> The Eucharist was regarded as the distinctively Christian sacrifice from the closing decade of the first century, if not earlier. Malachi's prediction (1:10f.) that the Lord would reject the Jewish sacrifices and instead would have 'a pure offering' made to him by the Gentiles in every place was early seized upon by Christians as a prophecy of the Eucharist. The *Didache* indeed actually applies the term *thusia*, or sacrifice, and the idea is presupposed by Clement in the parallel he discovers between the Church's ministers and the Old Testament priests and levites ... Ignatius's reference [*Philad.* 4] to 'one altar, just as there is one bishop', reveals that he, too thought in sacrificial terms. Justin speaks [*Dial.* 117:1] of 'all the sacrifices in this name which Jesus appointed to be performed, viz. in the eucharist of the bread

---

7 Philip Schaff, *History of the Christian Church*, Vol. 3, p. 492.

and the cup, and which are celebrated in very place by Christians.' Not only here but elsewhere [*ibid.* 41:3] too, he identifies 'the bread of the eucharist, and the cup likewise of the eucharist', with the sacrifice foretold by Malachi. For Irenaeus (*Heresies* 4:17:5) the Eucharist is 'the new oblation of the new covenant.'[8]

Contrary to the Catholic Church's consistent belief in the Real Presence and the Sacrifice of the Mass over two thousand years, Protestantism has ever been a house divided. In October 1529, Luther and Zwingli met in Marburg, Germany, to resolve their differences concerning the Eucharist. The two leaders failed to reach an agreement. The advent of Calvin only added another division within the ranks. Since the sixteenth century, hundreds of different interpretations of the words "This is my Body" have appeared. How paradoxical that the very gift God gave to the world as a sign of the visible unity of Christians has become the source of so much dissension and division. While lauding Luther and Calvin at any opportunity, Evangelicals nevertheless reject their respective Eucharistic teachings in favour of Zwinglian symbolism. This situation sadly brings to mind the words of St Ignatius quoted in the beginning of this section, *"They who deny the gift of God are perishing in their disputes."*

The development of doctrine concerning 'transubstantiation'

Galea's historical case is brief. Put simply, he asserts that the Catholic Church has not always accepted the "argument" of transubstantiation (p. 41). Rather, it was first put forward as a theory by Paschasius Radbertus in the ninth century, and was only declared to be official Church dogma by the Fourth Lateran Council in 1215. It is difficult to see why Galea thinks this is so significant. Perhaps he wants his readers to believe that because transubstantiation as a theory only emerged in the ninth century belief in the Real Presence is therefore not of Apostolic origin.

What Galea makes no attempt to discuss is the concept of *development of doctrine*. Development of doctrine does not involve the revelation of any new doctrine, but rather a deeper understanding of doctrine "once and for all delivered to the saints." According to Scripture, it is the Holy Spirit who works with the Church to effect development of doctrine:

---

8 J.N.D. Kelly, *Early Christian Doctrines*, 5th ed. rev., Harper & Row, New York, 1978, p. 196.

But the Advocate, the Holy Spirit, whom the Father will send in my name, will teach you everything, and remind you of all that I have said to you (Jn 14:26).

"When the Spirit of truth comes, he will guide you into all the truth; for he will not speak on his own, but will speak whatever he hears, and he will declare to you the things that are to come. He will glorify me, because he will take what is mine and declare it to you" (Jn 16:13-14).

There are a number of doctrines that have 'developed' over the centuries that both Catholics and Protestants agree upon. These include the divinity of Christ (Nicea AD 325), the divinity of the Holy Spirit (Constantinople AD 381) and the two natures of Christ (Chalcedon AD 451), just to name a few. Why should Protestants reject development that aims at getting a better understanding of the Eucharist?

Transubstantiation is simply a term formally accepted by the Church to explain *how* the bread and wine become the Body and Blood of Christ. For centuries it was not considered necessary to think about *how* the change to the Body and Blood of Christ was effected as the doctrine of the Real Presence was so widely believed by Christians both east and west; all that mattered was to believe that a change *had* taken place. However, when scholars began thinking, writing and debating about how the change occurred, it then became necessary for the Church to provide clarification.

The term 'transubstantiation' simply means 'change of substance.' Though it was only formally adopted in the first part of thirteenth century, eastern Fathers as early as the sixth century employed the Greek expression *meta-ousiosis*, or 'change of being', which expresses the same idea. This latter fact proves that transubstantiation is not dependent on or derived from Aristotelian philosophy as Aristotle was unknown to the early Fathers. However, the Church certainly did in later centuries rely upon the Aristotelian distinction between *substance* and *accidents* to explain how transubstantiation works. Is there any problem with this? No. Ever since St Paul's sermon on Mars Hill in Athens (Acts 17:22-31) Christians have utilised pagan philosophy and learning to explain and defend Christianity.

Nevertheless, transubstantiation is but the secondary issue; the primary issue is the Real Presence. The quotes from the Fathers of the Church outlined in the previous section are sufficient to settle beyond doubt that Christians both east and west have believed in the Real Presence from the first century AD onwards.

Miscellaneous issues
The Mass: Idolatrous?

Galea quotes Isaiah 46:3-7 and Psalm 115 in support of the idea that "God does not allow inanimate objects to represent him" (p. 40). Hence, as the Mass turns the eternal Son of God into an object to be worshipped the Catholic Church violates the second commandment. The reality is that Isaiah and the Psalm were concerned not with representing the true God through inanimate objects but with prohibiting the making of idols out of human hands: "hire a goldsmith, and he makes it into a god"; "Their idols are silver and gold, the work of human hands." In any case, it is Christ himself who wills to come to us under the forms of bread and wine as evidenced by John 6:51: "And the bread that I will give is my flesh for the life of the world." This is neither idolatrous nor disrespectful.

Cannibalism

Ironically, the charge of cannibalism (*thyestian feasts*) against Christians was first alleged by pagan Romans who had come into contact with the beliefs of the early Christians concerning the Eucharist. The Protestant Reformation regurgitated this old allegation.

Jesus is not cannibalised through the eating of the Eucharist simply because he is neither killed nor destroyed in the process. Furthermore, Christians do not eat or drink Jesus' flesh and blood as they normally appear but under the simple and palatable forms of bread and wine. Jesus chooses to come to us as a gift under innocuous forms so we can have a communion with him—a communion that unites us to him and nourishes us both spiritually and physically. As eloquently put by St Augustine (*Sermons* 57:7 [Inter AD 391-430]), "The Eucharist is our daily bread. The power belonging to this divine food makes it a bond of union. Its effect is then understood as unity, so that, gathered into his Body and made members of him, we may become what we receive..." It is only those who realise the significance of this gift but without excuse deny it that forfeit eternal life.

Martyrs

Galea quotes the unfortunate case of Andrew Hewet, who was ordered burnt to death for denying that the consecrated host was the actual Body of Christ during the reign of Mary Tudor. Introducing this event, however, only evidences that transubstantiation was a major battle ground between the Catholic Church and Protestants. It certainly does not go to prove that Hewet's convictions were true, or any more true than the convictions held by the 123 priests martyred for trying to keep the original faith of England alive during the Elizabethan persecution; nor is Hewet any more a hero than St Margaret Clitherow who was crushed under the weight of a 700 pound stone while eight months pregnant for having Mass said in her private home.

Conclusion

What more can be said about the priesthood, the Mass, and the Eucharist except to praise Christ for his wonderful gifts? When looked at together, the words of Christ, St Paul, Hebrews, and the Fathers of the Church blend together as a beautiful tapestry to provide a consistent and universal belief in the Eucharist stretching for fifteen centuries before the advent of the Protestant Reformation. Those who hold to Catholic beliefs know that they have certainty about the Eucharist, that theirs is the faith of generations of Christians going back to the Apostles. In contrast, what certainty can the Evangelical have concerning his or her views on the Eucharist as opposed to Catholic belief, or, indeed, the beliefs of other Protestants? In the final analysis, the Evangelical critique of the Church's teachings on the priesthood, Mass, and the Eucharist will always be deficient from the point of view of Scripture, the Church Fathers and history.

4
The Bible and the Church
Daniel Miller[1]

So then, brethren, stand firm and hold to the traditions which you were taught by us, either by word of mouth or by letter (2 Thes. 2:15).

If I am delayed, you may know how one ought to behave in the household of God, which is the church of the living God, the pillar and bulwark of the truth (1 Tim. 3:15).

At the beginning of Chapter 4 in his book Ray Galea correctly points out that before anyone can properly investigate the vital matters that divide Catholics and Protestants one really has to first resolve "some very important questions about authority" (p. 49). In a genuine concern to ensure the integrity of divine revelation, Galea asks three questions that outline the essential parameters of the debate (pp. 49-50):

Is the Bible the only place where God has promised to speak?
What authority should I rely on to determine whether something is from God?
What or who should be allowed to bind my conscience in matters of salvation and morality?

Despite what many may believe, the Catholic Church also shares Galea's concerns.

What should be the relationship between the Bible, Tradition and the Church? Galea answers this question by reiterating the classical Protestant position, namely, that "the final authority in all matters of faith and morals is found *only* in the written word of God" (p. 57), which for him of course is the Bible. Commonly known as *Sola Scriptura*, or "Scripture Alone",

---

[1] Daniel Miller is a lawyer who has worked in private practice, in house for public companies and in the government sector. He has a keen interest in apologetics and is currently a parishioner of Sacred Heart parish in Westmead. He is married to Deanne and currently has two children, Emily and Joseph.

this teaching stridently asserts that the Bible is the "one final authority" (p. 56) that rules, critiques and judges all other human authorities, teachings and traditions. Yes, Galea acknowledges that other authorities have their role to play but "the final and overruling authority belongs to God, as he speaks to us through the Scriptures" (p. 57).

There are various passages in the New Testament that Protestants consistently quote in support of *Sola Scriptura*, for example, Acts 17:11, 1 Cor. 4:6, Eph. 4:11-12, and 2 Tim. 3:16-17. Galea outlines only the last of these four, which reads:

> *from childhood you have been acquainted with the sacred writings which are able to instruct you for salvation through faith in Christ Jesus. All scripture is inspired by God and is profitable for teaching, for reproof, for correction, and for training in righteousness, that the man of God may be complete, equipped for every good work* (2 Tim. 3:16-17).

In defending the view that the Bible is the sole and final authority, Galea proceeds to argue three points (pp. 54, 57-59):

(i) Unwritten traditions possess the dangerous potential to "eventually overwhelm" and "undermine" obedience to God's word (pp. 54 and 57);
(ii) That the Bible itself is both "sufficient" (p. 57) and "clear" (p. 58) for any "humble, God-fearing heart" to be saved and lead a godly life;
(iii) As God has spoken "authoritatively, finally and clearly in the Scriptures" (p. 59) there is no need for the Catholic Church, without any biblical mandate, to insert and give itself power "to authorise teachings and traditions alongside Scripture" (p. 59).

In response to Galea, what is the actual Catholic position concerning the relationship between the Bible, Tradition and the Church?

Tradition

Contrary to opinion held by many Protestants, tradition *per se* is not condemned in Scripture. There are unwritten traditions that are specifically praised and commended to Christians to adhere: "So then, brethren, stand firm and hold to the *traditions which you were taught by us, either by word of mouth* or by letter" (2 Thes. 2:15). St Paul gives this exhortation because oral preaching (παράδοσις = handing down) was the original medium by which the Gospel spread before the New Testament was written (Acts 2:42; Rom. 10:17; 1 Cor. 11:2; 1 Cor. 15:3; 2 Tim. 2:2; 1 Pet. 1:25). We know that St Paul himself received the following words of Christ orally, "It is more blessed to give than to receive" (Acts 20:35), for such words are not recorded in the Gospels. Over time, the Holy Spirit inspired Apostles and Evangelists to pen the original oral Good News in writing, but *nowhere* do these same authors assert that they intended to record the *whole* original oral deposit of faith or to substitute it entirely. In fact, certain verses in the Bible indicate that the authors of Scripture never intended to crystallise all oral Tradition (Jn 20:30; Jn 21:25; 1 Cor. 11:34; 2 Jn 12; 3 Jn 13). Today, as in St Paul's time, the Word of God is one whole comprising both written and oral dimensions.

What was condemned by Christ in Matthew 15:6 (and by St Paul in Col. 2:8) were only those traditions, whether doctrines or practices, *which made God's word and commandments ineffective*. Christ himself observed all the noble traditions of the Jews, such as the Pasch and all the liturgical festivals with their appurtenances, songs and ceremonies. It is the Church, as the indefectible teaching authority established by Christ (Mt 16:19; 28:18-20), which determines what is or is not authentic Apostolic Tradition. Whether we realise it or not, *every* Christian, Protestant or Catholic, follows a particular tradition. Nobody, as Galea admits, reads the Bible in isolation or a vacuum (p. 58). We all bring a particular interpretation and perspective to our understanding and interpretation of divine revelation that is really a tradition. There is a Lutheran tradition, a Calvinist tradition, an Anglican tradition, and so on. Many Protestant converts to Catholicism remark that it is not so much that they had not previously read certain Bible verses in support of the Catholic position; rather they could not previously see the Catholic understanding because they were reading such verses through thick Protestant glasses (i.e., Protestant traditions).

Other verses in Scripture that speak positively of Christian tradition include:

> *Be imitators of me, as I am of Christ. I commend you because you remember me in everything and maintain the traditions even as I have*

delivered them to you" (1 Cor. 11:1-2).

"If any one is disposed to be contentious, we recognise no other practice, nor do the churches of God (1 Cor. 11:16).

"Now we command you, brethren, in the name of our Lord Jesus Christ, that you keep away from any brother who is living in idleness and not in accord with the tradition that you received from us" (2 Thes. 3:6).

Interestingly, Christ himself, as well as some of the Apostles, referred to *unwritten Old Testament tradition*:

(i) Christ says, "the scribes and the Pharisees sit on Moses' seat" (Mt 23:2-3). Nowhere is such a seat mentioned in the Old Testament.

(ii) St Matthew (Mt 2:22-23) refers to the prophecy that the Messiah would be "called a Nazarene." There is no Old Testament record of such a prophecy.

(iii) St Paul (Gal. 3:19) and St Stephen (Acts 7:52-53) refer to the Law being "put into effect through angels." Nowhere is this mentioned in the Old Testament.

(iv) St Paul refers to "Jannes and Jambres" who "opposed Moses" (2 Tim. 3:8-9). Neither of these two men is mentioned in the Old Testament.

(v) St Jude mentions the prophecy of Enoch, saying, "Behold the Lord came with his holy myriads" (Jude 1:14). This prophecy is nowhere to be found in the Old Testament.

(vi) St Jude mentions the struggle between St Michael and the Devil for the body of Moses (Jude 1:9). The only prior written account of such a struggle is contained in the apocryphal work, *The Assumption of Moses.*

(vii) The author of *Hebrews* mentions the Prophet Isaiah being "sawed in two" (11:36). Such a death for the Prophet is mentioned only in the apocryphal work, *The Ascension of Isaiah* 5:1-4).

In summary, by Tradition the Catholic Church means Apostolic Tradition, which ranks equally with the written word to complete divine revelation, not the 'traditions of men.' Tradition supplements the written Word of God; it does not contradict it. Furthermore, Tradition assists the

Church to fully understand and appreciate the whole written Word, and vice versa. Tradition embraces all those truths which have been passed on from age to age either orally, in the writings of the Church Fathers, in the Acts of the Martyrs, in early paintings and inscriptions, in the practices and customs of the Universal Church, and in the definitions of Councils and Popes. It is, therefore, not a question of Scripture *vs.* Tradition but rather Scripture *and* Tradition.

The Bible: its basis, sufficiency and clarity

After arguing that all Tradition is unreliable, Galea goes on to espouse his confidence in "God's own inspired word", the Bible, and the two resulting premises that he believes flow from this, namely that the Bible is sufficient (p. 57) and is clear for every believer (p. 58). However, what grounds, if any, exist for such confidence?

(i) How do we know that the Bible is the inspired Word of God?

The Bible is a collection of books. It did not simply fall from the sky. There were many writings in the early Church that were used by early Christians that are not part of the Bible now. How does Galea know for certain that the collection of writings he considers the Bible contains only divinely inspired writings?

Essentially, this is a question that touches simultaneously on two important controversies—the Canon of the Bible and *Sola Scriptura*. If *Sola Scriptura* as a doctrine is to be consistent then Scripture itself should be the sole authority to clearly tell Christians what writings/books should be part of the Bible. However, the Bible itself gives no answer to this question, either in the Old or New Testaments. This should leave all sincere Christians asking the question, where does the Table of Contents found in the front of every Bible come from? In reality, the Table of Contents is *extra-Biblical.* As one convert from Protestantism, James Akin, states:

> The Protestant apologist is in a fix. In order to use sola scriptura he is going to have to identify what the scriptures are, and since he is unable to do this from scripture alone, he is going to have to appeal to things outside of scripture to make his case, meaning that in every act of doing this he undermines his case. There is no way to escape

the canon of tradition.²

This then begs two further questions: Who gave us the Table of Contents and what authority did they have to determine it?

The Holy Spirit did not promise a revelation to any individual Christian concerning the authentic canon. Anglican Church historian, J.N.D. Kelly offers one possible solution as to how canonical Scripture came together and the criteria used to determine it:

> Unless a book could be shown to come from the pen of an apostle, or at least to have the authority of an apostle behind it, it was peremptorily rejected, however edifying or popular with the faithful it might be.³

But how could early Christians know whether a book was Apostolic? Certainly not simply by a book's claim to be so, since the Gospels were anonymous and there were numerous spurious gospels and epistles in circulation (for example, the Gospel of Thomas, the Secret Gospel of Mark, the Gospel of the Hebrews, the Acts of Peter, the Acts of John, etc.). Protestant Scripture scholar F. F. Bruce writes that:

> [The early Fathers] had recourse to the criterion of orthodoxy ... This appeal to the testimony of the churches of apostolic foundation was developed especially by Irenaeus ... When previously unknown Gospels or Acts began to circulate ... the most important question to ask about any one of them was: What does it teach about the person and work of Christ? Does it maintain the apostolic witness to him ...?⁴

In other words, a book was reckoned as Apostolic only if its contents were consistent with the teachings of the Apostles (i.e., Apostolic παράδοσις, or tradition) as handed on *by the Church*. Who, however, was to make such a determination? To assert that it was the Holy Spirit alone without men who determined such is neither historical nor correct. The Holy Spirit did do all the work of inspiration and collection but with and through men who were leaders and pillars of the Church divinely founded, that is, the infallible voice of St Peter and the Apostles and their

---
2 James Akin, *The Two Canons: Scripture and Tradition*, Website 1/18/99, p. 6.
3 J.N.D. Kelly, *Early Christian Doctrines*, 5th ed. rev., Harper & Row, New York, 1978, p. 60.
4 F.F. Bruce, *The Canon of Scripture*, Inter-Varsity press, 1954, p. 260.

successors. Thus came the decrees of Popes St Damasus (AD 382) and St Innocent I (AD 405), and the Councils of Hippo (AD 393) and Carthage (AD 397), which accepted as canonical the Greek Septuagint and all the books of the New Testament. In these pronouncements the Catholic has the way to certainty. Without such a voice the Protestant has only a fallible collection of infallible books.

However, Galea would not be comfortable with this result because as a Protestant he does not believe that the Catholic Church has any legitimate divine authority. Though Galea does not mention it himself, the traditional Protestant position to avoid a 'Catholic' conclusion is to argue that the Council of Carthage, etc., simply "rubber stamped" or formalised a canon that had already been determined by the 'people of God' under the influence of the Holy Spirit. This is both vague and a-historical. If such were really so then these councils would never have been convoked in the first place. The argument is settled by the great St Augustine of Hippo, who in AD 397 said:

> If you should find someone who does not yet believe in the Gospel, what would you answer him when he says: 'I do not believe?' Indeed, I would not believe in the Gospel myself if the authority of the Catholic Church did not influence me to do so (*Against the Letter of Mani* 5, 6).

(ii) The Bible: sufficient?

Now, is the Bible sufficient? On p. 57 Galea makes the following conclusions before quoting 2 Tim. 3:15-17 in support:

the final authority in all matters of faith and morals is found only in the written word of God.

the Bible contains all we need to be saved and to live a godly life.

However, is 2 Tim. 3:15-17 really a proof-text for Sola Scriptura? Reading the verse we find no words such as "alone" or "only" used with respect to Scripture. No one who claims to be Christian, least of all the Catholic Church, denies that Scripture is "inspired" and "profitable" to perfect a "man of God." But it is certainly different to assert that Scripture is "sufficient." "Sufficient" is not the word used by St Paul in 2 Tim. 3:15-17. He uses the Greek word ophelimos (ὠφέλιμος) which translates as "useful" or "profitable." Certain Protestants might argue that "profitable" means "sufficient." If so, then they would run into difficulties with Titus 3:8 which says, "The saying is sure. I desire you to insist on these things, so that those who have believed in God may be careful to apply themselves to good deeds; these are excellent and profitable (ophelimos) to men." Would any Protestant assert from this verse that good works are sufficient to get to heaven, thus rendering faith in Christ unnecessary? Similarly, St Paul in his letter to the Ephesians says that, "his gifts were that some should be apostles, some prophets, some evangelists, some pastors and teachers, to equip the saints for the work of ministry, for building up the body of Christ" (4:11-12). In others words, is the perfecting of the saints to be done through the leaders of the Church alone without the aid of Scripture?

Cardinal John Henry Newman, another convert to Catholicism from the Anglican Church, certainly saw the Protestant fallacy of employing 2 Tim. 3:16-17 in support of *Sola Scriptura*:

> It is quite evident that this passage furnishes no argument whatever that the Sacred Scripture, without Tradition, is the sole rule of faith; for, although Sacred Scripture is profitable for these four ends, still it is not said to be sufficient. The Apostle requires the aid of Tradition (2 Th. 2:14). Moreover, the Apostle here refers to the Scriptures which Timothy was taught in his infancy [i.e., the Old Testament].[5]

In any case, Scripture is clear that "the Word of God" is not simply something written, but includes what the early Christians *heard* from the Apostles (e.g., Acts 4:31). Stephen K. Ray, another convert from Evangelical Christianity, makes the following interesting point:

> As an Evangelical, when I read the phrase 'word of God' I would automatically plug in the word 'Bible'; this, however, is not at all the meaning usually intended in the Bible itself. Roughly nine out of ten times, 'word of God' is referring to the spoken word, not the written word (e.g., 1 Thes. 2:13). The *spoken* words, the oral tradition, were *also* the very 'words of God.'[6]

Finally, arguments against *Sola Scriptura* also make sense from a practical point of view. James Akin, the convert to Catholicism referred

---

5 John Henry Newman, *Inspiration in its Relation to Revelation*, 1884.
6 Stephen K. Ray, *Crossing the Tiber*, Ignatius Press, 1997 Ed., p. 30.

to earlier, explains this well.[7] First, for *Sola Scriptura* 'to work' every Christian in every age would need to have ready access to a copy of the Bible, especially for personal or group study. However, this was completely impossible until the invention of the printing press, which only occurred in 1456. Even after that date, printing remained rare and expensive. What did the average poor Christian do in the centuries before 1456 and all those who for centuries afterwards could not afford a Bible? Secondly, *Sola Scriptura* also assumes universal literacy. Not only literacy in a general sense, but a well developed sense of literacy, for as Galea says near the end of his book, one must not "take (his) word for it" but "Take up God's word and see for yourself" (p. 104). In other words, a Christian must not only be able to read but also possess the skill to understand difficult texts and evaluate different interpretations. This assumption is certainly not true of all Christians in history, nor even today.

(iii) Is the Bible sufficiently clear?

Galea's next argument in defence of *Sola Scriptura* is that the Bible is sufficiently clear. In other words, its message of salvation is clear and can be understood by humble God-fearing Christians without the need for interpretation "by the experts in Rome" (p. 58). At the same time, Galea concedes that "some parts of the Bible are obviously more difficult to understand than others" and that we should not always read the Bible "in glorious isolation, ignoring the wisdom and insights of other Christians, including the great saints of the past" (p. 58).

Galea admits that his position is that of "the Reformers (who) wanted to insist on the clarity of Scripture" (p. 57). Yet, these same 'reformers' privately admitted the fallacy of such a doctrine. Luther observed that because of private interpretation of Scripture …

> There are almost as many sects and beliefs as there are heads; this one will not admit Baptism; that one rejects the Sacrament of the altar; another places another world between the present one and the day of judgment; some teach that Jesus Christ is not God. There is not an individual, however clownish he may be, who does not claim to be inspired by the Holy Ghost, and who does not put forth as

---

[7] James Akin, *The Practical Problems of Sola Scriptura*, www.cin.org/users/james/files/practicl.htm

prophecies his ravings and dreams.[8]

Writing to Melanchton, Calvin had to concede,

> It is indeed important that posterity should not know of our differences; for it is indescribably ridiculous that we, who are in opposition to the whole world, should be, at the very beginning of the Reformation, at issue among ourselves.[9]

Furthermore, there are many Lutheran and Calvinist Christians who today would not agree with their founding fathers on a number of important points of belief. For example, most Protestants reject the Catholic belief in the perpetual virginity of Mary, citing principally Mt 1:25 in support. Galea does this himself on p. 86. However, the founders of Protestantism strictly defended the Catholic teaching. Martin Luther said:

> It is an article of faith that Mary is Mother of the Lord and still a virgin ... Christ, we believe, came forth from a womb left perfectly intact.[10]

> I am inclined to agree with those who declare that 'brothers' really mean cousins here, for Holy Writ and the Jews always call cousins brothers.[11]

Ulrich Zwingli, another major Protestant leader (1484-1531), even more adamantly stated:

> I firmly believe that Mary, according to the words of the gospel, as a pure Virgin brought forth for us the Son of God and in childbirth and after childbirth forever remained a pure, intact Virgin.[12]

Finally, John Calvin on Matthew 1:25 wrote:

> There have been certain folk who have wished to suggest from this passage (Matthew 1:25) that the Virgin Mary had other children than the Son of God, and that Joseph then dwelt with her later; but what folly this is! For the gospel writer did not wish to record

---

8 Cited by Leslie Rumble MSC, *Bible Quizzes to a Street Preacher*, Rockford, Ill.: TAN Books and Publishers, 1976, p. 22.
9 Cited by Patrick F. O'Hare, *The Facts About Luther*, rev. ed., Rockford, Ill.: TAN Books and Publishers, 1987, p. 293.
10 Weimer, *The Works of Luther*, Pelikan, Concordia, vol. 11, pp. 319-320.
11 Weimer, *The Works of Luther*, Pelikan, Concordia, vol. 22-23, pp. 214-215.
12 *Zwingli Opera, Corpus Reformatorum*, Berlin, 1905, in Evang. Luc., vol. 1, p. 424.

what happened afterwards; he simply wished to make clear Joseph's obedience and to show also that Joseph had been well and truly assured that it was God who had sent His angel to Mary. He had therefore never dwelt with her nor had he shared her company.[13]

Reading all this, as a Catholic I have to ask, "Who has the correct interpretation of Matthew 1:25?" On one side there is the Catholic Church, Luther, Zwingli, and Calvin; on the other there are modern-day Protestants, including Galea and all other Evangelical Anglicans. As for the next question, "Which Protestant privately reading Scripture has the correct interpretation of Matthew 1:25: Luther, Zwingli, Calvin or modern-day Evangelicals?" That is anyone's guess! From such an example we can understand what St Peter was worried about when he warned, "no prophecy of scripture is a matter of one's own interpretation" (2 Pet. 1:20).

St Peter also warned that the "ignorant and unstable" would "twist" the Scriptures "to their own destruction" (2 Pet. 3:16). One bitter fruit of *Sola Scriptura* and private interpretation of the Bible has been the spawning of over 35,000 different Protestant denominations all claiming to be "Bible-believing", yet agreeing on little more than their anti-Catholic tenets. The response will come that, despite the differences in interpretation and belief among Protestants, there is nevertheless agreement on the 'essentials.' Such a claim begs two important questions: Just what are the 'essentials'?; and who decides whether a disputed doctrine/belief is an 'essential' or not? The reality is that among the sincere advocates of *Sola Scriptura* and private interpretation there is no universal agreement on any number of 'essentials', for example, the Trinity, the divinity of Christ, the nature of the Eucharist, Church government (hierarchical or congregational), infant/adult baptism, baptismal regeneration, the number of sacraments, predestination, the necessity of works, women in ministry, the Rapture, divorce and remarriage, polygamy, same-sex relationships, masturbation, artificial contraception, in-vitro fertilisation, abortion, etc., etc. Furthermore, no amount of private study allegedly under the guidance of the Holy Spirit will ever bridge these disagreements.

Another reason why the Bible can never always be clear to the average reader arises from the Greek text of the New Testament (Nestle-Aland *Novum Testamentum Graece* (Stuttgart: Deutsche Bibelstiftung, 1979). An

---

13 Calvin, *Sermon on Matthew 1:22-25*, 1562.

exhaustive investigation of all ancient manuscripts, codices and minuscules reveals that of the 7,948 verses from Matthew to Revelation 6,176 contain textual variants. That equals 78% of the whole New Testament. These variations range from simple spelling mistakes, changes in tense, missing words, or whole sentences that are either missing or significantly different. How can the average reader in all these instances know what is the original uncorrupted text, let alone its meaning? Tradition and the Church working together are the only way out of this dilemma.

The bottom line is that an individual Christian will not always find the Bible sufficiently clear to guide him/her in the path to salvation. A person who builds his faith on private interpretation is akin to the fool in Matthew 7:24-27 who built his house on the grains of sand. As grains of sand tend to shift to the downfall of the house, so too do individual minds continually change the interpretation of Scripture to the downfall of faith. On the contrary, the wise man built his house on rock (*kepha*); likewise does the faithful Christian build his faith on St Peter (*Kepha*) and his successors. We will not always understand what we are reading; in such times we need someone to guide us with certainty (Acts 8:30-31). That brings us to the next part of the debate.

Bringing it all together—the Church

On p. 58 of his book Galea asks the following question: "if God had spoken authoritatively, finally and clearly in the Scriptures, why insert the Church into the process? Galea's question would be a valid one if the Church were a man-made institution that was established sometime after Christ. But it would be an altogether different scenario if the Church was a divine institution founded by Christ and endowed with power and authority to teach, govern and sanctify in his name. Does the Bible have anything to say about an authoritative Church? The following would say, *Yes!*:

(i) The Lord Jesus Christ established an authoritative Church of is own: "and on this rock I will build my Church" (Mt 16:18);

(ii) As founder of the Church, Christ is also its head: "Christ is the head of the church, his body" (Eph. 5:23);

(ii) The Church Christ founded is visible: "A city built on a hill cannot be hid" (Mt 5:14);

(iii) Christ established his Church with an hierarchical authority to govern it: "Truly, I say to you, whatever you bind on earth shall be bound in heaven, and whatever you loose on earth shall be loosed in heaven" (Mt 18:17-18). This hierarchical authority is appointed by the Holy Spirit (Acts 20:28). Cf. 2 Cor. 10:8; 2 Cor. 13:10; 1 Thes. 4:2; 2 Thes. 3:14; Acts 15:24.

(iv) Christ invested his Church with his own mission: "Jesus said to them again, 'Peace be with you. As the Father has sent me, even so I send you'" (Jn 20:21);

(v) Christ gave his Church the power to sanctify the faithful: "I chose you and appointed you that you should go and bear fruit and that your fruit should abide" (Jn 15:16);

(vi) Christ gave authority to his Church to baptise and teach all nations: "Go therefore and make disciples of all nations, baptising them in the name of the Father and of the Son and of the Holy Spirit, teaching them to observe all that I have commanded you; and lo, I am with you always, to the close of the age" (Mt 28:20);

(vii) Christ bestowed the Holy Spirit on his Church to forgive sins: "And when he had said this, he breathed on them, and said to them, 'Receive the Holy Spirit. If you forgive the sins of any, they are forgiven; if you retain the sins of any, they are retained'" (Jn 20:23);

(viii) Christ appointed St Peter as the visible head of his Church on earth: "You are Peter, and on this rock I will build my church" (Mt 16:18); "I will give you the keys of the kingdom of heaven, and whatever you bind on earth will be bound in heaven, and whatever you loose on earth will be loosed in heaven" (Mt 16:18-19);

(ix) St Peter and the Apostles, as rulers of the Church on earth, are to be obeyed: "Obey your leaders and submit to them, for they are keeping watch over your souls, as men who will have to give account" (Heb. 13:17); cf. 1 Thes. 5:12-13;

(x) To obey St Peter and the Apostles, and logically their successors, is to obey Christ: "Truly, truly, I say to you, he who receives any one whom I send receives me; and he who receives me receives him who sent me" (Jn 13:20);

(xi) The power and authority given to the Apostles was intended to be handed down to subsequent generations through the laying of hands: "and what you have heard from me before many witnesses entrust to faithful men who will be able to teach others also" (2 Tim. 2:2). Cf. Acts 13:2; 1 Tim. 4:14; Tit. 5-10;

(xii) Those wishing to belong to Christ's Church are required to be formally baptised in the name of the Trinity: Mt 28:19; cf. Mk 16:16;

(xiii) There are consequences for those who willingly refuse to listen to the voice of Christ's Church "if he refuses to listen even to the church, let him be to you as a Gentile and a tax collector" (Mt 18:17); "He who hears you hears me, and he who rejects you rejects me" (Lk 10:16). Cf. 1 Thes. 5:12-13;

(xiv) Christ promised the Holy Spirit to guide and protect his Church for all time: "And I will ask the Father, and he will give you another Advocate, to be with you forever" (Jn 14:16);

(xv) It is Christ's Church which is the bulwark of Christian truth: "if I am delayed, you may know how one ought to behave in the household of God, which is the church of the living God, the pillar and bulwark of the truth" (1 Tim. 3:15);

(xvi) Christ promised that he would always be with his Church and that it would survive until the end of time: "the gates of hades will not prevail against it" (Mt 16:18); "And remember, I am with you always, to the end of the age" (Mt 28:20).

Acts 15 provides us with a biblical/historical example of the authoritative Church at work. The Council of Jerusalem took place about AD 49 or 50. In the first phase of the Council of Jerusalem there was much discussion and debate over the entry of Gentiles into the Church: "But some believers who belonged to the party of the Pharisees rose up, and said, 'It is necessary to circumcise them, and to charge them to keep the law of Moses'" (vv. 6-7). In the second phase St Peter got up and spoke authoritatively on the issue: "And God who knows the heart bore witness to them, giving them the Holy Spirit just as he did to us; and he made no distinction between us and them, but cleansed their hearts by faith" (vv. 8-9). Then there was silence as the multitude contemplated St Peter's words. In the third phase Sts Paul and Barnabas spoke, relating ... "what signs and wonders God had done through them among the Gentiles" (v. 12). Next, St James asked to be heard and echoed what St Peter had first said: "Therefore my judgment is that we should not trouble those of the Gentiles who turn to God, but should write to them to abstain from the pollutions of idols and from unchastity and from what is strangled and from blood" (vv. 19-20).

The Council of Jerusalem displayed features later ecumenical councils in the history of the Church would emulate: the rulers of the whole Church attended the Council; there was an assessment of the issues in light of Tradition (Acts 15:7-9) and some references to Scripture (St James quotes the prophet Amos); it promulgated decisions under the guidance of the Holy Spirit relating to faith and morals binding on all Christians ("For it seemed good to the Holy Spirit and to us..." [Acts 15:28]); and its decisions were recorded in written form and proclaimed universally as the final word on the matter: "As they went on their way through the cities, they delivered to them for observance the decisions which had been reached by the apostles and elders who were at Jerusalem" (Acts 16:4).

In the face of the above one would have to concede that Christ certainly intended to establish an authoritative Church that would exist in all ages until the end of time. However, does it necessarily follow that that Church today is the Church of Rome?

The true Church of Christ is identifiable by certain 'marks.' To qualify as a mark the means of identification must possess two aspects: (i) it must be an outwardly visible sign objectively evident to everyone, including non-Christians; (ii) it must be an essential characteristic without which the Church would not be the Church of Christ.

According to the Presbyterian minister Loraine Boettner:

The marks of a true church are:
1. The true preaching of the Word of God.
2. The right administration of the sacraments. And,
3. The faithful exercise of discipline.[14]

One obvious difficulty with Boettner's marks is that they do not include a test to determine whether the church in question was actually founded by Christ. Furthermore, his criteria (based on Calvin's) do not aim to discover "the true Church" but "a true church." Any man-made institution could therefore claim to be a true church so long as it fulfils the three above outlined points. We would soon end up with the absurd situation of having many true churches each considering themselves to be teaching the truth concerning the word of God, the sacraments and discipline, while

---

14 Loraine Boettner, *Roman Catholicism*, Presbyterian and Reformed Publishing Co. (Phillipsburg, NJ), 1962, p. 20.

having no unity of belief, government or discipline between themselves. This absurd situation is what some hope to replace the Catholic Church with.

The real marks of the true Church, which are visible and essential, number four. They are: *one, holy, catholic and apostolic*. These marks are found in Scripture, are based on reason and can be defended by it.

One

> *I will build my Church* (Mt 16:18).

The true Church is founded and built by Christ. Christ founded one Church, not many. Protestantism is not one united body in doctrine and discipline, but a series of disparate organisations antagonistic not only to Catholicism but also often to each other.

> *One flock, one shepherd* (Jn 10:16).

The central authority of the Pope of Rome has kept the Catholic Church united in doctrine and discipline since the days of the Roman Empire. Protestantism continues to splinter with the advent of each new self-appointed 'prophet' or minister who claims to hold the true meaning of Scripture.

Holy

> *And for their sakes I sanctify myself, so that they also may be sanctified in truth* (Jn 17:19).

The true Church will be holy in her founder, teachings and worship. There is no guarantee that all its members will practise what she preaches as is gathered from Our Lord's images of the sower of the seed (Mt 13:18-23), the net enclosing the fish (Mt 13:47-52), and the sheep and the goats (Mt 25:31-46). The survival of the Catholic Church—despite the examples of half a dozen bad Popes (out of 265), and other scandals—only reinforces the fact that the holiness of the Church derives from Christ and him alone. In any case, Protestantism is far from free when it comes to scandal, and none of its founders can claim to match the holiness of any Catholic saint, let alone Christ himself.

Catholic

Go therefore and make disciples of all nations (Mt 28:19).

Remaining essentially one and the same, the Church adapts to all times, places and people. No nation or race is excluded from her fold, no language from proclaiming her Gospel. Christ opened his arms on the Cross for all peoples and nations, hence the true Church must be universal, not simply a national church based on race, or subject to a particular king or parliament.

Apostolic

The true Church will trace its history, episcopal succession and doctrine right back to the Apostles themselves: "I am with you always" (Mt 28:20). It was not established in 1517, 1534, 1540, in the nineteenth century, or last week in California. It must have existed since the Apostles, exist now, and continue until the end of the world.

Only the Catholic Church can show herself to be One, Holy, Catholic and Apostolic.

Finally?

On pp. 58-59 of his book Galea asserts that God has "spoken authoritatively, *finally* and clearly in the Scriptures." By his use of the word "finally" Galea implies that God has spoken for the last time through the Scriptures and so there is no other authoritative teaching forthcoming or even possible after AD 100. Therefore, what need do Christians have for a teaching Church?

Formally, there is a great need. Since the first century AD there have been many heresies, many controversies that have arisen concerning faith and morals. More often than not Scripture verses were cited by either side in support of their respective arguments (as is the case still today). Such was the case in the 4th century with the Arian heresy and its denial of the divinity of Christ. From Scripture alone the Arian controversy could not be definitively resolved, especially as the Arians based their arguments solely on Scripture. In many other cases new developments have given rise to controversies that were completely unforseen by the Gospel writers. For example, nuclear weapons use, the contraceptive pill, embryonic stem cell research, therapeutic cloning, surrogacy, in-vitro fertilisation, just to name a few. Many Bible-believing Christians have no problem with one or more of these practices, while others do have objections. The Bible provides no obvious or certain answer as to their legitimacy. On the other hand, the Bible contains much 'material' from which clear-cut answers can be deduced, but this material is not always clearly evident and is open to being ignored or misinterpreted by private individuals. Such material often needs to be 'teased out', translated, interpreted and pasted together. This is where an authoritative teaching Church guided by the Holy Spirit is absolutely necessary if one desires a once and for all definitive decision rather than an academic opinion.

As a final point, Galea makes another accusation that the Catholic Church believes herself to be "the standard of truth and there is no authority to which she must submit and by which she must be judged" (p. 53). However, as the *Catechism of the Catholic Church* states, the Church is not superior to the Bible, but its servant (CCC #86). A servant always plays a subservient role to his/her Lord. In teaching and guarding the Gospel the Catholic Church only interprets, defines, or declares what was delivered once and for all by Christ to the Apostles; she does not engage in the creation of new teaching. Essentially, this is a negative, or reactive role. This does not involve the Catholic Church "taking the focus off the Bible's teaching and on to the Church's teaching and traditions" (p. 59), but rather setting the correct parameters and boundaries so that the faithful can be guaranteed a correct understanding of Christ's teachings. After all, it is the Church established by Christ, and no other, that is "the pillar and bulwark of the truth" (1 Tim. 3:15).

Conclusion

In conclusion, it can be stated unequivocally that *Sola Scriptura* is not revealed by God, least of all in the Scriptures. It is itself a human tradition, one that, sadly, damages the complete Word of God by divorcing the oral from the written Word, discarding the oral Apostolic tradition, and taking the remaining written Word out of the safe interpretative hands of the one divine teaching authority established by Christ, that authority which he promised to sustain till the end of the world (Mt 28:20).

5

The Way of Salvation

Thomas Waugh[1]

Introduction

In this chapter Ray Galea examines the differences between Catholics and Protestants concerning the issue of salvation—the most important issue that any person must address in his or her life. By way of introduction, Galea makes specific reference to the "Day of the Lord", or Judgement Day, when, in his words "(w)e will be saved or damned" (p. 61). Thereafter, Galea asks the following questions: "How will (God) decide whether I am in or out? What is the way of salvation?" (*ibid.*) Galea, quite correctly, points out that "Protestant theology and Catholicism give very different answers to this most basic of questions" (*ibid.*). The task I have set for myself in writing this chapter is to show how and why the Catholic 'way of salvation' is not only more reflective of the Bible than the Protestant way (or ways) but is entirely one and the same as the Biblical 'way of salvation.' I will also highlight the various instances in which Galea does not correctly represent the Catholic position and provide the necessary rectification.

Justification and Salvation

In the next part of his chapter, Galea discusses the relationship between the important notions of *justification* and *salvation*. From the Catholic perspective, while these two concepts are connected they have distinct definitions. According to the Council of Trent "justification" is:

> ... a translation, from that state wherein man is born a child of the
> first Adam, to the state of grace, and of the adoption of the sons of

---

[1] Thomas Waugh and his wife are both converts from Anglicanism of the Evangelical and High Church branches respectively. Together with their children they currently reside in the northern suburbs of Sydney. Thomas spent 2009 as Convener of the Catholic Chaplaincy in the University of Sydney and is currently the Director of the Catholic Adult Education Centre.

God, through the second Adam, Jesus Christ, our Saviour.[2]

In most probability, this is *not* a definition with which Galea or any other Protestant Christian would have difficulties. Both Catholics and Protestants agree that man is born without the requisite righteousness to enable him to dwell with God forever and that Jesus Christ provides the only means by which we are transferred from a state of unrighteousness to a state of righteousness involving being reborn as sons of God (i.e., justification). However, though both Catholics and Protestants agree that salvation is directly tied to justification, they would disagree about whether justification includes sanctification. In Catholic language, justification includes sanctification, which in turn equals being in a 'state of grace.' If one dies in a state of grace one is destined to be with God forever, and hence saved. In Catholic theology, sanctification involves an *increase of righteousness or holiness,* which usually is a process spanning one's whole life. In contrast, Galea believes that justification and sanctification are entirely separate events, processes or issues.

With the above in mind, one would well be justified (pardon the pun) in wondering what the actual differences between the Catholic and Protestant views are. It is to this enquiry that Galea attempts to bring some clarity on p. 62:

> Put simply, the Catholic view of justification is a process, beginning with baptism and continuing throughout our lives, by which God acts to forgive us and then with our cooperation change us by his Spirit to become more righteous and acceptable to himself. He makes us righteous, infusing justice and righteousness into us over time, with our own efforts and good works, and the sacraments of the church playing key roles in how this happens. Thus, when we arrive at Judgement Day, the basis upon which God will judge us is in part what *Christ did on our behalf to take away our sins but also whether we have become sufficiently righteousness in our own character to be worthy of salvation* ... By contrast, Protestants point to what the Bible *says very clearly in numerous places about justification–that justification is an event not a process.* It's a once-off declaration by God that the sinner is cleared of all guilt, and is thus completely blameless and righteous in his sight ... when we put our faith in

---

[2] Council of Trent, Chapter IV, Sixth Session.

Christ" (emphasis added).

Does Galea represent the Catholic position accurately? The short answer is an emphatic *No!* Firstly, Galea asserts that the Catholic Church teaches that God infuses justice and righteousness into us over time, *"with our own efforts and good works."* However, what about mentioning the Catholic teaching that God infuses justice and righteousness *in one instant* with baptism to achieve *initial* justification? Subsequent to this initial and instantaneous justification the faithful Catholic will through their *"own efforts"* engage in meritorious *"good works"* but, again, Galea does not mention that these "efforts and works" are themselves the product of God's (prevenient or actual) grace which is made available *solely* through the merits of Christ's death and resurrection *and nothing else*. To quote the great St Augustine, *"Only grace works every one of our good merits in us, and God, when he crowns our merits, crowns nothing other than his own gifts"* (Epistle 194:5:19). The conclusion that could be drawn from Galea's incomplete exposition of Catholic teaching is that Catholics are Pelagians or semi-Pelagians who believe that they can attain salvation entirely through their own efforts. Nothing could be further from the truth.

Secondly, does the Catholic Church really teach that God will judge us on the basis of whether we have become *"sufficiently righteous"* through our own efforts separate from Christ's Passion? To the contrary, the Church teaches that it is *solely on account of Christ's passion* that we can be reborn (justified) *through faith and baptism* thereby entering into relationship with God and thereby achieving salvation–period. To quote the Catholic Apologist and convert to Catholicism, James Akin:

> There is no magical level of works one needs to achieve in order to go to heaven. One is saved the moment one is initially justified. The only things one then does is good works because one loves God (the only kind which receive rewards) and not choose to cast out God's grace by mortal sin.[3]

The Catholic Church during the Council of Trent stated as much when speaking on the effects of baptism:

> In those who are born again God hates nothing, because there is no condemnation to those who are truly buried together with Christ by

---

[3] *Righteousness and Merit* www.cin.org/users/james/files/righteou.htm

baptism unto death ... but, putting off the old man and putting on the new one who is created according to God, are made innocent, immaculate, pure, guiltless and beloved of God, heirs indeed of God, joint heirs with Christ; so that there is nothing whatever to hinder their entrance into heaven (Fifth Session, Fifth Decree).

... while the efficient cause is a merciful God who washes and sanctifies gratuitously, signing, and anointing with the holy Spirit of promise, who is the pledge of our inheritance; but the meritorious cause is his most beloved only-begotten, our Lord Jesus Christ, who, when we were enemies, for the exceeding charity wherewith he loved us, merited justification for us by his most holy Passion on the wood of the cross, and made satisfaction for us unto God the Father (Chapter VII, Sixth Session).

The above should be sufficient to dispel the assertion that Catholics are required to make themselves *"sufficiently righteous"* in order to attain salvation. Nevertheless, Galea, as we shall see, would still disagree with the assertions that (i) through baptism we are born again (ii) we are actually made righteous when justified and not simply declared righteous and (iii) that we can forfeit our salvation should we subsequently turn our back on God. We will now address these three matters in further detail.

Baptism—necessary for Justification and Salvation?

The short answer to this question is *Yes!* Baptism in the name of the Father and of the Son and of the Holy Spirit is necessary for justification and salvation because:

(i) Christ commanded it and all Christians are obliged to obey the Lord in all things for salvation;
(ii) Baptism washes away sins, Original and actual;
(iii) Baptism infuses the Holy Spirit into the soul of the new Christian.

The following Scriptures vindicate belief in these three points:

Go therefore and make disciples of all nations, baptising them in the name of the Father and of the Son and of the Holy Spirit (Mt 28:19).

He who believes and is baptised will be saved; but he who does not believe will be condemned (Mk 16:16).

Jesus answered, 'Truly, truly, I say to you, unless one is born of water and the Spirit, he cannot enter the kingdom of God' (Jn 3:5).

And Peter said to them, 'Repent, and be baptised every one of you in the name of Jesus Christ for the forgiveness of your sins; and you shall receive the gift of the Holy Spirit' (Acts 2:38).

And now why do you wait? Rise and be baptised, and wash away your sins, calling on his name (Acts 22:16).

There is one body and one Spirit, just as you were called to the one hope that belongs to your call, one Lord, one faith, one baptism (Eph. 4:4-5).

Husbands, love your wives, as Christ loved the church and gave himself up for her, that he might sanctify her, having cleansed her by the washing of water with the word (Eph. 5:25-26).

let us draw near with a true heart in full assurance of faith, with our hearts sprinkled clean from an evil conscience and our bodies washed with pure water (Heb. 10:22).

Baptism, which corresponds to this, now saves you, not as a removal of dirt from the body but as an appeal to God for a clear conscience, through the resurrection of Jesus Christ"(1 Pet. 3:21).

The necessity of water baptism, however, does not exclude the efficacy of substitutes such as *Baptism of Desire* and *Baptism of Blood*. A person has a baptism of desire when he or she has perfect contrition for their sins and desires to do whatever is necessary for salvation. Baptism of desire resembles sacramental Baptism in producing sanctifying grace in the soul and forgiving original sin and serious actual sin. This belief is proved from the following words of Christ: "he who loves me will be loved by my Father, and I will love him" (Jn 14:21); "her sins, which are many, are forgiven, for she loved much" (Lk 7:47); "Truly I tell you, today you will be with me in Paradise" (Lk 23:43).

A person has a baptism of blood when he or she willingly dies as a martyr. Christ has promised salvation to those who give their lives for him: "he who loses his life for my sake will find it" (Mt 10:39); "every one who acknowledges me before men, I also will acknowledge before my Father who is in heaven" (Mt 10:32).

Justification—a once-off declaration by God?

We now turn to treat in detail the issue of whether in justification one is actually made righteous by God or whether justification is simply a once-off declaration by God that the sinner is now completely blameless and righteous in his sight. Is it true, as Galea asserts, that the Scriptures indicate "very clearly that justification is an event not a process"?

In the face of Protestant objections the Catholic Church has consistently maintained that:

> ... justification is not only the remission of sins, but also the sanctification and renewal of the inner man.[4]

The Protestant Reformers conceived of justification in *forensic terms*. At the end of his or her life, the individual Christian comes before God in his role as Judge. Due to his/her fallen state this Christian is in breach of the laws of God and is therefore sentenced to condemnation. However, according to *forensic justification* God has provided a substitute:

> ... who will stand in place of the accused criminal? The substitute is Christ. Christ stands before the bar of God's justice in place of the sinner and takes the full wrath of God for the latter's crimes. Prior to taking the punishment for the sinner, Christ shows the judge by his perfect obedience to the law that he himself is not a criminal ... this righteousness of Christ is "imputed" to the sinner, that is, the righteousness is transferred or credited to the sinner so that God's scrutiny as judge is directed towards the transferred righteousness, not the sinner himself. Having the perfect righteousness of Christ given to him, the accused criminal, though still a sinner within his nature, can be set free from the court of law. Once freed, the justification process is over.[5]

The means by which the righteousness of Christ is applied or "imputed" to the individual is *through faith alone*. As a corollary, Protestants advocate the doctrine of penal atonement. Just as the righteousness of Christ is imputed to the sinner, the sin and guilt of humanity is said to be imputed to Christ on the cross where he underwent the *specific punishment for that sin and guilt*.

---

[4] Council of Trent, Chapter VII, Sixth Session.
[5] Robert A. Sungenis, *How Can I Get to Heaven?—The Bible's Teaching on Salvation Made Easy to Understand*, 1998, Queenship Publishing, p. 229.

Not surprisingly, in contrast to this position the Catholic Church sees justification in *covenantal terms*. Justification is not simply a forensic declaration but a *rebirth* whereby man enters into a *grace based relationship* with God and becomes his adopted child. As with any relationship, man is required to be faithful thereto and can, by his own choosing, break or forfeit the relationship at any time. Man enters the relationship through baptism and faith and expresses the relationship in works of obedience and charity. *Importantly, one does not perform works in order to enter the relationship but to grow and maintain the relationship.*

Likewise, Catholicism sees the nature of the Christ's atonement on the cross in *covenantal* rather than purely forensic terms. Accordingly, Christ did not merely take upon himself the sin and guilt of humanity and suffer the specific punishment due for that sin and guilt but rather in willing obedience sacrificed himself (i.e., *"propitiated"*) to the Father on behalf of the family of Adam thereby making it possible for humanity to re-enter relationship with him. As 1 John 2:2 states: *"He is the atoning sacrifice [or propitiation] for our sins, and not only for ours but also for the sins of the whole world."*

This is not the place to undertake an in-depth critique of the doctrine of penal atonement, however there are at least three reasons as to why this doctrine is erroneous:

(i) If Christ had paid the actual price for our sins, then it follows that *every single individual should attain heaven*. Otherwise, God would, in effect, be requiring a double payment for the same offence from those condemned to hell;
(ii) If the paradigm for justification is conceived purely in forensic terms, there is no requirement for faith; and,
(iii) If the atonement were conceived in terms of a once-off forensic event, there would be no requirement for Christ's ongoing role as our heavenly priest.

While Catholics can agree with Galea that God declares us righteous, Catholics quite correctly point out that God does not declare what is not actual fact. Accordingly, Catholics assert that man is not only declared righteous but is actually made righteous, and that he can grow in righteousness or holiness throughout his life. God's declarations of righteousness can therefore occur at any stage in the process.

That man is made and not simply declared righteous is evident upon an examination of the Scriptures. We begin by turning to Romans 6:1-7:

What shall we say, then? Shall we go on sinning so that grace may increase? By no means! We died to sin; how can we live in it any longer? Or don't you know that all of us who were baptised into Christ Jesus were baptised into his death? We were therefore buried with him through baptism into death in order that, just as Christ was raised from the dead through the glory of the Father, we too may live a new life. If we have been united with him like this in his death, we will certainly also be united with him in his resurrection. For we know that our old self was crucified with him so that the body of sin might be done away with, that we should no longer be slaves to sin—because anyone who has died has been freed from sin.

Note that the passage clearly states that as a result of the death undergone by the Christian through baptism, the Christian has *"died to sin"* and that, as a result, he may *"live a new life."* Furthermore, the Christian's old self has *"been crucified with him [i.e., Christ] so that the body of sin might be done away with."* St Paul indicates that anyone who has died has been *"freed"* from sin. Notably, however, upon examination of the Greek, we find the words *"has been justified"* (δεδικαίωται) instead of the word *"freed."* As the context clearly contemplates a change in the Christian's very being, it is clear that, for St Paul, to be justified includes *being freed from sin* and is not simply a declaration that bears no relationship to reality.

Therefore, since we have been justified through faith, we have peace with God through our Lord Jesus Christ, through whom we have gained access by faith into this grace in which we now stand. And we rejoice in the hope of the glory of God. Not only so, but we also rejoice in our sufferings, because we know that suffering produces perseverance; perseverance, character; and character, hope. And hope does not disappoint us, because God has poured out his love into our hearts by the Holy Spirit, whom he has given us"(Rom. 5:1-5).

For just as through the disobedience of the one man the many were made sinners, so also through the obedience of the one man the many will be made righteous (Rom. 5:19).

he saved us, not because of deeds done by us in righteousness, but in virtue of his own mercy, by the washing of regeneration and renewal in the Holy Spirit, which he poured out upon us richly through Jesus Christ our Saviour, so that we might be justified by his grace and become heirs in hope of eternal life (Tit. 3:5-7).

The next question is whether justification is a process. Citing Scripture, the Council of Trent declared:

> Having, therefore, been thus justified, and made the friends and domestics of God, advancing from virtue to virtue, they are renewed, as the Apostle says, day by day; that is, by mortifying the members of their own flesh, and by presenting them as instruments of justice unto sanctification, they, through the observance of the commandments of God and of the Church, faith co-operating with good works, increase in that justice which they have received through the grace of Christ, and are still further justified, as it is written; He that is just, let him be justified still; and again, Be not afraid to be justified even to death; and also, Do you see that by works a man is justified, and not by faith only. And this increase of justification holy Church begs, when she prays, "Give unto us, O Lord, increase of faith, hope, and charity."[6]

Now, note two things: firstly, the increase in justification is preceded by the fact that an individual has *"been thus justified, and made the friends and domestics of God."* One does not perform good works to *attain or enter into relationship with God* but to grow in that relationship. Secondly, Protestants would agree that, following one's conversion to Christ, one can grow in sanctification thereby becoming more like him. This is precisely what the Catholic teaching on progressive justification is.

Is there any Scripture to support progressive justification? According to the following passages, the answer must be *Yes!*:

> *For it is not the hearers of the law who are righteous before God, but the doers of the law who will be justified* (Rom. 2:13).

> *Do you not know that if you yield yourselves to any one as obedient slaves, you are slaves of the one whom you obey, either of sin, which leads to death, or of obedience, which leads to righteousness?* (Rom. 6:16).

> *So we do not lose heart. Though our outer nature is wasting away, our inner nature is being renewed everyday* (2 Cor. 4:16).

---

[6] Council of Trent, Sixth Session, Chapter X.

work out your own salvation with fear and trembling (Phil. 2:12).

But grow in the grace and knowledge of our Lord and Saviour Jesus Christ (2 Pet. 3:18).

He that is just let him be justified still (Rev. 22:11).

Furthermore, let us examine Romans 4:3 where St Paul, quoting Genesis 15:6, asserts that Abraham "believed God and it was reckoned to him as righteousness" against the background of God's promise (Gen. 15:5) that Abraham's descendants would be as the stars of the sky. Clearly, Abraham was justified at the time he believed the promise concerning the number of his descendants. Accepting for the moment Galea's argument, this should be the one and only point in Abraham's life when he became justified, as justification is "a once-off declaration by God that the sinner is cleared of all guilt" (p. 62).

Scripture, however, indicates otherwise. In Hebrews 11:8 we are told "By faith Abraham obeyed when he was called to set out for a place that he was to receive as an inheritance, not knowing where he was going." Noting that recognition is given to this act of faith within the context of Old Testament exemplars that placed their faith in God, it is reasonable to assert this act of faith was justifying faith. The difficulty for Galea's view of justification is that the call of Abraham to leave Haran is recorded in Genesis 12:1-4, that is, *prior to his justification in* Genesis 15:6. Furthermore, in James 2:21-23, we are told "Was not our ancestor Abraham justified by works when he offered his son Isaac on the altar? You see that faith was active along with his works, and faith was brought to completion by the works. Thus the scripture was fulfilled that says, 'Abraham believed God, and it was reckoned to him as righteousness,' and he was called the friend of God."

Again, the difficulty for those who hold the "justification as a once-off declaration only" position is that the offering of Isaac is recorded in Genesis 22:1-18, that is, *after his justification* in Genesis 15:6. Therefore, according to Scripture Abraham was justified on at least three different occasions: (i) when he first left Haran and went to the promised land; (ii) when he believed the promise concerning his descendants; and (iii) when he offered his son Isaac on the altar.

Can one lose their justification?

Notably, and in keeping with the forensic model adopted by the Reformers, Galea states:

> *We constantly remain justified or 'right with God' throughout our Christian walk, regardless of how we happen to be going at the time.* It's a bit like being married—some days I'm a great husband, and some days I'm not, but ... I am always married because of the complete change in relationship and status that happened at the beginning, at the wedding (p. 62). (Emphasis added).

Is this consistent with what St Paul taught? Certainly, as indicated above, no amount of works can *"gain"* a relationship with God or entitle us thereto. This does not, however, mean that one cannot do damage to the relationship and such damage that, in the absence of reconciliation, the relationship is severed. One might agree with Galea's marriage analogy if justification was *solely* a forensic event, however, as we have seen, this is, at best, only part of the picture. In the Old Testament, the relationship between God and the people of Israel is conceived of in terms of a marriage to which, more often than not, Israel was less than faithful:

> *During the reign of King Josiah, the Lord said to me, 'Have you seen what faithless Israel has done? She has gone up on every high hill and under every spreading tree and has committed adultery there'* (Jer. 3:6).

The claim that *"we constantly remain justified ... regardless of how we happen to be going at the time"* is reminiscent of the Baptist belief of "once saved always saved" (OSAS). According to OSAS, no sin subsequent to justification can separate the saved Christian from the love of God and future eternal life. The Calvinist belief goes one step further, claiming that the 'saints' are assured of heaven after death because they are assured of perseverance in grace during life. In contrast, the Catholic Church teaches neither assurance of perseverance in grace during life nor certainty of heaven after death. What does Scripture have to say? The following passages provide overwhelming evidence that despite being chosen by God some Christians fall away and will finally be lost:

1. In Luke 8:13, Jesus tells us that there are some who receive the word with joy but, because they have no root, they believe for a while and in time of temptation fall away.

2. In Luke 15:11-32, Jesus tells the parable of the prodigal son, in which one of the sons of the father leaves home, is subsequently twice described by his father as being "dead" and then returns home and is spoken of by the father as being "alive again."
3. In Romans 8:13, St Paul warns his audience of Christians that if they live according to the flesh they will die.
4. In Romans 11:20-33, St Paul states: *"Granted. But they were broken off because of unbelief, and you stand by faith. Do not be arrogant, but be afraid. For if God did not spare the natural branches, he will not spare you either. Consider therefore the kindness and sternness of God: sternness to those who fell, but kindness to you, provided that you continue in his kindness. Otherwise, you also will be cut off. And if they do not persist in unbelief, they will be grafted in, for God is able to graft them in again."*
5. In 1 Corinthians 9:23-27, St Paul states: *"I do all this for the sake of the gospel, that I may share in its blessings. Do you not know that in a race all the runners run, but only one gets the prize? Run in such a way as to get the prize. Everyone who competes in the games goes into strict training. They do it to get a crown that will not last; but we do it to get a crown that will last forever. Therefore I do not run like a man running aimlessly; I do not fight like a man beating the air. No, I beat my body and make it my slave so that after I have preached to others, I myself will not be disqualified for the prize."*
6. In 1 Corinthians 15:1-2, St Paul states: *"Now, brothers, I want to remind you of the gospel I preached to you, which you received and on which you have taken your stand. By this gospel you are saved, if you hold firmly to the word I preached to you. Otherwise, you have believed in vain."*
7. In Galatians 5:1-4, St Paul states: *"It is for freedom that Christ has set us free. Stand firm, then, and do not let yourselves be burdened again by a yoke of slavery. Mark my words! I, Paul, tell you that if you let yourselves be circumcised, Christ will be of no value to you at all. Again I declare to every man who lets himself*

be circumcised that he is obligated to obey the whole law. You who are trying to be justified by law have been alienated from Christ; you have fallen away from grace."

8. In Colossians 1:21-23, St Paul states: *"Once you were alienated from God and were enemies in your minds because of your evil behaviour. But now he has reconciled you by Christ's physical body through death to present you holy in his sight, without blemish and free from accusation—if you continue in your faith, established and firm, not moved from the hope held out in the gospel."*

9. In 1 Timothy 1:19-20, St Paul states: *"By rejecting conscience, certain persons have made shipwreck of their faith, among them Hymenaeus and Alexander, whom I have delivered to Satan that they may learn not to blaspheme"* (1 Tim. 1:19-20).

10. In 2 Timothy 4:10, St Paul states: *"For Demas, in love with this present world, has deserted me and gone to Thessalonica."*

11. In Hebrews 3:12, the inspired author states: *"See to it, brothers, that none of you has a sinful, unbelieving heart that turns away from the living God."*

12. In Hebrews 6:4-6, the author states: *"It is impossible for those who have once been enlightened, who have tasted the heavenly gift, who have shared in the Holy Spirit, who have tasted the goodness of the word of God and the powers of the coming age, if they fall away, to be brought back to repentance, because to their loss they are crucifying the Son of God all over again and subjecting him to public disgrace."*

13. In Hebrews 10:23-29, the author states: *"Let us hold unswervingly to the hope we profess, for he who promised is faithful. And let us consider how we may spur one another on toward love and good deeds. Let us not give up meeting together, as some are in the habit of doing, but let us encourage one another—and all the more as you see the Day approaching. If we deliberately keep on sinning after we have received the knowledge of the truth, no sacrifice for sins is left, but only a fearful expectation of judgment and of raging fire that will consume the enemies of God. Anyone who rejected the law of Moses died without mercy on the testimony of two or three witnesses. How much more severely do you think a*

man deserves to be punished who has trampled the Son of God under foot, who has treated as an unholy thing the blood of the covenant that sanctified him, and who has insulted the Spirit of grace?"

14. In 2 Peter 2:20-22, St Peter states: *"If they have escaped the corruption of the world by knowing our Lord and Saviour Jesus Christ and are again entangled in it and overcome, they are worse off at the end than they were at the beginning. It would have been better for them not to have known the way of righteousness, than to have known it and then to turn their backs on the sacred command that was passed on to them. Of them the proverbs are true: 'A dog returns to its vomit', and, 'A sow that is washed goes back to her wallowing in the mud.'"*

15. In Revelation 22:19, St John states: *"And if anyone takes words away from this book of prophecy, God will take away from him his share in the tree of life and in the holy city, which are described in this book."*

As a result of these and many other passages, the Council of Trent rightly declared:

> In opposition also to the subtle wits of certain men, who, by pleasing speeches and good words, seduce the hearts of the innocent, it is to be maintained, that the received grace of Justification is lost, not only by infidelity whereby even faith itself is lost, but also by any other mortal sin whatever, though faith be not lost; thus defending the doctrine of the divine law, which excludes from the kingdom of God not only the unbelieving, but the faithful also (who are) fornicators, adulterers, effeminate, liars with mankind, thieves, covetous, drunkards, railers, extortioners, and all others who commit deadly sins; from which, with the help of divine grace, they can refrain, and on account of which they are separated from the grace of Christ.[7]

Is this an important difference?

Galea then turns his attention to the question of whether the differences between Catholicism and Protestantism concerning the Justification debate are important. Galea concludes that the differences have "massive

---

[7] Council of Trent, Chapter XV, Sixth Session.

implications" resulting in "two different kinds of Christian life" and "two different churches" (p. 64). Why? Principally because of Catholicism's rejection of "any belief in assurance of salvation" as "arrogant and presumptuous" (p. 64).

To emphasise his point Galea recalls a time when he was asked to give a talk to a class of 13-year-olds at a Catholic school. He opened with two questions:

(i) *"How many of you are certain that if you died tonight you would go to heaven?"* (p. 64): To this question apparently, not one child answered in the affirmative; and,

(ii) *"If you were to die tonight, and stand before Jesus and he were to say to you, 'Why should I let you into my kingdom?', what would you say?"* (p. 64): To this question, Galea reports that an array of answers were given, including *"I don't know"* and *"No reason why he should let me in."* Regarding the majority, according to Galea, *"Not one child mentioned that their hope or trust was in Christ's death for their sins. They all appealed to their good works to save them—which is the very thing that the Bible rejects"* (pp. 64-65).

Galea readily admits that these students did not have a perfect knowledge of Catholic theology or ability to express their beliefs properly, but that *"It's where the Roman Catholic ship ends up, given the direction chartered by the Church. It ends up with no assurance possible that you are actually going to be saved, and a reliance on your efforts and good works to get you over the line"* (p. 65).

How does the Catholic respond to this? Perhaps, by beginning with the first of the two questions posed by Galea above. For clarity's sake the question of assurance can be framed in two ways:

(i) Whether an individual can be certain that, *at any particular moment*, he or she is in a state of grace before God such that if he or she were to die at that moment, they would be welcomed into heaven; and,

(ii) Whether an individual can be certain that he *will persevere in the Christian Faith*, or, maintain his or her relationship with God until the end of his or her life such that when they die they will be welcomed into heaven.

In relation to (i), it is by no means clear that St Paul himself had such assurance. Prior to his execution for the Christian Faith he stated:

> *I am not aware of anything against myself, but I am not thereby justified [Gk., dedikaiomai]. It is the Lord who judges me* (1 Cor. 4:4).

Therefore, at least in relation to his present justification, St Paul did not claim an *infallible* assurance. Nor did St Paul have infallible certainty about the fate of his Christian friend Onesiphorus: *"May the Lord show mercy to the household of Onesiphorus, because he often refreshed me and was not ashamed of my chains. On the contrary, when he was in Rome, he searched hard for me until he found me. May the Lord grant that he will find mercy from the Lord on that day! You know very well in how many ways he helped me in Ephesus"* (2 Tim. 1:16-18). Consequently, the Council of Trent was right to declare the following:

> For even as no pious person ought to doubt of the mercy of God, of the merit of Christ, and of the virtue and efficacy of the sacraments, even so each one, when he regards himself, and his own weakness and indisposition, may have fear and apprehension touching his own grace; seeing that no one can know with a certainty of faith, which cannot be subject to error, that he has obtained the grace of God.[8]

This of course does not mean that that we cannot have a confident *moral assurance of salvation* based upon an examination of our response to God's grace. Indeed, St Paul urged believers at Corinth to *"Examine yourselves to see whether you are in the faith; test yourselves. Do you not realise that Christ Jesus is in you—unless, of course, you fail the test?"* (2 Cor. 13:5). It is after such a self-examination that St Paul could confidently exclaim the following:

> *I have fought the good fight, I have finished the race, I have kept the faith. Henceforth there is laid up for me the crown of righteousness, which the Lord, the righteous judge, will award to me on that Day* (2 Tim. 4:7-8).

Likewise, St John states in 1 John 3:18-22:

> *Dear children, let us not love with words or tongue but with actions and in truth. This then is how we know that we belong to the truth, and how we set our hearts at rest in his presence whenever our hearts condemn us. For God is greater than our hearts, and he knows everything. Dear*

---

[8] Council of Trent, Chapter IX, Sixth Session.

friends, if our hearts do not condemn us, we have confidence before God and receive from him anything we ask, because we obey his commands and do what pleases him.

In relation to (ii), it is also clear that St Paul had no absolute assurance that he would persevere until the end of his life and was frank in admitting that even he could fall away: *"I pummel my body and subdue it, lest after preaching to others I myself should be disqualified"* (1 Cor. 9:27). The same fear of falling from grace prompted St Paul to open the following warning to the Philippians: *"Therefore, my beloved, as you have always obeyed, so now, not only as in my presence but much more in my absence, work out your own salvation with fear and trembling"* (Phil. 2:12).

At this point, it may be well worth positing the following scenario: Many Protestants of the Reformed persuasion believe that if one has a genuine saving faith, one will certainly persevere until the end of one's life. If one does not persevere, the logical conclusion is that one never had a genuine saving faith. The question that naturally arises is how then is one to know at any given point in one's life whether one will persevere until the end thereof? Furthermore, assume one falls into grievous sin and leaves the Christian Faith. Presumably the logical conclusion one is to draw is that despite any confidence or assurance that one may have had in his or her salvation at an earlier point in one's life, *in fact*, one's faith was not genuine. Finally, assuming one decides to make a *subsequent* act of faith, how is one to know that the subsequent act is a genuine act of saving faith which will cause one to persevere until the end of one's life?

In other words, how is one to know with certainty that he or she may not fall into a sinful pattern of living in the future, thereby demonstrating that a true faith was not possessed to begin with? In contrast, the Catholic can be certain that he or she has received the disposition of faith and is also certain that it can be lost and, furthermore, knows what to do if and when it is lost.

How then would the Catholic respond to the second question Galea posed to the children? To begin with, it should be pointed out that there is *absolutely no evidence* in Scripture that Jesus will ask such a question at anyone's judgement. Rather, *every judgment scene depicted in Scripture indicates that the faithful will be judged according to their works*. The following passages are but a small sample of the Biblical data:

Not everyone who says to me, 'Lord, Lord,' will enter the kingdom of heaven, but only he who does the will of my Father who is in heaven (Mt 7:21).

For the Son of Man is going to come in his Father's glory with his angels, and then he will reward each person according to what he has done (Mt 16:27).

Then he will say to those at his left hand, 'Depart from me, you cursed, into the eternal fire prepared for the devil and his angels; for I was hungry and you gave me no food, I was thirsty and you gave me no drink, I was a stranger and you did not welcome me, naked and you did not clothe me, sick and in prison and you did not visit me.' Then they also will answer, 'Lord, when did we see thee hungry or thirsty or a stranger or naked or sick or in prison, and did not minister to thee?' Then he will answer them, 'Truly, I say to you, as you did it not to one of the least of these, you did it not to me.' And they will go away into eternal punishment, but the righteous into eternal life (Mt 25:41-46).

Do not be amazed at this, for a time is coming when all who are in their graves will hear his voice and come out—those who have done good will rise to live, and those who have done evil will rise to be condemned (Jn 5:28-29).

But because of your stubbornness and your unrepentant heart, you are storing up wrath against yourself for the day of God's wrath, when his righteous judgment will be revealed (Rom. 2:5).

So we make it our goal to please him, whether we are at home in the body or away from it. For we must all appear before the judgment seat of Christ, that each one may receive what is due him for the things done while in the body, whether good or bad (2 Cor. 5:9-10).

and, once made perfect, he became the source of eternal salvation for all who obey him (Heb. 5:9).

Make every effort to live in peace with all men and to be holy; without holiness no one will see the Lord (Heb. 12:14).

You see that a person is justified by what he does and not by faith alone. In the same way, was not even Rahab the prostitute considered righteous for what she did when she gave lodging to the spies and sent them off in a different direction? (Js 2: 24-25).

And I saw the dead, great and small, standing before the throne, and books were opened. Another book was opened, which is the book of life. The dead were judged according to what they had done as recorded in the books (Rev. 20:12).

Behold, I am coming soon! My reward is with me, and I will give to everyone according to what he has done (Rev. 22:12).

Indeed, in 1 Corinthians 13:12-17, St Paul sheds some light on the nature of the judgement to be had by Christians:

If any man builds on this foundation using gold, silver, costly stones, wood, hay or straw, his work will be shown for what it is, because the Day will bring it to light. It will be revealed with fire, and the fire will test the quality of each man's work. If what he has built survives, he will receive his reward. If it is burned up, he will suffer loss; he himself will be saved, but only as one escaping through the flames.

Romans and Justification

Galea next turns to the books of Romans and Ephesians. Citing Romans 4, Romans 6 and Ephesians 2, Galea makes the following claims (pp. 67-68):

- Justification is "a gift and not a wage."
- Justification is freely given out of God's generosity, not earned.
- The one justified "simply trusts in 'him who justifies the ungodly.'"
- Luther and the Reformers faced with Roman Catholicism a similar problem to that faced by Paul.
- The "works which will never justify" include any human law or work, including those imposed by the Church.
- While works "play no part" in our justification and salvation, they are still important as part of "all the holy and good things (Christ) has already prepared for us to do!"

It should be evident from what has been written already, that the Catholic says a hearty *"Amen"* to the proposition that justification is a gift freely received from God. It is this reception of grace St Paul speaks of in Romans and Ephesians. Nevertheless, for the sake of completeness, it is apt to quote from the Council of Trent again:

… none of those things which precede justification—whether faith or works—merit the grace itself of justification. For, if it be a grace, it is not now by works, otherwise, as the same Apostle says, grace is no more grace.[9]

However, and as stated above, while Catholics recognise the Biblical principle of justification by grace, they also recognise the Biblical principle that *justification is ongoing because justification is an ontological reality as well as a declarative one.*

Justification in this *"ongoing"* sense does not denote entry into relationship with God that ultimately determines our eternal destiny but *growth in* and *maintenance of* that relationship. Furthermore, the Catholic Church teaches that works are meritorious not in the sense of *"strict merit"*—which obliges God to reward as a debtor—but in the sense of what is termed *"condign merit"*, which is the reward God in his graciousness promises to bestow for good works performed by those in friendship with him.

That Christians are able to please God and graciously merit reward in this secondary sense is evident from the following Scriptures:

But when you give to the needy, do not let your left hand know what your right hand is doing, so that your giving may be in secret. Then your Father, who sees what is done in secret, will reward you" (Mt 6:3-5).

Do not store up for yourselves treasures on earth, where moth and rust destroy, and where thieves break in and steal. But store up for yourselves treasures in heaven, where moth and rust do not destroy, and where thieves do not break in and steal (Mt 6:19-20).

He who receives a prophet because he is a prophet shall receive a prophet's reward, and he who receives a righteous man because he is a righteous man shall receive a righteous man's reward. And whoever gives to one of these little ones even a cup of cold water because he is a disciple, truly, I say to you, he shall not lose his reward (Mt 10:41-42).

And every one who has left houses or brothers or sisters or father or mother or children or lands, for my name's sake, will receive a hundredfold, and inherit eternal life (Mt 19:29).

And a poor widow came, and put in two copper coins, which make a penny. And he called his disciples to him, and said to them, 'Truly, I say to you, this poor widow has put in more than all those who are contributing

---

[9] Council of Trent, Chapter VIII, Sixth Session.

to the treasury. For they all contributed out of their abundance; but she out of her poverty has put in everything she had, her whole living' (Mk 12:42-44).

But when you give a feast, invite the poor, the maimed, the lame, the blind, and you will be blessed, because they cannot repay you. You will be repaid at the resurrection of the just (Lk 14:13-14).

About the ninth hour of the day he saw clearly in a vision an angel of God coming in and saying to him, 'Cornelius.' And he stared at him in terror, and said, 'What is it, Lord?' And he said to him, 'Your prayers and your alms have ascended as a memorial before God' (Acts 10:3-4).

knowing that whatever good any one does, he will receive the same again from the Lord, whether he is a slave or free (Eph. 6:8).

I have received full payment and even more; I am amply supplied, now that I have received from Epaphroditus the gifts you sent. They are a fragrant offering, an acceptable sacrifice, pleasing to God (Phil. 4:18).

For this reason, since the day we heard about you, we have not stopped praying for you and asking God to fill you with the knowledge of his will through all spiritual wisdom and understanding. And we pray this in order that you may live a life worthy of the Lord and may please him in every way: bearing fruit in every good work, growing in the knowledge of God (Col. 1:9-10).

Finally, brothers, we instructed you how to live in order to please God, as in fact you are living. Now we ask you and urge you in the Lord Jesus to do this more and more (1 Thes. 4:1).

And do not forget to do good and to share with others, for with such sacrifices God is pleased (Heb. 13:16).

The man who plants and the man who waters have one purpose, and each will be rewarded according to his own labour (1 Cor. 3: 8).

Do not be deceived: God cannot be mocked. A man reaps what he sows. The one who sows to please his sinful nature, from that nature will reap destruction; the one who sows to please the Spirit, from the Spirit will reap eternal life. Let us not become weary in doing good, for at the proper time we will reap a harvest if we do not give up. Therefore, as we have opportunity, let us do good to all people, especially to those who belong to the family of believers (Gal. 6:7-10).

Behold, I am coming soon! My reward is with me, and I will give to everyone according to what he has done (Rev. 22:12).

What about the Ten Commandments?—Is observance of such necessary for salvation?

According to the minds of Jesus, St John and St Paul the answer is *Yes!* This is so not because Christians are required to pile up a certain amount of good works in order to please God but because those who are in Christ are required to consistently *love their neighbour as themselves.* Love is the necessary *fruit* of a genuine Christian life. Christians show such love through obeying the Commandments. The following Scriptures unequivocally teach the necessity of obeying the Commandments as a law of love for salvation:

> *Whoever then relaxes one of the least of these commandments and teaches men so, shall be called least in the kingdom of heaven; but he who does them and teaches them shall be called great in the kingdom of heaven* (Mt 5:19).
>
> *If you would enter life, keep the commandments* (Mt 19:17).
>
> *And behold, a lawyer stood up to put him to the test, saying, 'Teacher, what shall I do to inherit eternal' life?' He said to him, 'What is written in the law? How do you read?' And he answered, 'You shall love the Lord your God with all your heart, and with all your soul, and with all your strength, and with all your mind; and your neighbour as yourself.' And he said to him, 'You have answered right; do this, and you will live'* (Lk 10:25-28).
>
> *And as he was setting out on his journey, a man ran up and knelt before him, and asked him, 'Good Teacher, what must I do to inherit eternal life?' And Jesus said to him, 'Why do you call me good? No one is good but God alone. You know the commandments: Do not kill, Do not commit adultery, Do not steal, Do not bear false witness, Do not defraud, Honour your father and mother.' And he said to him, 'Teacher, all these I have observed from my youth.' And Jesus looking upon him loved him, and said to him, 'You lack one thing; go, sell what you have, and give to the poor, and you will have treasure in heaven; and come, follow me'* (Mk 10:17-22).

And whenever you stand praying, forgive, if you have anything against any one; so that your Father also who is in heaven may forgive you your trespasses (Mk 11:25).

Every branch of mine that bears no fruit, he takes away, and every branch that does bear fruit he prunes, that it may bear more fruit ... If you keep my commandments, you will abide in my love, just as I have kept my Father's commandments and abide in his love. These things I have spoken to you, that my joy may be in you, and that your joy may be full. This is my commandment, that you love one another as I have loved you' (Jn 15:2 & 10-12).

He who says 'I know him' but disobeys his commandments is a liar, and the truth is not in him; but whoever keeps his word, in him truly love for God is perfected. By this we may be sure that we are in him: he who says he abides in him ought to walk in the same way in which he walked (1 Jn 2:4-6).

And this is his commandment, that we should believe in the name of his Son Jesus Christ and love one another, just as he has commanded us. All who keep his commandments abide in him, and he in them. And by this we know that he abides in us, by the Spirit which he has given us (1 Jn 3:23-24).

For neither circumcision counts for anything nor uncircumcision, but keeping the commandments of God (1 Cor. 7:19).

What is "faith", etc?

Galea then turns to consider the Biblical definition of faith. Among other things he states (pp. 68-69):

- Faith is more than just an intellectual assent that something is true, "it is a personal trust that something is true."
- Faith trusts in God's promises in the Bible.
- Faith is "an open hand" that "offers nothing and contributes nothing"; faith simply "receives salvation" from God "as a free gift."
- Abraham became justified in God's sight by believing in God's promise that "he would have a son and be a father to many nations"; likewise, Christians are made righteous by placing their "trust in the death of Jesus."

How does a Catholic respond to the above? Firstly, by quoting what the sacred author says in Hebrews 11:1:

> Now faith is the assurance of things hoped for, the conviction of things not seen.

In other words, it firstly believes in things unseen, namely God and heaven. However, it does not end there for the Christian. Christians must also believe that God "raised from the dead Jesus our Lord, who was put to death for our trespasses and raised for our justification" (Rom. 4:24-25). Finally, an authentic faith is only complete if Christians are willing to believe in all the truths revealed by Christ. A 'cafeteria faith' (one in which we are free to pick and choose our articles of faith) is no real faith at all. Such persons are traditionally known as *heretics*.

Personal trust" in the salvific work of Christ is vital for the Christian but it does not pertain to faith; rather the virtue of hope. Likewise, love of Christ is not within the virtue of faith but within the virtue of charity. Though all three work together to perfect the Christian life they are distinct. This is why St Paul can say, "So faith, hope, love abide, these three; but the greatest of these is love" (1 Cor. 13:13).

On the basis of such, the Catholic Church declared in the Council of Trent:

> If any one saith, that justifying faith is nothing else but confidence in the divine mercy which remits sins for Christ's sake; or, that this confidence alone is that whereby we are justified; let him be anathema.[10]

Rather than being a *"tragedy"* (p.71) and flying *"in the face of what Paul teaches in Romans"*, the teaching of Trent is a most apt and comprehensive summary of not only the teaching of the Apostle but also the teaching of Scripture as a whole.

Furthermore, however, the Catholic would point out the contradiction between the assertion that *"faith offers nothing and contributes nothing"* and *"Abraham believed God's promise that he would have a son and be a father to many nations, and this rendered him 'righteous' in God's sight..."*. Ironically, the meritorious nature of the faith exercised by Abraham is referred to in the very passage (Rom. 4:20-25) quoted by Galea on p. 70 to illustrate his

---

[10] Council of Trent, Canon XII.

point. I shall now reproduce the same quote together with the previous two verses to demonstrate the meritorious value of the faith exercised:

> *Against all hope Abraham in hope believed and so became the father of many nations, just as it had been said to him, 'So shall your offspring be.' Without weakening in his faith, he faced the fact that his body was as good as dead—since he was about one hundred years old—and that Sarah's womb was also dead. Yet he did not waver through unbelief regarding the promise of God but was strengthened in his faith and gave glory to God, being fully persuaded that God had power to do what he had promised. That is why 'it was credited to him as righteousness.' The words 'it was credited to him' were written not for him alone, but also for us to whom God will credit righteousness—for us who believe in him who raised Jesus our Lord from the dead. He was delivered over to death for our sins and was raised to life for our justification* (Rom. 4:18-25).

For this reason the author of Hebrews tells us that by virtue of Abraham's faith and the faith of those referred to in Hebrews 11 *"the men of old received divine approval"* (Heb. 11:2).

Notably, and in further contradiction to the concept of *"imputed"* or *"declared"* righteousness, we see that Abraham was *"rendered 'righteous'"* (to use Galea's words) *precisely because* of the act of faith. That is, his crediting with righteousness followed up an actual act of righteousness. Interestingly enough, the phrase *"credited to him as righteous"* is used in only one other place in Holy Scripture, namely, Psalm 106:

> *But Phinehas stood up and intervened, and the plague was checked. This was credited to him as righteousness for endless generations to come.*

This passage is referring to the incident recorded in Numbers 25 in which some of the men of Israel engaged in cultic sexual intercourse with Moabite and Midianite women. For this sin, the Lord ordered Moses to kill them. In defiance, an Israelite man brought a Midianite woman into his tent, most likely to engage in sexual intercourse. The priest Phinehas saw this happen, grabbed a spear, and went into the tent and killed the man and the woman. For this act God praised him. Accordingly, and again, the phrase *"credited as righteousness"* was *employed to convey the fact that the act in question was inherently righteous and pleasing to God, rather than in a purely declarative manner.*

Finally, the Catholic would point out that the assertion *"we also are* 'counted righteous' by putting our trust in the death of Jesus" (p. 70) does not follow from the Biblical text cited in support thereof. Rather Romans 4: 23-25 states that:

> The words 'it was credited to him' were written not for him alone, but also for us to whom God will credit righteousness—for us who believe in him who raised Jesus our Lord from the dead. He was delivered over to death for our sins and was raised to life for our justification.

Finally, Galea asserts that,

> God wants us to know with certainty that if we too trust the promise that Christ died for our sins and was raised for our justification, then we too are justified now ... That is why a Bible-believing Christian can put his hand up in class and say, 'Yes, I'm quite certain that if I died tonight God would accept me into his eternal kingdom'—not because I think I'm particularly good, or measure up to his standards, or have earned it, but because I'm placing my trust in Christ and his blood, and I know that God will definitely accept me on that basis, because he has promised to (pp.70-71).

A Catholic would agree with the passage cited and, in particular Romans 5:9, which states: *"Since we have now been justified by his blood, how much more shall we be saved from God's wrath through him!"* Drawing upon the entirety of Scripture, however, a Catholic would urge the following caution:

> *Do not be deceived: God cannot be mocked. A man reaps what he sows. The one who sows to please his sinful nature, from that nature will reap destruction; the one who sows to please the Spirit, from the Spirit will reap eternal life. Let us not become weary in doing good, for at the proper time we will reap a harvest if we do not give up* (Gal. 6:7-9).

Conclusion

The basic thesis of Galea and most of the Protestant world is that Christians are justified by 'faith alone.' In contrast, these same Protestants claim that the Catholic Church teaches a 'works salvation' or, at best, that it is necessary to add something to Christ's work in order to be saved.

Let us summarise the Catholic position. Christ is the only Saviour; his death on the Cross is the only means through which humanity was reconciled to the Father. The Cross of Christ alone effects the objective redemption of the whole of humanity. This same self-sacrifice is infinitely meritorious and cannot be added to. How, though, is each individual saved? This question is vitally important for while Christ's atoning sacrifice is more than sufficient for the salvation of all humanity, not all of humanity will be saved. The reason? God's offer of salvation through Christ is open to everyone, yet everyone is, at any moment, at liberty to accept or reject the offer. Each person is asked to do the following: have faith, hope, love and obedience.

Faith in God and the risen Christ is the beginning of the Christian life; hope is trusting in the grace of Christ for all the help we need to persevere and reach our final destination, heaven; love is charity—the love of God/Christ above all things and our neighbour as ourselves; and finally, obedience to all Christ and his Church commands (for example, "He who hears you hears me, and he who rejects you rejects me, and he who rejects me rejects him who sent me" [Lk 10:16]). There is no assurance of perseverance; rather, the Christian must correspond every moment with God's grace to remain in grace. I am not certain that I will go to heaven if I die tonight even if "I am not aware of anything against myself"; rather, I live in confident hope for "It is the Lord who judges me" (1 Cor. 4:4).

If the Christian life were a tree, faith would be the roots, hope the trunk, and charity the fruit. Christ cursed the tree that had life but no fruit.

One therefore receives new birth, justification, salvation and eternal life by:

- Christ's Cross (Eph. 2:16) and Christ's Blood (Rom. 5:9).
- Grace (Eph. 2:8) and faith in Christ (Jn 3:16; Acts 16:31).
- Repentance (Acts 2:38; 2 Pet. 3:9) and Baptism (Jn 3:5; 1 Pet. 3:21).
- Confessing publicly with our mouths (Rom. 10:9).
- Knowing and adhering to the truth (1 Tim. 2:4).
- Obeying the Commandments (Mt 5:19 and 19:17).
- The doing of good works in faith (Js 2:24).

In this chapter we have shown that *"The way of salvation"* is most fully embodied within the Catholic Church and not the teachings of those whose rebellion divided and weakened Christendom. Ironically, Galea finishes his chapter by quoting Martin Luther, who stated *"I felt that I was a sinner before God with an extremely disturbed conscience."* Sadly, it was this *"extremely disturbed conscience"* and not Scripture that was responsible for the doctrines subsequently espoused by Luther.

6

It's Just Grace

Glenn Bolas[1]

Introduction

In his chapter *"It's Just Grace"* Ray Galea states that justification is a free gift given by God in Christ. We do not deserve to be justified or saved. All we have to do in response is hold out "an open hand ... in trust" to grasp onto this gift. In no way do our merits or works save us. It's all grace (pp. 74-75). As a Catholic, I can add to that a hearty 'Amen!' However, such a response would seem odd to Galea and many Evangelical Protestants[2], who regard the above as one of the fundamental differences between Protestant Evangelicalism and Catholicism. Having once worshipped as a Protestant Evangelical and now as a Catholic, that view seems curious to me. Since I first started investigating the Catholic Church several years ago, my beliefs about many things have changed in subtle and not-so-subtle ways. Considering the many differences between Protestants and Catholics, I think I can safely say that it is on the matter of grace that my beliefs have changed the least.

How could that be? Have I not fully swallowed Catholic dogma? Or was I perhaps not really a full-fledged Protestant Evangelical previously? Surely grace is, if anything, what the Reformation was all about? The doctrines can't be that similar, can they?

Perhaps some bona fides is in order then. My relationship with Jesus Christ has been formed and nourished principally from two sources. One

---
1 Glenn Bolas is a former Baptist and graduate in English Literature from the University of Sydney. Glenn currently teaches English in central Sydney.
2 It will be noted that I refer throughout this chapter to Protestant Evangelicals and Protestant Evangelicalism. While the terms may be unwieldy, I use them for the sake of precision. I do not believe that Evangelicalism, with its emphasis on evangelism, a personal relationship with Christ and devotion to and knowledge of the Bible, is necessarily or irrevocably bound up with any of the doctrines where Protestants differ from other Christians. In becoming Catholic, I do not believe I have ceased to be Evangelical—I simply stopped protesting.

was the Baptist church where I worshipped for the better part of my life, a small but loving church community whose members I yet count as very dear friends. There I sat under the expository preaching of successive pastors, learned what a Christian community, characterised by fraternal charity, is supposed to look like, and was nourished by the fruitful marriage of poetry and theology that is nineteenth century hymnody. The second source was the Sydney University Evangelical Union (S.U.E.U.). To them I owe too many things to name—a solid tertiary-level theological formation, a greatly broadened and deepened understanding of and appreciation of Scripture, an unwavering missionary instinct, a consciousness of the responsibility of all Christians to evangelise in season and out of season, and the example of a multitude of souls, all with very different personalities and expectations of life but all with a passion to share the good news, to know it ever better themselves and thereby to know Jesus Christ.

Never once did I feel disillusionment in this environment or feel like something was missing and needed to be sought elsewhere. Instead, something else happened. Through a set of circumstances during my university studies, which I won't go into here, I discovered by chance that St Ignatius of Antioch, one of the early Christian martyrs, had believed that the Lord's Supper was the literal Body and Blood of Jesus Christ (*Letter to the Smyrnaeans* 7). This was an anomalous discovery. If you're going to change fundamental aspects of the Christian faith and suffuse it with weird pagan-esque elements (and St Ignatius was too early—immediately sub-apostolic—for anyone else to have tampered with his doctrine), why die for it rather than sacrifice to Caesar? Rather like a liberal bishop who believes Jesus' body was actually eaten by wild dogs, but then is ostracised by the liberal establishment for his staunch defence of the Virgin Birth. It doesn't quite add up. Befuddled by this contradiction, I began a whirlwind tour of the writings of the Early Church and discovered that many of the beliefs I took for granted as being classically Christian were in fact peculiar only to Evangelical Protestantism and would have been foreign to the immediate successors of the Apostles.[3] Frantic and confused, but at the same time fascinated and a little elated, for several months my Bible and one or other of the Church Fathers was never far from my hand, the writings of Luther and Calvin also being frequent companions, though in lesser amounts and mostly for comparison. This, and a specifically Protestant desire to recover and imitate the faith of the early Church, ultimately set me on the road to Catholicism.

What is Grace?

So what of grace? My Evangelical instincts were and are fantastically sensitive to anything that would limit or diminish the efficacy of the Cross of Christ. The mere suggestion of merit gets my hackles up—one of the great blessings bestowed upon me by the S.U.E.U. Like most Protestants, I knew that the Catholic Church taught that you could earn your salvation, that this was why the Reformation happened, and that Luther had, rightly, said that the Church stands or falls on the doctrine of free grace. Well, if that was the case, my loyalties were clearly with the Reformers. But it was only fair for me to check for myself that these things were so. The Church Fathers were no help here—I had to seek out what the modern Catholic Church taught, and I wasn't sure what I would find (though I did rather hope that it would be blatant works-righteousness so I could be absolved from having to join the Catholic Church—a prospect I did not particularly relish at the time). Naturally, rather than trusting secondary sources, I went to the most primary one there could be on the matter—the Council of Trent. There, from the heart of the Catholic Church in the very heart of the Reformation years, I found this:

> If anyone says that man can be justified before God by his own works, whether done by his own natural powers or through the teaching of the law, without divine grace through Jesus Christ, let him be anathema.

---

[3] I was somewhat bemused to read Galea's statement, "I could have been a Catholic in the fourth century." In fact, his present beliefs are far more in conflict with those of fourth-century Catholics than perhaps he realises, as a cursory reading of a few sermons, commentaries and other writings from the fourth century would soon indicate. If it were true that Galea could have been a Catholic in the fourth century, I would certainly have been able to avoid becoming one in the twenty-first.

If anyone says that divine grace through Christ Jesus is given for this only, that man may be able more easily to live justly and to merit eternal life, as if by free will without grace he is able to do both, though with hardship and difficulty, let him be anathema.

If anyone says that without the predisposing inspiration of the Holy Ghost and without his help, man can believe, hope, love or be repentant as he ought, so that the grace of justification may be bestowed upon him, let him be anathema (Session 6, Canons 1-3).

One can hardly find a more thorough statement of the doctrine of *sola gratia* than that.[4]

So, if we all agree on this, what was the Reformation really all about, and why does Galea single out the Catholic Church's teaching on grace for a whole chapter's worth of critique in his book? The first question is, perhaps, beyond our scope here. To find out the answer to the second, on the other hand, let us examine Galea's own critique of Catholic teaching on these matters.

Galea's first problem is a difference over what grace is. He himself defines grace at the beginning of the chapter as "generosity", when God gives something out of his goodness despite our unworthiness (p. 73). Here, grace is not the thing given but the act of giving or, alternatively, the attitude of the giver. Galea contrasts this definition of grace with the Catholicism's "complex" understanding, which he notes sees grace also as "a kind of power or assistance which God gives to help us" (pp. 76-77).

Let us see then how the Bible uses the term.

The Greek for 'grace' is χαρις. *Thayer's Lexicon* defines the word as meaning, among other things, "good-will, loving-kindness, favour", going on to add "Moreover, the word χαρις contains the idea of kindness which bestows upon one what he has not deserved." This is borne out by such texts as Romans 5:15 (*"But the free gift is not like the offence. For if by the one man's offence many died, much more the grace of God and the gift by the grace of the one man, Jesus Christ, abounded to many"*), 2 Corinthians 8:9 (*"For you know the grace of our Lord Jesus Christ, that though he was rich, yet for your sakes he became poor, that you through his poverty might become rich"*), 2 Thessalonians 2:16 (*"may our Lord Jesus Christ himself, and our*

---

4 Indeed, I found almost nothing in the Council of Trent's decree on justification that I had not long believed as an Evangelical.

God and Father, who has loved us and given us everlasting consolation and good hope by grace") and, on a human level, Colossians 4:6 (*"Let your speech always be with grace, seasoned with salt, that you may know how you ought to answer each one"*). Each of these texts clearly refer to an attitude on the part of the giver, a spirit of generosity despite, not because of, the state of the recipient.

However, this is not the only way in which Scripture uses the term. Thayer's offers another possible meaning: "what is due to grace; the spiritual condition of one governed by the power of divine grace ... a token or proof of grace ... a benefit; a gift of grace, benefaction, bounty ..."; in other words, the gift which is the result of the attitude of the giver. On a human level, St Paul uses the word with this meaning in 1 Corinthians 16:3 when speaking of the monetary gift he plans to send to the Church in Jerusalem. When speaking of the salvation of God, he uses the same word in the same sense in Romans 4:4 (*"Now to him who works, the wages are not counted as grace but as debt"*). This, moreover, is the only possible way to understand texts like 1 Peter 4:10 (*"As each one has received a gift, minister it to one another, as good stewards of the manifold grace of God*—how can one be a steward of somebody else's regard for one, and how could such an attitude be 'manifold'?) or 2 Corinthians 9:14 ("*... and by their prayer for you, who long for you because of the exceeding grace of God in you"*—how can one speak of God's generosity being in you?—"towards you", perhaps, but "in you"?) and 2 Corinthians 8:6 (*"So we urged Titus, that as he had begun, so he would also complete this grace in you as well"*; again, this passage makes no sense if we limit the meaning of 'grace' to generosity or favour). Also, in James 4:6, St James tells us, *"But he gives more grace."* If we read grace here to mean generosity, does it not imply that God has not been as generous or loving towards us as he could be, that his mercy towards us has not been total? Such a reading would call into question the efficacy of Christ's sacrifice, for how could God give more than what he has already given on the Cross?

Clearly, Scripture speaks of grace, both in the sense of divine favour and generosity, and to denote that which God gives us because of

his favour towards us. Moreover, what exactly is it that he gives, according to Scripture? Ranging over the few passages above, we can come up with, in addition to God's attitude of gracious benevolence towards us in spite of our sins, the divine life of the Holy Spirit within us (2 Cor. 9:14), the reservoir of spiritual gifts we have through the same Holy Spirit (1 Pet. 4:10), and divinely granted strength in the face of temptation (Js 4:6—this, it is worthwhile noting, is what Galea is referring to when he describes 'Catholic' grace as being "assistance which God gives to help us"). These correspond to what Catholics refer to as sanctifying grace, charisms, and actual graces, respectively. In the Bible, χαρις can mean all these things. To limit the definition is to be false to Scripture. Indeed, the Catholic Church does not limit it. In the *Catechism of the Catholic Church* (CCC ##1996, 1997, 2003), we find all these meanings: "Grace is favour", then a paragraph later, "Grace is a participation in the life of God", then further on, "There are furthermore special graces, also called charisms after the Greek term used by St Paul ... [which] are oriented toward sanctifying grace and are intended for the common good of the Church." It is therefore unfounded to assert that the Catholic Church's "understanding of the word ... is often different from what the Bible means by it." On the contrary, Catholicism gives the word the full range of Scriptural meanings.

Of course, Evangelical Protestants do not necessarily disagree with the Catholic Church about any of this. They simply use different words to express the same ideas. So sanctifying grace corresponds, in the Evangelical lexicon, to 'the indwelling of the Holy Spirit', charisms are 'spiritual gifts', while actual graces are 'promptings of the Spirit.' So I believe this dispute is a bit of a red herring.

The Sacramental Economy

There may, upon examination, be no material difference between Catholic and Evangelical Protestant ideas about grace, and certainly no biblical foundation for any difference anyway. But there are other issues relating to grace that Galea raises that are far less cosmetic. These too deserve a response. Several issues are here interrelated and are difficult to disentangle and treat in their own space, but I shall attempt to do this as well as possible. Firstly, let us examine briefly one difference that in some ways is relatively ephemeral as far as differences go (especially upon examination) but also drives at something profound.

On several occasions throughout *Nothing in My Hand I Bring*, Galea speaks critically of the Catholic Church's[5] sacramental system. For Galea, belief in sacraments as channels of grace inevitably leads one to deny God's free generosity, forgiveness and justification by faith alone in favour of a life "of ritual obligation and performance" (p. 80). Galea continues, "The message I received growing up, and which Catholics all over the world receive, was: Keep going to Mass, keep going to confession, be a good Catholic, and you'll give yourself the best chance of going to heaven. The focus was all on what *I had to do*, and this seems to be the inevitable result of the Catholic sacramental system" (p. 80).

There are legitimate concerns at work here. But I'm not certain that Evangelical Protestantism is as immune from a similar characterisation as Galea would like it to be. For Evangelical Protestantism has its own 'sacraments', if you will. They are simply different from the Catholic ones. When I was growing up, we had the Sinner's Prayer. If a person prayed it, that meant that they had become a Christian and now had 'Jesus in their heart.' I myself prayed it when I was five one day after our family Bible reading during breakfast, to the supreme joy of my parents, and despite later (mostly unvoiced) concerns on my part as to whether I had really meant it or understood sufficiently what I was saying at the time. Now as a Catholic, I can look back on that morning and regard it as a truly graced moment in my childhood and thank God for it. Indeed, I still see the Sinner's Prayer being used, in various forms and permutations, at the end of tracts and at the close of evangelistic services. I don't wish at this point to argue with the theology of this practice, but to point out that the focus was all on what *I had to do*. If I hadn't prayed the Sinner's Prayer or some similar form of prayer, I wasn't a Christian and Christ had no part in me. Nor does becoming a Christian put an end to it. Someone has written somewhere that Evangelical Protestants have two sacraments: prayer and Bible study. I think this is a not inaccurate insight.

In an Evangelical church, if I wish to have a closer walk with Jesus, and express this desire to my pastor, his recommendation will invariably be

---

[5] It is perhaps worth noting that the criticism also implicates all the Orthodox Churches, the Lutheran Church and what up until relatively recently were substantial numbers of Anglicans (including, for instance, pillars of Anglican orthodoxy such as Taylor, Hooker and Cranmer)—in other words, most Christians. No doubt, Galea and others would retort that truth is not established by a majority vote, and in that they would be quite right; still, it is worth realising that the Catholic Church is far from alone in proposing sacramentalism as a fundamental part of the Christian faith.

more prayer and Bible study. If I am going through difficulties in my life, I will be advised to pray and study my Bible more (possibly with particular texts or other resources recommended as aids to this). If I am having doubts about my faith, the advice will be that I need to pray and study my Bible more (again with appropriate texts and resources recommended). If there's a problem in the Church, perhaps a dispute or two warring parties or a difficult decision to make, what should be done to find a way forward? Invariably (if the Church members are strong in their faith and serious about following Jesus) the answer will come back: the best way to resolve this situation is to pray and study the Bible. This is how we get God involved in the process. Further, there is the act of coming to church itself. Evangelicals will (rightly) become worried about a person's relationship with Jesus if they haven't been seen at church for a few Sundays. Church-going is not regarded in practice as simply a worthwhile but optional aid to faith, but as something of faith's essence and inextricably bound up with it. Looking at these kinds of practices, I could easily echo Galea and say, "In practice, this means that the life of the devoted Evangelical is one of ritual obligation and performance. The message I received growing up, and which Evangelicals all over the world receive, was: Keep praying, keep reading the Bible, keep going to church on Sunday (and get involved in as many activities as possible), keep evangelising your colleagues, fellow students, etc., and you'll stand a pretty good chance of having been saved (otherwise, you might not have been saved in the first place)."

Am I engaging in an argument which might be summarised, "Oh yeah? Well, you're no better!" Though it might seem that way at first glance, the point I am trying to make is quite different. It should be clear that both Catholics and Evangelical Protestants have different ways of 'doing religion.' Whatever our words, we don't behave in practice as if salvation is a free ride, but rather oblige believers to do things, whether it be to fulfill and complete the work of grace in us (as Catholics do) or to justify a total justification already received (as Protestant Evangelicals do). But does that mean that we are as bad as each other, and both in effect undermining the free grace of Jesus' redemptive sacrifice? There might be some Christians (for example, from the Emerging Church) who would argue that, but I think that conclusion is too easy. There is more going on here than that.

The fundamental question is, "Given that God's grace has been poured out through the saving death and resurrection of Christ, how is that grace applied to the individual?" This is a non-partisan question. Neither Catholics nor Evangelical Protestants believe in universalism, that everyone will inevitably be saved. But Christ has died for all (2 Cor. 5:14), and did so more than two thousand years ago, and this does not mean that everyone alive after the resurrection was automatically saved. Human individuals are not saved the moment they are born (not even Calvinists believe that!). So how is the grace from that once-for-all act to be made effective to each individual? The Catholic replies that Christ's death and resurrection is applied primarily by the Holy Spirit in baptism, and then grows through the believer's participation in Christ through the sacraments and the life of sanctification, coming to its fulfillment in heaven. The Evangelical Protestant replies that Christ's death and resurrection is applied primarily by a single act of volitional faith at a particular moment, usually taking the form of a prayer, and then grows as the believer seeks to follow Christ and bear fruits worthy of repentance, coming to its fulfillment in heaven. These theologies are not so dissimilar as has been supposed, but merely assign the same roles to different things. Nor does either theology deny grace, for both Catholics and Evangelical Protestants believe firmly in prevenient grace—the doctrine that we do not seek after God unless he has first sought after us and planted the desire and power to seek him in our hearts.

So how is this not 'works-righteousness'? If I have to do something, doesn't that mean that I am *de facto* adding to the work of Christ? This question must apply, as we have seen, to both Catholics and Protestants and it is no idle question. I recall, while still a Protestant, having sophisticated and heated discussion with my fellow believers at an Evangelical Union Conference about why faith did not qualify as a work. In the end, none of us reached a satisfactory conclusion. Indeed, aren't all of these things, in the end, 'works'?

In fact, this is not the case. The reason is this. In all the above cases, I am not doing but receiving. I am not trying to push water upstream; I am clearing the rocks away so it can flow freely downstream and into me. I can't do anything to make Christ forgive me and renew me to my pre-Fall condition. But nor do I have to. He has already done it. Now it's just a matter of letting that reality affect, consume and transform me. Salvation is not about doing something but about not doing something, not about earning or obtaining salvation but about receiving salvation.[6]

Given that we all agree on that much, what is to be said for Galea's critique of the sacramental system? It should be clear now that if the sacraments are condemned on the basis of a mistaken *grace vs. works* polemic, there is nothing to prevent Protestant practice falling under the same condemnation. But, in fact, the criticism won't fly in either case, as we have just seen.

So why does the criticism seem to get so much traction? What *is* the difference between Baptism and the Sinner's Prayer?

If we assume for the moment that we are talking about adult baptism, the sole real difference is that one is a physical act said to bestow a spiritual reality, while the other is a mental act said to bestow a spiritual reality. I would propose that it is this that bothers Evangelical Protestants most about the sacramental system. It involves actions and words and objects. A simple prayer seems somehow more direct, simpler, unmediated.

And perhaps it is. But is it authentically Christian for all that?

An atheist or agnostic might inquire why God had to become man and die for us to be forgiven. Could not God simply forgive without the elaborate set-up of the Incarnation? Could he not simply have taken our sins upon himself without bothering about details like Jewish maids, bumbling disciples and cowardly Roman politicians? Several answers could be offered to such an inquiry. God wanted to reveal himself fully in a manner that was accessible to man. Without the shedding of blood there is no remission for sins. The old Patristic battle-cry of "What was not assumed is not redeemed." But surely a redemption without an incarnation would be a far more direct, simpler and unmediated way of salvation? Far more spiritual.

Perhaps, but I am reminded of Mr Bingley's response to his sister in Austen's *Pride and Prejudice* when she suggests that "[Balls] would surely be much more rational if conversation instead of dancing made the order of the day." "Much more rational," he replies, "but it would not be near so much like a ball." Likewise, a direct redemption without the bother of

---

6 Indeed, many Christian groups preserve this truth by continuing the hallowed practice of infant baptism. For a baby certainly can do nothing towards its salvation; and neither can it put up any obstacle to God's grace. It is precisely for this reason that Christians have since ancient times baptised infants, and the practice is a powerful testament to the doctrine of *sola gratia*.

the Incarnation would seem on the face of it much more direct, simpler, indeed more rational, but it would not be a genuine redemption. In the same way, a simple mental prayer seems a great deal more sensible than a sacrament requiring things and people and actions, but there is something vital, something essential, missing. For all its directness, it is a lot less human. It would fit the angels better.

That, at any rate, is the complaint that the early Christians would have made. Listen to St Cyril of Jerusalem in the mid-4th century:

> Since man is of a twofold nature, composed of body and soul, the purification is also twofold: the corporeal for the corporeal and the incorporeal for the incorporeal. The water cleanses the body, and the Spirit seals the soul. Thus, having our heart sprinkled by the Spirit and our body washed with pure water (cf. Heb. 10:22), we may draw near to God. When you go down into the water, then, regard not simply the water, but look for salvation through the power of the Holy Spirit. For without both you cannot attain to perfection. It is not I who say this but the Lord Jesus Christ, Who has the power in this matter. He says, *'Unless a man be born again of water and the Spirit, he cannot enter the kingdom of God'* (Jn 3:3 and 5). (*Catechetical Lectures* 3:4)

One of the misrepresentations that was sometimes used or bandied about by Catholic apologists during the Reformation was that the Protestants believed in salvation by intellect alone, that the Protestants taught that God required merely a mental acceptance of doctrine to be saved, or that Protestants believed one was saved by believing one was saved. This of course was and is false, and the Protestants rebutted the accusation by distinguishing *frigida opinio*, a simple belief that something is true, from *fiducia* or *fide vera*, that is, trust in a person. It is by trust in the person of Jesus Christ that we are saved, they said. In this they spoke the truth. Grace can only be received by faith and faith is, as Galea says, "an open hand ready to receive what God promises to give through Jesus Christ … It simply trusts another and receives salvation from him as a free gift. Faith points away from itself and says, 'I can't take away my own sins, or atone for them. Christ alone can do that for me'" (p. 69). So it is and so it does. But faith must be an act of the whole person, a truly open hand, not one half-closed, with only the mind and will ready to receive. One might venture a paraphrase of the Patristic Christological maxim and suggest that "what has not been offered in faith cannot be redeemed."

In fact, Protestant Evangelicals already know this. I have sat under many sermons in which I was urged to "write God a blank cheque", to examine myself to see if "there are any rooms in your life that you haven't let Jesus into." John Stott famously described his own conversion in similar terms:

> Intellectually speaking, I had believed in Jesus all my life, on the other side of the door. I had regularly struggled to say my prayers through the key-hole. I had even pushed pennies under the door in a vain attempt to pacify him. I had been baptised, yes and confirmed as well. I went to church, read my Bible, had high ideals, and tried to be good and do good. But all the time, often without realising it, I was holding Christ at arms length, and keeping him outside. I knew that to open the door might have momentous consequences (John Stott, quoted in Timothy Dudley-Smith, *John Stott: The Making of a Leader*, Inter-Varsity Press, Leicester, 1999, p. 95).

Faith, as the Reformers rightly said, must be a disposition of the whole person, not just of the intellect or, for that matter, of any other aspect of the human person taken in isolation. Those were challenging sermons that I sat under (they must have been—I can still remember them!), and there is a sense in which such openness to God's grace must be a lifelong thing, continually fought for, as I find myself constantly putting up obstacles on the road of discipleship. Yet it may be truly said that it is not really I who fight to clear such obstacles, even as I erect them, but Christ himself who lives in me and whose grace in me is being constantly renewed. The concept, as a concept, is not foreign to Evangelical Protestants, but this is precisely what the sacraments are. In accordance with my human nature (which is now shared by God himself in Christ), God has instituted that my whole person—body, soul, mind, emotion and will—receive his grace. Is this unbiblical? Hardly. For we are commanded to *"put on Jesus Christ, and make no provision for the flesh to fulfill its lusts"* (Rom. 13:14), for *"He who began a good work in you will carry it on to completion until the day of Christ Jesus"* (Phil. 1:6).

On the one side, then, it is claimed the sacramental economy makes salvation look "piecemeal", as J.I. Packer says and Galea reiterates (p. 80).

But this is not a just criticism, because the Christian life must, on that view, always be regarded as piecemeal and incomplete. Even St Paul did not see it "as a complete package" received all in one go. On the contrary, he wrote to the Philippians, *"Not that I have already obtained all this, or have already been made perfect, but I press on to take hold of that for which Christ Jesus took hold of me. Brothers, I do not consider myself yet to have taken hold of it. But one thing I do: Forgetting what is behind and straining toward what is ahead, I press on toward the goal to win the prize for which God has called me heavenward in Christ Jesus"* (Phil. 3:12-14).[7] Even Martin Luther himself would agree, for he says, "The sin, it is true, is wholly forgiven, but it has not been wholly purged. If the Holy Spirit is not ruling men, they become corrupt again; but the Holy Spirit must cleanse the wounds daily. Therefore this life is a hospital; the sin has really been forgiven, but it has not yet been healed."[8]

To summarise, rejection of the sacramental economy as a bit of "earning salvation by works" will not work. The same criticism can be too easily levelled at Evangelical practices on the same grounds. In fact, the only thing that separates them is that sacraments, which are received by faith, must be received as such by the whole person, whereas Protestant Evangelical 'sacraments' are only received by the will and intellect. On that ground, the Christian sacramental economy comports better with Scripture, the Creeds, the Reformers and even common exhortations heard from Evangelical pulpits.

There is also more on this matter that may be said from the Catholic side. To the Catholic (and no doubt to many other Christians as well), the Protestant Evangelical distrust of sacraments as channels of God's grace strikes one as symptomatic of a broader problem—a desire or belief that God should not get too involved. This is reflected in other beliefs commonly held by Protestant Evangelicals but not by other Christians, such as the imputation of the alien righteousness of Christ and, for those of a Calvinistic bent, monergism (the belief that God works to effectually bring about the salvation of individuals through spiritual regeneration without cooperation or consent from the individual). Common to all

---

[7] Notice also here that there is no contradiction between Christ's free gift and my striving to take hold of it. "Lord, ... You have indeed done for us all our works" (Is. 26:12).
[8] *Final Sermon at Wittenberg*, 1546, AE 51:373.

of these is the feeling that God's grace shouldn't get its hands dirty; it should always act externally, never from within. As such, the fact of the Incarnation is seen more as a singular event, almost a bit out of character for God, a one-off act on his part, rather than as an act of God thoroughly in keeping with his character, establishing an eternal principle. Christianity means that in Jesus, God became man and bore humanity's sin and death, destroying them, as it were, from the inside. In Jesus, God is still man and, by uniting myself with that man through faith (of the whole person, not just the will and intellect), my sin and death is also being destroyed from the inside. To Protestant Evangelicalism, grace can only be an external agent, and anything that comes from within me must be a 'work', an attempt at 'merit', something wholly unconnected to and necessarily opposed to grace. But classical Christianity does not make this false dichotomy. Neither does Scripture, for Our Lord himself tells us, *"Remain in me, and I will remain in you. No branch can bear fruit by itself; it must remain in the vine. Neither can you bear fruit unless you remain in me. I am the vine; you are the branches. If a man remains in me and I in him, he will bear much fruit; apart from me you can do nothing"* (Jn 15:4-5). This, likewise, is the only way to understand St Paul's talk of believers as members of Christ's Body. To this, it will be replied, "But what I do is merely a symptom of what has already been done. I do good works not in order to be redeemed, but because I have been redeemed." Indeed. But even if we were to accept the Protestant distinction between justification and sanctification (which the Catholic Church, together with the Eastern Orthodox, does not, though this again is less consequential than may at first appear—for which see below), redemption does not refer only to the former. When I am perfect, when I fully reflect Christ, then shall my redemption be brought to its completion. To deny this is to fall under the condemnation of 1 John 1:8. Redemption, from beginning to end, in my participation in it as much as its external action upon me, is the work of grace.

By rejecting the sacramental economy, by trying to draw a too sharp distinction between incorporation into Christ (justification) and the work of the Holy Spirit in the believer (sanctification), and by relegating the action of grace to something necessarily extrinsic to my soul, Protestant Evangelicalism inadvertently minimises our union with God in Christ, limiting the ways God is allowed to approach humanity to more 'spiritual' and non-incarnate methods, and thereby it places strictures on what his grace is allowed to do. But these limits are no necessary part of biblical Christianity; in fact, they signify a departure from it.

Galea writes that grace in Catholicism comes through human activity (i.e., the sacraments) in stages over a lifetime, "with the uncertain hope that sufficient righteousness will have been imparted and earned to merit salvation at the end." To this, we may now safely say that the accusation will not hold since sacraments are no more mere human activity than the Sinner's Prayer.

Assurance

In fact, it is worth pointing out that within Galea's statement above lies an implicit assumption in relation to assurance of salvation.

Indeed, the Evangelical Protestant will often lament that Catholics have no assurance of salvation. The question is often put, "Do you know where you'll spend eternity?" Any hesitation or confusion in answering the question is taken as confirmation of the respondent's status as one of the lost, and, with a flurry of biblical citations, it is soon impressed upon such a person that faith in Jesus will secure for them a certain and blessed afterlife. It doesn't seem to occur to those who use such evangelistic techniques that a respondent might have a personal relationship with Christ already and have chosen to leave it up to him where he/she spends eternity.[9] Indeed, I was surprised and not a little bemused to find that this very objection formed the core of the evangelical response to World Youth Day in 2008.

Now it should be said that assurance of salvation is by no means a foreign concept for Catholics. Here is what one Catholic wrote on the subject, for example:

The penitent thirsting for God feels the compunction of fear at first; later on, he experiences the compunction of love. When he considers

---

9 It is one of the symptoms of the cultural as well as doctrinal differences that stand between Catholics and Evangelical Protestants that, in the situation described above, the Evangelical Protestant is likely to think, "What a shame it is that Catholics are so uncertain of their salvation when, if they only read their Bibles, they would see what blessed assurance is available through faith in Christ," whereas the Catholic is likely to think, "Why is this Protestant talking to me as though the Last Judgment will be like a quiz where I have to know the right answer? And why is he acting like being able to quote the Bible without looking and cite chapter and verse is evidence of faith?"

his sins he is overcome with weeping because he fears eternal punishment. Then when this fear subsides through prolonged sorrow and repentance, a feeling of security emerges from an assurance of forgiveness, and the soul begins to burn with a love for heavenly joys. Now the same person, who wept out of fear of punishment, sheds abundant tears because his entrance into the kingdom of heaven is being delayed.[10]

This would not sound so strange coming from a Methodist preacher. In fact, it comes from the pen of Pope Gregory I.

So, it is baseless to accuse Catholics of having no assurance of salvation at all, of living their Christian lives in a perpetual state of uncertainty and fear. However, while recognising a place for assurance, the Catholic Church avoids turning it into a good in itself, much less a requirement of every believer. It is conscious that the Scriptures depict a Day of Judgement which sees individuals who are assured of their salvation but end up damned, as well as individuals who have no such assurance yet end up saved (Matt. 7:21-23; Matt. 25). Here we find a warning for Christians who are tempted to be complacent about their salvation. It is not up to us to judge either our souls or those of others.

At Protestant funerals, if the departed was a Christian, it is not uncommon for the people and the minister to speak of that person's presence in heaven as a given, and to turn the funeral into an act of thanksgiving for the departed's newfound place among the blessed. Informed Catholics know not to do this. They recognise that to speak in this way is to have judged the person's soul, and that to do so is to usurp a prerogative that belongs to Jesus Christ and him alone. Likewise, Catholics are conscious of the temptation to presumption, of assuming that I will be saved no matter what I do, of judging my own soul rather than committing my soul and its judgement to Jesus. On this matter, St Paul said, *"I care very little if I am judged by you or by any human court; indeed, I do not even judge myself. My conscience is clear, but that does not make me innocent. It is the Lord who judges me. Therefore judge nothing before the appointed time; wait till the Lord comes. He will bring to light what is hidden in darkness and will expose the motives of men's hearts. At that time each will receive his praise from God"* (1 Cor. 4:3-5).

---

10 Pope St Gregory the Great, *Dialogues*, 3.34, AD 593-594.

Our Lord's words in Matthew 25 provide, moreover, not just a warning for the complacent but good news for the scrupulous. For assurance of salvation is not a requirement for salvation. There will be, it seems, those who on the Last Day do not expect to be saved and yet will be. What is salvation's requirement, then? Matthew 25 provides an answer, and it is love of Christ, particularly in his less obvious guises.

In this connection, I believe it needs to be emphasised that, as the great preacher A.W. Tozer said, "God must be loved for himself."[11] I believe a paradigm shift needs to be made here, and it needs to be made by a vast number of Christians, both Protestant and Catholic. Salvation, redemption, justification or whatever we choose to call it is not a means to an end. As Christians, we do not commit ourselves to Jesus to get to heaven, as though he were the means to some other end. We do not receive salvation as some kind of insurance policy for the afterlife or the end of the world (whichever comes first). Our relationship with Jesus is not a ticket for something else. Heaven is precisely that relationship in its fullness: contemplation and communion with Jesus for eternity.

Jesus Christ will not suffer himself to be a means for any man. He will not tolerate being used. He *is* the end. He is the goal. He is the destination. He intends to be all in all (1 Cor. 15:28). He does not exist for me—I exist for him. So the mentality that sees—or offers—salvation in terms of, "I get something in exchange for something else" is fundamentally misguided. There is no transaction, no exchange. Jesus (much less faith or works or anything else) is not a ticket we present at the door in order to get in. Rather, we are, through the Holy Spirit, learning to breathe in a new atmosphere. We are being courted in preparation for a marriage. So, even faith or a relationship with Jesus, if it becomes simply a means to some other end, will do us no good.

Much preaching gives the impression that eternal life is a thing in itself, with Jesus attached as a necessary but arbitrary corollary. "Jesus died for you so that you could have eternal life" (indeed, far too often John 3:16 is quoted with this—presumably unintentional—subtext). But eternal life is not a thing in itself. Salvation is precisely a relationship with Jesus Christ,

---

11 The title and subject of one chapter in A.W. Tozer, *Man—The Dwelling Place of God*, Christian Publications, 1992. The chapter is also available online at http://www.worldinvisible.com/library/tozer/5j00.0010/5j00.0010.14.htm

nothing less. They are the same thing. Redemption (which ultimately, to be complete, must include the resurrection of the body; the soul free of guilt and sin, the body free of corruption and decay) is that relationship taken to its natural and necessary conclusion. Eternal life is no more or less than total and lasting union with God in Jesus Christ, a participation "in the divine nature" (2 Pet. 1:4). This is the goal of evangelism, and all our evangelistic efforts should impel and guide toward that end. As such, I worry that the preoccupation with assurance, which necessarily causes me to examine my own feelings rather than contemplate and pursue the Saviour, is simply unhelpful. As Pope St Gregory points out above, assurance may well come, but it generally comes to the mature Christian and it comes as a corollary of a total focus on and pursuit of Jesus. It is certainly not a right to be demanded, much less a litmus test of salvation, as far too many Protestant evangelists treat it. And, to return to Galea's statement quoted earlier, language like "sufficient righteousness will have been imparted and earned to merit salvation at the end" is not only incorrect when used to describe Catholic theology, but also inherently problematic because it completely ignores the whole concept of personal relationship that is so vital to any understanding of the sacraments, much less soteriology in general.

What I must seek after, and what I must press upon those whom I evangelise, is not assurance of salvation (which, as the Scriptures show [Matt. 7:21-23], may turn out to be mistaken) but Jesus Christ, who is himself our salvation. Both my personal evangelising and my own Christian life should have this in view: that through prayer, Scripture, the Church community and most particularly in the sacraments he instituted, I meet and commune with Jesus Christ and am formed through that union, by grace and the Holy Spirit, into his likeness until, at last, on the Day of Resurrection, I shall stand before him redeemed, recreated, as the creature that he always intended I should be, united with him in cross-shaped love.

I believe the above answers sufficiently Galea's chief objections on the subject of grace. However, there are other issues that he mentions or touches on briefly in the same chapter, and these too deserve some explanation in response, lest Galea's rejection of them and (in some cases) ridicule be regarded as unanswerable.

Purgatory

At the end of the previous section we considered how Jesus Christ is not simply the doorway to, but *is*, our eternal destiny as Christians. Thinking thus about the Parousia and the destiny of "righteous men made perfect" (Heb. 12:23) brings us within range of the doctrine of Purgatory, and at this point I must make a curious confession. I believed in Purgatory as a Protestant Evangelical.

Don't misunderstand me. I don't mean to say that I came to believe in Purgatory and that this was my first step on the road towards Catholicism. On the contrary. I believed in Purgatory years before Catholicism was even on my radar. It was during my university years, when one pushes the envelope of ideas, testing and experimenting with thought and doctrine, a process that ideally culminates in making the faith once delivered ultimately one's own (that is, at any rate, how it worked for me, thanks in no small part to a supportive Christian community on campus in the form of the Evangelical Union). At the time, I knew no Catholics, or if I did I didn't know them as such, and Catholicism was nothing but vague rumours of works-righteousness and transubstantiation, about which I knew roughly as much as I did about Mormons or Buddhists. However, it seemed to me, in my reading of Scripture and my thinking about doctrine, that two things were quite clear. One was that *"nothing impure shall enter"* the heavenly Jerusalem (Rev. 21:27). The other was that it seemed very doubtful that every Christian was fully sanctified by the time they died (possibly any Christian—I recalled that St Augustine had somewhere mentioned how, even years later, images and memories of his past deeds were still the cause of temptations for him). Given these two facts, it was logically necessary to suppose that the process of sanctification is brought to its completion for the vast majority of believers at some point after death, but before they enter the heavenly Jerusalem, i.e., into the fullness of God's presence. Rummaging around the dregs of half-remembered conversations and general knowledge, I recalled that there was a word for such post-mortem completion of sanctification: Purgatory.

Of course, that was as far as I went. I had heard that Catholics believed you could spend years in Purgatory and that people could use various methods to shorten their time there. I had heard that it was a place, like Heaven and Hell will be places after the General Resurrection. But I didn't feel any need to subscribe to any of that. As far as I was concerned, in all likelihood, the completion of sanctification is probably instantaneous and takes place the moment after death, and I found agreeable the thought that it would be the very gaze of God upon my soul that would bring to an end every skerrick of fallenness in me. In this sense, one would speak of being "in Purgatory" in the same way one speaks of being "in love"— not a place, but an event, an experience. I imagined that this was a rather different idea from what the Catholic Church taught and, unlike the dread and fear which I imagined that medievals had felt towards Purgatory, I found myself looking forward to it with great longing. Of course, several of my fellow Evangelicals raised their eyebrows when I spoke of my ideas, but I thought (and think) them perfectly defensible from Scripture, and no less biblical than the doctrine of the Trinity or the Hypostatic Union. Like these two latter doctrines, they follow on naturally and logically from the biblical data (Lk 12:59; 1 Cor. 3:13-15; Heb. 12:22-23; 2 Tim. 1:16-18). I imagined that the Catholic Church had, as with so many other doctrines, merely allowed Purgatory to become overgrown with a lot of later accretions and that Protestants, in their zeal to prune things back to allow biblical truth to shine through, had lopped off one branch too many; as though, eager to deny the Immaculate Conception, someone had inadvertently denied the Virgin Birth.

Much, much later, when I began to investigate the truth of Catholicism on the basis of entirely different issues (as I have already described), I supposed I should take a look at what the Church taught about Purgatory and to what extent it lined up with what I already believed. Surprisingly, I found that there was precious little dogma about Purgatory, and a great deal of freedom and room for speculation. The *Catechism of the Catholic Church* states, "All who die in God's grace and friendship, but still imperfectly purified, are indeed assured of their eternal salvation; but after death they undergo purification, so as to achieve the holiness necessary to enter the joy of heaven" (CCC 1030). That's it. Not a physical place. No time limits. Just a completion of the Spirit's work of sanctifying the believer. Unwittingly, I had derived from Scripture and a bit of logical deduction a Catholic doctrine whole and entire, completely independently of the Catholic Church!

For this reason, I still find it remarkable when Evangelical Protestants go out of their way to reject Purgatory, and I sometimes suspect such reactions owe much to a knee-jerk rejection of anything bearing the faint odour of "Romish-ness." Galea says that the teaching of Purgatory clearly assumes that the death of Jesus is insufficient to wash the believer of sin and its consequences. However, when the Catholic who actually knows his or her faith is asked, "What sanctifies us after death?" He or she will reply, "The same thing that sanctifies us while we are alive: Jesus' death and resurrection."

Two things follow from this, which hadn't occurred to me previously but had occurred to the Catholic Church. One is prayers for the dead. Which, as it turns out, is not a Catholic practice *per se*, but a Jewish one[12], which the early Christians simply continued to practise (as evidenced by inscriptions in the Catacombs). If one accepts Purgatory in some form (as I think one must from Scripture), prayer for the dead makes complete sense. Even if final sanctification is instantaneous, my prayers are still worthwhile, in the same way that I may pray for my brother if he is going for a job interview, even if the interview happened this morning and I am praying for him this afternoon (before I have heard from him how it went) and even if I am quite sure that he will get the job. It may be objected that we can ask nothing for the dead because they are dead, their race is run, their course finished, and besides, God has already done everything for them and to pray for the dead implies that the once-for-all sacrifice of Christ is somehow insufficient. To this objection, C.S. Lewis once replied, "But don't we believe that God has already done and is already doing all that he can for the living? What more should we ask? Yet we are told to ask" (C.S. Lewis, *Letters to Malcolm: Chiefly on Prayer* 20). To deny the possibility of prayer for the dead on the basis of the finished work of Christ must logically also call into question prayer for the living. I think there are few Christians who would go down that road.

The second thing is indulgences, that much-maligned and much-

---

12 Part of the Yizkor, one of the Jewish prayers of mourning, runs, "Have mercy upon him; pardon all his transgressions . . . Shelter his soul in the shadow of Thy wings. Make known to him the path of life." The practice of praying for the dead was certainly common in Judaism during and before the time of Christ and the Apostles also, as may be seen from 2 Maccabees 12:43-45. It is worth noting the explicit connection made in 2 Maccabees 12 between prayers for the dead and the doctrine of the resurrection of the body. Given the absolute centrality of the latter to Christian faith, it is hardly surprising that Christianity continued the practice.

misunderstood doctrine. To get to indulgences, though, requires a bit of theological legwork. Firstly, it must be pointed out that the Catholic Church teaches that we can help fellow believers on the path of discipleship, not only by our prayers but also by our actions. This ought to be an obvious point, except that the concept of doing any kind of work that is not intellectual but more hands-on tends to raise the bogeyman of 'works-righteousness' in the Evangelical mind. But let us have done with such irrational reactions. If I am mentoring someone in my church (as, say, an assistant minister), doing marriage counselling, running the Sunday school, leading a Bible study, going to visit the elderly or doing street evangelism, I am helping people towards Christ. This much, I hope, all parties will accept. This is the first point.

The second point is this. Part of the essential work of the Holy Spirit in my sanctification is cleansing me of the effects of my past sins, both external and internal. Thus, if I, newly converted, have long had a terrible temper, though my sins are forgiven through the Blood of Christ, there still remains (a) my reputation for having a temper in the eyes of family and friends, the hurt I have caused them on numerous occasions and their long-standing habit of giving me a wide berth if they sense I am stressed and (b) the effects on my personality, the difficult-to-break habit of flying off the handle at the slightest provocation; in a word, a near-total lack of self-control. My conversion doesn't instantly fix all of these things. However, that doesn't mean that the Blood of Christ is insufficient; it simply means that some of its effects are instantaneous (my relationship with God is now as it should be) and some of them take time. This is what sanctification is. Of course, this does not preclude my co-operating in the process. If the Spirit prompts me to hold my tongue when I would very much like to give someone a tongue-lashing, I should take the hint. If I know that tiredness makes me irritable, I should ensure I get to bed at a decent hour each night. I may even go and get anger management counselling. None of these things involve me adding to the work of the Spirit since they are all done in the power of the Spirit anyway, i.e., by grace. Indeed, if I didn't do these things, saying, "I don't want to earn my salvation; God will make me Christ-like on his own", I think both Protestants and Catholics would tell me not to be stupid, and quite probably both would quote Philippians 2:12-13 at me. Thus, all the work of sanctification, including whatever I bring to it, is done through the Holy Spirit, solely by the grace flowing from Christ's death and resurrection. This also, I think, we can all agree on.

The Catholic Church takes all of this one step further, allowing these two points to dovetail with each other. We are all, by virtue of our union with Christ, members of one Body, bound together in the Spirit, and therefore connected to each other in a profound sense that transcends race, family and even gender (Gal. 3:28; Our Lord also hints at this in Mt 12:49-50). Therefore, the Church reasons, in the same way that I can help fellow believers towards Christ by my actions and prayers, I can contribute to their sanctification by participating in the work of the Spirit in my own life. Because of our profound connection in Christ, and solely through that connection, such things will in fact sanctify them. This is, of course, a theological leap, and not one Protestants of any stripe tend to make, but it is not for that reason an unbiblical one, as evidenced by the mysterious phrase of St Paul in Colossians 1:24 *("Now I rejoice in my sufferings for your sake, and in my flesh I complete what is lacking in Christ's afflictions for the sake of his body, that is, the church").*

An indulgence, then, is simply such an act of participation in the sanctifying work of the Spirit. It may be for my own sanctification or, as noted here, for the purification of a soul in Purgatory. On the small-scale, it could be something as simple as reading Scripture for fifteen minutes with a proper mindset (i.e., a mind fixed on Christ and detached from any sinful desire or impulse). Alternately, it could be patient endurance in the face of an ongoing adversity in one's life. By attaching an indulgence to such things, the Church declares them to be inherently sanctifying if done with the right motives (that latter element is crucial), and that the sanctification from these things can be passed on, through our union with Christ, to someone else. It should be pointed out that all of this presupposes that the person attaining an indulgence has repented and is already firm in their life of discipleship. Thus the Church 'indulges' such persons, not in their sin, but in mitigating or removing the concrete consequences of sin. It is, one might say, a sanctification boost.

All the chief ideas upon which the doctrine of indulgences rest is found in Scripture: the Church's power to bind and loose, vicarious sanctification between members of the Church, and my participation in the Spirit's work of sanctifying. Although the doctrine has developed over the centuries it is not in the least unbiblical.

The Reformation controversy over indulgences owed to the fact that one such method of 'gaining an indulgence' (i.e., contributing to someone else's sanctification after death) was by giving to the poor or to the Church—what would be called nowadays tithing. This, not entirely surprisingly, led to abuses and corruption on the part of those collecting the money and popularising this particular form of indulgence, and Luther was right to decry the abuses (such abuses were previously condemned in Church Councils as far back as 1215, 1245, 1274 and 1312). Indeed, the Catholic Church took many of his criticisms seriously and it was during the Reformation that the Church forbade Church-sponsored indulgences involving money. Weirdly, the indulgences controversy had surprisingly little to do with his later doctrinal disagreements with the Church.

The connection of this with Purgatory should be obvious. If I can assist in the sanctification of a living fellow believer by virtue of our union with Christ, then I can do the same for one who is dead. The same concept applies here as it does to prayer. Obviously, if their sanctification *is* complete, whatever I do, be it Scripture reading, patient endurance in a time of adversity, an unseen act of charity, prayer or anything else, God will apply the merit to some other soul who needs it, according to his wisdom and mercy.

Frankly, I don't see any particular reason why any of these things should be problematic for the average Protestant Evangelical. There is nothing particularly offensive about the theology involved, and, as I said before, I suspect most of the problems are simply due to the stigma of Catholicism. On the other hand, I can see why a Protestant Evangelical wouldn't want to commit to them necessarily. Many, though willing to accept such possibilities as interesting biblical speculation, might wish to reserve them for the liberty of the believer, rather than turning them into dogma on the level of statements in the Creed. To be honest, that position makes a certain amount of sense to me. Certainly, the Eastern Orthodox never made such speculations even if their practice does include, as it always has, prayers for the dead. Still, our souls long for Purgatory (certainly mine does), for the final cleansing, the complete healing, to have all our fallenness repaired, our prelapsarian natures restored, our eyes adjusted to gaze at last on the light of the Almighty in a rapture of undiluted love and joy. To quote C.S. Lewis again: "Would it not break the heart if God said to us, 'It is true, my son, that your breath smells and your rags drip with mud and slime, but we are charitable here and no one will upbraid you with these things, nor draw away from you. Enter into the joy.' Should we not reply, 'With submission, sir and if there is no objection, I'd *rather* be cleaned first.' 'It may hurt, you know.' 'Even so, sir'" (C.S. Lewis, *Ibid.*).

Confession

Galea singles out confession (the Sacrament of Penance or Reconciliation, to give it its proper name) as an example of the problems he sees in the sacramental economy, which I treated in a more general sense earlier; and thus it would perhaps be proper to say a few things on this subject specifically also. Indeed, quite proper, as it looms large in the Protestant Evangelical mind and seems in many ways to encapsulate so much of what Evangelicals find objectionable about Catholicism.

I would like to come at the subject from two different but complementary angles. The first regards the nature of sin. For human beings in general sin has three effects, and for sin to be dealt with each of these effects must be addressed. The first and most important, and indeed most fundamental, is our relationship with God. Sin, even in its most minor, habitual and inadvertent forms, distorts and weakens our relationship with God. When the person commits a serious or mortal sin, that relationship is broken utterly. Indeed, every human is born into that position because of the sin of Adam.

The second is in our relationship with others and, on a larger view, with the whole of creation. Sin distorts and destroys every relationship I have, even if the sin is a secret one and is not known to anyone but myself.

Finally, it damages and distorts my own nature. By sinning, I become less human, less like the creature I was created to be. My members war within me, my passions rage against my reason, my imagination rages against my intellect, my body rages against my soul. For the Christian, the stakes are higher. By grace I am cleansed from Original Sin, but the ever-present tendency to sin, the fallenness of my broken human nature remains. Thanks be to God for the power of the Holy Spirit whose transforming power is at work in me! But if I do sin, the consequences are, if anything, more far-reaching. By doing so, I reject the grace of God and grieve the Spirit, introducing barriers into my relationship with God. I weaken the Body of Christ, whose member I am. I also profane the temple of the Holy Spirit—myself. What is to be done for the Christian in this situation? The Protestant Evangelical would advise me to pray a prayer of repentance. That is good as far as it goes—in fact, it is absolutely necessary!—but it only deals with one of the effects of sin: its effect on my relationship with God. What about the other two effects—especially given that my relationship with God is so intimately bound up with my relationship with the rest of the Church, since it is, after all, his Body?

The Catholic Church (not to mention all the other Christian denominations that practice confession[13]) in its theology and practice, allows God to deal with all three effects. Through repentance, contrition and prayer, my relationship with God is restored. Through the ministry of the Church, embodied in the priest, my relationship with my fellow believers (which is part of my relationship with God, after all) is restored. By being forced to confront my sin verbally and without excuse, I am, in a sense, restored to myself.[14] In this way, God deals with the specific sins of believers, both holistically and with surgical precision. In addition, the Church makes a part of this practice acts of satisfaction, more commonly known as penances. These are what were discussed earlier: my participation in the Spirit's work of sanctifying me and undoing the temporal (as opposed

---

13 It is worth remembering, here as earlier, that Galea, in singling out the Catholic Church, has set himself in opposition against the majority of Bible-believing Christians, both historically and currently, including all the Orthodox Churches and not a few Protestants, most notably the Lutherans, from Luther to the present day, and the Anglican Reformers and divines.

14 This element bears emphasising. It is too easy, when all one has to do is say a quick mental prayer, to whitewash one's sins. This, of course, is never one's intention. But the tendency is almost ineluctable. Having done so for the better part of one's life, the sudden duty of verbalising one's sins—unspeakable thoughts and deeds, long-standing habits and vices, things on which one's conscience has been progressively and imperceptibly dulled—articulating such things with words which one had perhaps never articulated before even to oneself, laying them out clinically and systematically, without excuse or justification, long after the pleasure of the thoughts and deeds themselves has evaporated—let me say here, having had long experience of both approaches, that the latter is far more terrifying, more arresting, more humiliating and ultimately more beneficial. My own relationship with Jesus Christ is better for going to confession. The irony is, having a clearer vision of my own sinfulness than ever before, I am far more aware of my own need for grace, and more inclined to seek it in him alone, apart from my own mental strivings and self-imposed emotionally cathartic guilt-trips.

to eternal) effects of sin. This might take the form of returning something if I have stolen it or apologising to a wronged party. More often, the priest will ask me to pray a prayer or series of prayers, knowing that the most damaging effect of sin is to take my focus off God and place it on created things. Prayer counters that tendency effectively by placing my focus back on God, where it should be.

The second angle from which I want to come at this subject is that of the Body of Christ and mediator-ship. Probably the most common objection Evangelical Protestants bring against the Christian practice of confession is that it appears to them to place someone between the believer and Jesus Christ in the realm of forgiveness. "I don't need a priest to stand between me and Jesus," it is declared, "I can go to Jesus directly." Invariably, (sometimes in a tone of eager zeal and joy-filled freedom, occasionally in a tone of triumphalism) 1 Timothy 2:5 will be quoted: *"For there is one God, and one mediator between God and men, the man Christ Jesus."* The simplest reply to this is that the objection betrays the lack of a coherent ecclesiology.

Of course, such a reply won't suffice on its own, unexplained. Some detail will have to be gone into. To begin with, the thing that is ignored by the recourse to 1 Timothy 2:5 is all of St Paul's language throughout his letters about the Church as the Body of Christ, with Christ himself as its Head. This, it should be observed, is not simply a metaphor or symbol. St Paul is talking about a reality. In Ephesians 5, he calls it a mystery, something hidden from the understanding but nonetheless real. We are, in a mysterious but true sense, incorporated into Christ and made one with him and, thereby, with each other. Now, let us suppose, one weekend, you had decided to do some handy work around the house and, weighing up your options and coming to the clear conclusion that a new bookshelf was needed, you proceeded to pick up your hammer and some nails and get to work; and then suppose a passer-by (or perhaps a relative) saw you hard at work and commented, "What is your hand building with that hammer?" An odd turn of phrase. Or, stranger still, the aforementioned person inquired, "Why are your hands building that bookshelf? Why aren't *you* doing it? You look capable enough." Most probably, you would think your interlocutor was either a bit soft in the head or was having a joke. Of course, it is true that your hands are building the bookshelf. But setting your hands up in opposition to you yourself—to your brain or to your creative mind or whatever—is idiotic. I believe the objection, "I don't need a priest to stand between me and Jesus—I can go to him directly," makes exactly the same nonsensical dichotomy.

Jesus Christ *is* the sole mediator. The *"mediator of a new covenant, [of] the sprinkled blood that speaks a better word than the blood of Abel"* (Heb. 12:24). His actions through his Body can hardly be said to be mediated through a third party, anymore than my hands mediate for me if I build a bookshelf with tools. Yes, it is true to say that my hands build it. But it is equally, if not more, true to say that I build it. Myself. Directly. In the same way, one may say with accuracy that the priest forgives sins in confession. But it would be equally, if not more, accurate to say that Jesus Christ forgives my sins there, and that he does so directly.

Why should Jesus forgive the specific sins committed by Christians in this fashion? It comes back to the whole reason behind the sacramental economy, and that is that, consonant with our nature, the Passion and Resurrection of Christ were at once spiritual and physical events and therefore the way their benefits are applied to us must likewise be at once spiritual and physical, thereby addressing the whole person and applying the mercy of Christ to the whole person. Thus, rather than isolating the will and intellect, Christ instituted a method whereby all the faculties are engaged and thereby healed.

Why should it be priests that one must confess to and be absolved by? St Paul tells us, *"There are different kinds of gifts, but the same Spirit. There are different kinds of service, but the same Lord. There are different kinds of working, but the same God works all of them in all men ... The body is a unit, though it is made up of many parts; and though all its parts are many, they form one body. So it is with Christ"* (1 Cor. 12:4-6, 12). Moreover, the gospels tell us that Jesus bestowed authority to forgive sins, not on all believers, but on those he had set aside for public ministry—*"And when he had said this, he breathed on them, saying, 'Receive the Holy Spirit. If you forgive the sins of any, they are forgiven; if you retain the sins of any, they are retained'"* (Jn 20:22-23). I recall an incident some time ago when an Anglican pastor friend of mine asked me for the scriptural basis for confession. When I responded with this verse, he said, "That's a very long bow you're drawing there." There are, perhaps, many who would agree with him. But the alternative—attempting to explain the verse away by saying that what Jesus really means is "If you *preach* the forgiveness of sins to any ..."—is, I think, a far longer bow to draw. It is far easier, and makes more sense theologically, historically and exegetically, to simply take the text literally.

Odd and End

A final point. All too often, I suspect, many differences between us that we think major turn out, upon examination, to be either minor or even illusory. But there are other subtler differences to which our attention is rarely drawn but which are nonetheless of greater consequence.

One of these is the Protestant habit, strengthened by the tendency to speak of our redemption primarily, and sometimes exclusively, in legal and forensic terms, of regarding both sin and grace as titles or decrees and nothing more. This habit of mind, I feel, is active in much of Galea's critique. On this view, one sits under a sentence of condemnation—that is what sin is. Then one receives a pardon and is declared acquitted—that is what grace is. There is, naturally, plenty of Scriptural warrant for this view. But it is not the only image provided by Scripture, nor even the principal one.

Another such, to take an example, is poison to denote sin (Deut. 29:18; 32:32; Amos 6:12), a substance whose effects are deadly but slow-acting. To adapt the metaphor to a modern context, we might speak of sin as a drug addiction.

There is a moment when you cease to take a drug, when you have your last bong or whatever. But then you've got the consequences to deal with, the damage the drug has done to your body, the cravings, etc. Sin is poison. It is an acid. It eats away at our souls. It cripples us, emotionally, mentally, spiritually and sometimes even physically. That doesn't go away in an instant. Human beings are creatures of time and process. God's grace in Christ does not treat us as though we were not. God did, after all, create us like that.

Grace is not magic. It builds on nature, as the Fathers were so fond of saying; it doesn't obliterate it. It is like yeast in bread (cf. Lk 13:20-21). The poison must be sucked out. The burns must be healed, not just bandaged over. Grace alone can do it—I certainly can't do it on my own, any more than I could do my own open-heart surgery. But grace is not simply a diploma, a title. It is life itself. It is the Blood of Christ in my veins; the sap of the True Vine; the antivenin. It has to be pumped through my system, get to where the poison is and nullify it.

The cravings may one day diminish. There may come a day when, through the work of grace, I will have little desire for the drug of sin, that everything contrary to the will of God will repulse me. However, that day is not yet. I'm still in rehab. My system is still being purged, my soul still being cleansed. But grace *is* a reality. It is effective. It effects real change in me. As long as I submit to it, the work will continue apace. This is redemption.

Conclusion

To wrap up, I think the theological problems highlighted in Galea's objections may be roughly summarised under two propositions: God, save in the exceptional case of the Incarnation, does not work through matter or intrinsically in the human person, but only extrinsically via man's 'spiritual' faculties; and, sin and grace are not primarily realities but titles.

I do not believe that either of these propositions is of the essence of Evangelicalism. As we have seen, in subtle and not-so-subtle ways the theology of the Catholic Church can frequently be found reflected in the practice of Protestant Evangelicals. The abysses that we imagine exist between us, certainly as regards the subject of grace, are neither so yawning nor so insurmountable as we might have supposed. In a few cases, they are merely perception. In many others, the gaps narrow between Catholic theology and Evangelical praxis, even if new gaps seem to appear between Evangelical praxis and Protestant rhetoric. In those cases where there is genuine insurmountable disagreement, it may be hoped that, aided by the grace of the Holy Spirit, we at least understand each other's reasoning better. In all things it is to be remembered that, as important as doctrinal orthodoxy is (and it is, for our beliefs ought to be in line with spiritual reality), we are never absolved from the obligation to love one another. I hope that, in this response to Galea's criticisms, I have not failed to do so.

In the meantime, we may offer up praise to God that, despite appearances, we do agree on the sheer gratuitousness of God's love for us in Christ. May we therefore come before our crucified and risen Lord with empty hands, ready to receive.

7

Mary

Kiran Newman[1]

Introduction

Nothing in *Nothing in my Hand I Bring* resonated with me quite as much as what Ray Galea says on page 21: "The truth really does matter. And the truth about Jesus matters most of all. Ask and it will be given to you, said Jesus. Seek and you will find."

For I too, like Galea, am a convert, and that several times over. I was born a Hindu, became an atheist at the age of ten, receded into agnosticism at the age of sixteen, became an Anglican in 2002, and finally became a Catholic on December 2, 2003. I too, like him, have felt God drawing me here, and have had to leave a "culture and community" and face accusations of arrogance in order to come home to God and his Church. To this day, most of my family do not understand my Christianity as anything but a betrayal of my heritage. Now, this leaves us in a bit of a bind, because the Church which I call home, and into which Jesus has led me and continues to lead me, is that which Galea left because he (in his own words) "could no longer remain within the Catholic Church and be true to the Lord Jesus" (p. 20). Needless to say, it is profoundly sad that, growing up Catholic, Galea possessed no sense of "Jesus' complete authority" over his life, or that Jesus was the "focus of [his] spirituality" (p. 16).

From what one reads in Galea's book, it is almost as though such things as the Society of Jesus, or indeed of Catholic devotion to the Sacred Heart of Jesus, or the Holy Name of Jesus, or the Stations of the Cross, or to the Divine Mercy, or to the Holy Spirit, or the ancient practice of *Lectio Divina*, involving slow and meditative reading of the Scriptures, were non existent. Nor is any mention made of the 'Jesus Prayer' (*Lord Jesus Christ,*

---

[1] Kiran Newman is a convert from High Anglicanism. He recently completed his doctorate at The University of Sydney (studying the scientific revolution of the 12th century) and is currently discerning his vocation with the Order of Preachers (Dominicans).

Son of God, have mercy on me, a sinner), or in more recent times, Pope John Paul II's great affirmation:

> Christ, the Redeemer of the world, is the one Mediator between God and men, and there is no other name under heaven by which we can be saved (cf. Acts 4:12) ... Jesus Christ is the recapitulation of everything (cf. Eph. 1:10) and at the same time the fulfilment of all things in God: a fulfilment which is the glory of God. The religion founded upon Jesus Christ is a religion of glory; it is a newness of life for the praise of the glory of God (cf. Eph. 1:12).[2]

I digress, but I wish to make a point, which needs to be clarified before we get to Mary, that whatever can be said about other Catholic devotions, they are not intended to take away from, but to enhance devotion to Our Lord Jesus Christ. The same principle applies here as to any other normal healthy intimate relationships: they deepen our relationship with God, and are gifts to us from God to lead us to himself. A relationship with Mary should lead us to Jesus, just as a healthy relationship with our parents should, if they are Christians, lead us to Jesus. Indeed, under normal circumstances, such relationships are an essential part of our relationship with God. An assumption that a relationship with Mary is to be excluded is bizarre, and unreal. It is bizarre because no one behaves as if a normal relationship with my brother or my mother will get in the way of a normal relationship with my father. Indeed, each of us depends on a whole network of relationships within our relationship with God, with a pastor, or a minister, with friends, but also with great Christians who have gone before us, both those immediately in the past, and those from a long time ago. I would imagine that such a list for any Christian would include people like St Augustine, St Paul, St John, St Jerome, C.S. Lewis, and G.K. Chesterton. Such relationships bring us closer to God, and do not take us away from him, because in all of these cases, one could say (more or less) that they point us to God. Mary, I would like to suggest here, is one such, indeed the greatest such, pointer to Christ and, therefore, God.

---

2 Pope John Paul II, *Apostolic Letter Tertio Millenio Adveniente* 6, 1994.

To Jesus through Mary?

My own journey might, I hope, serve as an interesting example. When I decided to give Christianity a go, I started attending an Anglican Church. It was as an Anglican, and within the tradition of Anglicanism, that I came to believe in the Real Presence of Jesus in the Blessed Sacrament, which Luther had held in some form, and which had been defended within the Anglican Communion by such wonderful preachers as the great 17th century divines Lancelot Andrewes, John Pearson, and John Donne. I was and am immensely grateful to the Anglican Communion for teaching me about the Real Presence, and thus sustaining my faith. I could tell you a story about how I moved from this to reading about the great Anglican Bishops' devotion to Mary, but fortunately or unfortunately, I did not discover the Anglican writings on Mary until well into my Catholic life. I came to Anglican Mariology rather as one might find a chocolate hidden in a schoolboy's lunch, having no idea I'd had it there all along. What did happen next was my baptism, which on the one hand pushed me out into a deeper search: I had reached thus far, but on the one hand, was deeply disquieted by the fact that quite a lot of my evangelical Anglican brethren seemed not to be quite in line with Anglican tradition on the Real Presence, and on the other hand, that mainstream Anglicanism seemed in many respects moving away from Christian orthodoxy, suggesting abandonment, for instance, of such basic elements of the Christian Faith as the bodily resurrection, and the Divinity of Christ, or divinely given moral precepts. I had finally run up against the fact that within the womb of Anglicanism were two rival nations, neither of which seemed to hold on to what had attracted me to Christianity in the first place: the conviction of the reality of Christ— the conviction which historically had been found within the Anglican Communion, but which had evaporated under the pressure of controversy, or the needs of the age.

For the first time, around this time, I met Catholics at the University of Sydney. Soon afterwards, after an initial reluctance, I started exploring Catholicism. One thing that changed during my journey into the Church was that, where I had previously struggled with conforming my actions to my morality, now, I found a supportive community within which goodness was presented not as an ideal, but as a real possibility. Indeed, this had been part of what drew me to the Catholic Church, that it put goodness within reach of ordinary human beings. It confirmed what I knew, and what gave me hope in the search for God: the potential for graced but nonetheless genuine and observable goodness in other human beings. This is not, I should clarify, about the "human creature participating servant-like in its own redemption", or about earning salvation by good works, but in knowing and seeing the work of God on earth, the sort of thing, for instance, that is involved in responding to something good with "Praise God!"

Within a Catholic context, I discovered personal prayer. Of course, I had prayed before, and gone to services, but it was Catholics who taught me to have a personal relationship with the God I worshipped, to speak to him, not just to ask him for things, but also to thank him, and to get to know him. The first prayer I was introduced to was the Divine Office, which consists of psalms, a reading, and a gospel canticle, either the Canticle of Zechariah (Lk 1:68-79) in the morning, the Canticle of Mary (Lk 1:46-55) in the evening, the Canticle of Simeon (Lk 2:29–32) at night. Note that all of these canticles are from the Gospel of Luke. One can see from this the devotion of Catholics to the Incarnation. All prayer takes place in light of God's completely unmerited reaching out to humanity. It was in this context then that I first came upon Mary. It is Mary's prayer of thanksgiving to God that I recited every evening. Later still, I discovered the Rosary, which I did not always feel comfortable praying, not because I had any objection to Mary, or to the repetitiveness, but because the Rosary forced me to actually pray, to actually engage in the act of contemplating God and what he had done for me.

The Rosary reveals something quite profound about Christian prayer: that it is ultimately an act of contemplating God. More particularly, it is an act of contemplating God as God has revealed himself to us in the life, death and resurrection of Jesus Christ. It is much easier to read a psalm (with inner commentary and appreciation of phrasing and so on) than it is to simply contemplate God in his wonderfulness. The Rosary by its very repetitiveness forces the issue, but it also provides with it its own solution. The Rosary is a series of meditations upon specific things that God has done for humanity. But is not the Rosary all about Mary? Well, simply, no. The focus is never primarily upon Mary but on our need for God, and on God's response to that need in Jesus Christ. Mary was part of God's plan for the redemption of humanity, and most significantly, the closest human being to Jesus. As such, she occurs repeatedly in the Rosary, but the entire logic of the Rosary is to focus on the figure of Jesus, and to do so relentlessly. To focus on Jesus is not, and ought not to be, entirely easy. After all, we are sinful and unworthy persons, and he whom we worship bore in his own body the consequence of our sins. Besides, few escape the temptation to focus on the most important person in the world–oneself. To this day, the Rosary (which I say almost every day) is not an easy prayer for me. Yet, I persist in it precisely because it brings me closer to Jesus, when my own natural instinct is to run away from him into myself. Sometimes this can be very disconcerting. The Rosary includes within it, not only a meditation upon Mary's child, but also upon Mary's God, teaching us the austere lessons of his rejection, so that he is known of ox and ass, but not of men, and of the continuation of that rejection in his trial and his Cross, leading ultimately towards his triumphal resurrection and ascension back to the Father.

However, is it not the case that there is one Our Father to ten Hail Marys, and do the mysteries not involve what Mary does, or what happens to Mary? Both of these are true. But in order to put both of these in context, we need to explore why the Hail Mary is a prayer, given that any prayer is a conversation with God. A Catholic would see the Hail Mary as a prayer, firstly because it begins with a recognition of what God has done for us, the incarnation. Thus, just as the term Mother of God, as Barth explains, is a Christological definition[3], so too the Hail Mary begins with a recognition of God's work for us in echoing the salutation of the Angel to Mary (Lk 1:28) and St Elizabeth's greeting of Mary (Lk 1:42), is transporting us back to the moment of the Annunciation, and St Elizabeth's recognition of her Saviour, and his mother. With the Angel and St Elizabeth, we celebrate God's work. And the second part of the Hail Mary, similarly recognises our sinful condition, and asks for the prayers of one who is closer to God than are we, joining always our own prayers to hers. I explore the Hail Mary in particular in greater detail below. But moving beyond this, the Hail Marys themselves form the background to the meditation upon God's work in

---

3 Karl Barth, *Church Dogmatics, I, 2*, "The Mystery of Revelation", pp. 138-139. All references to Barth are from Barth, *Church Dogmatics*, (ed.) G.W. Bromiley and T.F. Torrance London: T&T Clark, 1961.

and for humanity, which is the purpose of the Rosary. So too, then the point of the meditation on Mary is simply the recognition that Mary was part of God's choice for the redemption of humanity.

Mary and Scripture

If one wants to understand from the source how Mary has been viewed within the Catholic Church, and what aspects of Mary have been considered worth imitating, rather than rely on uninstructed prejudice, one fruitful avenue to investigate is to see how Mary has been depicted in Catholic art through the ages. It is curious then (on the Protestant view of the Catholic ignorance of Scripture) that Mary is consistently shown, in painting after painting spanning multiple centuries, doing what Protestants often accuse Catholics of ignoring: reading the Scriptures. This is not one or two stray pictures, but the common iconography spanning two millennia. The Angel visits Mary as she reads the Scriptures. The Holy Spirit indeed is not uncommonly depicted as entering through the ear of Mary, as Karl Barth notes with approval[4]:

> ... it is essentially right when John of Damascus describes Mary's ear as the bodily organ of the miraculous conception of Christ. 'The operation of the Holy Spirit at the conception of Jesus is one mediated through Mary's faith. Mary believes ... and by believing in the Word of God spoken by the angel she is thereby enabled to take the eternal Word into herself.[5]

This point is highly significant, and demonstrates how Catholics have traditionally regarded Mary and her ongoing role in the life of the believer– Mary is a woman of the Scriptures *par excellence*, one who hears the word of God, and brings forth the enfleshed Word. Unsurprisingly then, Mary led me back to the Scriptures.

In recognition of this, I propose that we examine some of the Scriptures keeping in mind Mary, who bore the Word as she meditated on the word of God in the Scriptures. In John 1:12-14, we are told that "But as many as received him, to them he gave power to become the sons of God, even to them that believe in his name: Which were born, not of blood, nor of

---
4 The image, as Barth notes, is from St John of Damascus. See St John Damascene, *An Exact Exposition of the Orthodox Faith*, Book IV, 14, AD 743.
5 Karl Barth, *Church Dogmatics*, I, 2, "The Miracle of Christmas", p. 201.

the will of the flesh, nor of the will of man, but of God. And the Word was made flesh, and dwelt among us, and we beheld his glory, the glory as of the only begotten of the Father full of grace and truth." Now the Word's becoming flesh does not just mean that he takes our sins upon himself so that we can go to heaven, which is a place of eternal happiness (though this is true as far as it goes). Rather, the Word's becoming flesh gives us *the power* to become sons of God. Further, becoming a child of God is not just something external, but does and must lead us to the beholding of the glory of God, the glory even as of the only begotten of the Father. Now Mary, as she who receives the Word pre-eminently, is the prime exemplar of this receiving and beholding God.

Behind much of what Galea says would appear to be the notion that Mary is the object of *independent* veneration for Catholics, and that she thus detracts from Christ. In reality, Mary, like any of the saints, living or dead, is only valuable insofar as she points to Christ. But just like all the saints, living or dead, but to a supereminent degree, she is an example of what is now possible to those who live in grace. Mary shows us that, indeed, Jesus does make all things new, including everyone who receives the Word.

With this in mind, we might go back and look at the annunciation, the actual taking of flesh by the Word when the angel visits Mary. Now, the clear implication of Luke 1:38 is that the *kecharitomene*[6] of Luke 1:28 assents to the plan of God and believes in his promise, and because of this, she is blessed. One can speculate as much as one likes about what would have happened had Mary not believed, but that would be idle speculation. Further, as Barth rightly points out,[7] this "*fiat mihi* of Mary is preceded by the resolve and promise of God." Catholics are entirely in agreement with this. The concept of Mary meriting to bear the Blessed One is completely foreign to Christian thought, and is contradicted by the Council of Trent, Session VI, on Justification, which affirms that we are saved gratuitously. Indeed, Trent goes further than this by saying that without the predisposition given by the Holy Spirit, a man cannot believe, hope, love, or repent. Further, this granting of grace to men occurs only

---

6 The word has traditionally been translated as "full of grace" which agrees better with the Greek. The King James has "thou that art highly favoured." The discussion of grace has been done in an earlier chapter. Allowing for that discussion, either will serve my purpose here.
7 Barth, *Church Dogmatics*, IV, 2, "The Homecoming of the Son of Man", p. 45.

through the life, death, and resurrection of Jesus Christ.[8] How did Mary respond positively to God? By grace, certainly, for we are not Pelagians or semi-Pelagians. Yet, how did she respond to grace if the means of giving that grace had not yet condescended to be incarnate of her? It would seem that God gave grace before and in lieu of the Incarnation (not just to Mary, but to all Old Testament figures). That being so, Mary's 'yes' to God is a yes "preceded by the resolve and promise of God", evidencing her total dependence on Christ.

With this in mind, we can revisit John's Gospel to the episode that Galea quotes: the wedding at Cana. He represents Mary as asking Jesus to do something. In my respectful submission, this is not substantiated by the text. Rather, she simply approaches Jesus, and brings a problem to his attention. Jesus' answer is "Woman, what concern is that to you and to me? My hour has not yet come" (Jn 2:4). She then turns to the servants and says, "Do whatever he tells you" (Jn 2:5). This is the only imperative that she is shown as issuing in the Scriptures, apart from "Let it be to me according to your word." (Lk 1:38) in response to the Angel Gabriel's message. Everywhere else, she is described as asking questions, pondering and so on (e.g., Lk 2:19). Then, Jesus tells them what to do and performs his very first miracle. There is no good textual reason to suppose that Mary knew what he was about to do (indeed, the "whatever" of her own statement suggests that she was in the dark as to precisely what he was going to do, though she trusted in him). I will argue that herein lies both the key to why Catholics (and the Orthodox, and the Classical Reformers, especially Lutherans and Anglicans) believe what they do about Mary, and how Mary relates to us. But before we proceed to that, let us draw out the implications of reading the Scriptures the way Galea does. John's Gospel is unlike any of the other Gospels in that the narration of Jesus' life is subordinated to its main purpose: to demonstrate that Jesus is God; to manifest his Divinity and his glory: "Jesus did this, the first of his signs, in Cana of Galilee, and revealed his glory; and his disciples believed in him" (Jn 2:11). Notice here the echo of John 1:14. The miracle is done to manifest his glory. If one were to say, with Galea, that he scolded his mother, and then did what she asked, then indeed, we would be over-emphasising Mary. His manifestation of his glory becomes accidental, something he is

---

8 Council of Trent, Session VI, Canons 1-3.

reluctant to do, but he does anyway. Now, this is not only to do violence to the internal logic of John's Gospel, where Jesus is perfectly in control, but also to the divinity of Jesus. Rather, Jesus manifests his glory as God at the time he chooses. Mary merely brings something to his attention. But why does God need to have it brought to his attention? The obvious answer is that he did not, any more than he needs us to bring our own problems to his attention. Nonetheless, he wishes us to pray. This is what Mary did, and it is quite significant that God, who inspired all the Scriptures, chose Mary to show us the validity of Christian prayer, and how he will answer our prayers, manifesting his glory.

How then do we make sense of Jesus' use of "woman" here? Rather than reading a rebuke into Jesus' words, we must note that Jesus addresses his mother as "woman" on several other occasions, last of all while hanging upon the Cross, when his "hour" *has* come (Jn 19:26). Now, unless we are to deny that Jesus was made "under the law" (Gal. 4:4) as St Paul puts it, we must acknowledge that Jesus was bound to honour his mother, just as all human beings are, though for reasons more than the norm, since his humanity is derived from his mother alone. Now, I am sure the boundaries of honouring one's mother are very wide indeed. But it would hardly be in keeping with it to insult her when she is faithfully weeping over his painful death. We can therefore rule out the idea that Jesus intended by "woman" to insult his mother. So, what was he doing on the Cross in describing her as "woman", and handing her over to his beloved disciple as her son, and her as his mother? The traditional answer is given by one Anglican priest, Sir Edwyn Hoskyns:

> Because Mary is the mother of Jesus, she will become the mother of those who believe in him. The second motherhood of Mary is anticipated, whose hour will come when the sacrifice on the cross has been offered. 'Woman' is a far better translation than 'Lady.' When, therefore, the fathers say that Mary is the new Eve, they have caught the meaning of the passage far better than modern commentators; for while Eve was the mother of a sinful people who ceased to have real contact with God, Mary is the mother of believers, who, redeemed from sin, are reborn and abide with God.[9]

---

9 Sir Edwyn Hoskins, *The Fourth Gospel*, London: OUP, 1940, p. 530 as quoted by Dr E.L. Mascall, "Theotokos", in *The Blessed Virgin Mary: Essays by Anglican Writers* (ed.) E.L. Mascall and H.S. Box, London: Darton, Longman & Todd, 1963, p. 21.

Mary is the mother of Jesus and "of the members of Christ", as St Augustine puts it.[10] But all Christians are members of the body of Christ. Thus, Mary assumes the place which once was Eve's, that of the Mother of all the Living. Nor was Hoskyns the first Anglican to recognise this theme or indeed to unite the two uses of "woman." That is already implicit, for instance, in the *Wedding Sermon* of the 17th century Anglican divine, John Cosin, where he says, "Jesus sent his mother before himself, and if she finds the place fit for her, then good, he will come after; if otherwise, there is no place for him."[11] Nor is this said out of any affection for Rome. After all, Cosin had "lost a son to Rome", whom he disinherited on that account.[12] He wrote several, some times quite bitter, controversial works against "Rome". Similar considerations apply to the poet John Donne, a convert from Catholicism and a consorter with the Calvinists, if not a "moderate Calvinist" himself,[13] who writes:

> If on these things I durst not look, durst I
> On His distressed Mother cast mine eye,
> Who was God's partner here, and furnish'd thus
> Half of that sacrifice which ransom'd us?[14]

What then are these Anglicans, for assuredly they are Anglicans, getting at? As Hoskyns rightly identifies it, this is an old patristic theme, going back to the earliest Christians, such as St Irenaeus, who writes:

> And just as through a disobedient virgin man was stricken down and fell into death, so through the Virgin who was obedient to the Word of God man was reanimated and received life. For the Lord came to seek again the sheep that was lost; and man it was that was lost: and for this cause there was not made some other formation, but in that same which had its descent from Adam he preserved the likeness

---

10 St Augustine, Sermon 72a, in *Augustine: Essential Sermons*, Daniel E. Doyle, O.S.A., (trans.) Edmund Hill, O.P., (ed.) Boniface Ramsey. Hyde Park, NY: New City Press, 2007, p. 119.
11 John Cosin, Sermon III, *A Marriage Sermon preached at Datchet near Windsor, on the second Sunday after Epiphany, A.D. MDCXXIV.*
12 John William Packer, *The Transformation of Anglicanism: 1643-1660*, Manchester: Manchester University Press, 1969, p. 72.
13 On Donne's Calvinism, see *John Donne and the Protestant Reformation: New Perspectives*, Detroit: WSUPress, 2003, passim., particularly D.W. Doerksen "Polemist or Pastor: John Donne and Moderate Calvinist Conformity."
14 John Donne, *Good Friday 1613, Riding Westward*. The language might shock modern Protestant ears, but Donne's Calvinist friends never disputed this poem.

of the (first) formation. For it was necessary that Adam should be summed up in Christ, that mortality might be swallowed up and overwhelmed by immortality; and Eve summed up in Mary, that a virgin should be a virgin's intercessor, and by a virgin's obedience undo and put away the disobedience of a virgin.[15]

Nor was this a theme peculiar to St Irenaeus. St Irenaeus, as Jaroslav Pelikan notes, states it "matter-of-factly, without arguing or having to defend the point because he could assume his readers would willingly go along with it." Indeed, Pelikan makes the further point that St Irenaeus "regarded himself as the guardian and transmitter of a body of belief that had come to him ... from the very apostles."[16] One can find a large number of similar passages in other early Fathers.[17] Indeed, Barth recognises the validity of this, and sees it (like the title *Theotokos*) as essentially a Christological recognition.[18] Thus, we have an original couple, Adam and Eve, denying God's plan for them, by going out of their way to do what God forbad them to do. As a result, they are punished and cast out of paradise. Since the second century, Christians have traditionally tended to see Adam and Eve paralleled with the New Adam and the New Eve. Just as Christ, the New Adam, recapitulates humanity, in opening to us the gates that were closed off by the sin of Adam, so too, Mary, the New Eve, consents to the plan of God and reverses the "no" of Eve, or as Pelikan puts it, there is here a "contrast between a calamitous disobedience by someone who was no more than human, Eve, and a saving obedience by someone who was no more than human, who was not 'from heaven' but altogether 'of the earth,' Mary as the Second Eve."[19] As Pelikan rightly goes on to note, "it was absolutely necessary to the integrity of both narratives that both the disobedience of Eve and the obedience of Mary be seen as actions of a free will, not as the consequences of coercion, whether by the devil in

---

15 St Irenaeus of Lyons, *The Demonstration of the Apostolic Preaching* 33, Inter AD 190-200.
16 Jaroslav Pelikan, *Mary through the Centuries: Her Place in the History of Culture*, New Haven: Yale University Press, 1996, p. 43.
17 Borrowing from another list, one could cite, for instance, St Justin Martyr, *Dialogue with Trypho* 100; Tertullian, *On the Flesh of Christ* 17; the *Epistle to Diognetus* 12; St Cyril of Jerusalem, *Catechetical Lectures* 12:15, and the most renowned Biblical scholar of his time, St Jerome, *Epistle to Eustochium* 22:21, ranging from St Justin in the 2nd century to St Jerome in 4th century, when Galea imagines he could have been a Catholic [Galea, p. 14].
18 Andrew Louth, *Mary and the Mystery of the Incarnation: an essay on the Mother of God in the theology of Karl Barth*, Oxford: SLG Press, 1977, p. 11.
19 Pelikan, *Mary through the Centuries*, p. 43.

case of Eve or by God in case of Mary."[20] In other words, Mary's will was not forced. She said yes freely, and consequently, as Donne puts it, she became her "Maker's maker, her Father's mother."[21]

Mary in the Reformation

Occasionally, Galea makes comments to the effect that "even Catholic authors" find this or that Catholic doctrine impossible to believe, or unsubstantiated by the Scriptures (p. 88). The authors he cites in these cases are people very much on the fringe of Catholicism.[22] It is rather as if I had taken this or that view of John Shelby Spong and said, "See? Anglicans don't believe Jesus Christ rose from the dead!" However fine a debating technique that may be (and I do not think it is at all), it is completely unfair in my view and out of place in a conversation supposedly between two Christians, and even less in a book seeking genuinely to put the case against a group of other Christians. But for all his deciding to make his stance on "Luther and the rest of the Reformers", even a cursory acquaintance with the historical Reformers and Reformed thinkers, up to and including Barth, would shed a rather different light upon Mary. Indeed, some extremely interesting insights on Mary come not from Rome, or even Italy, but Germany, from that doughty Reformer, Martin Luther, who spoke of Mary in the following terms addressing her in the first person: "No woman is like you. You are more than Eve or Sarah, blessed above all nobility, wisdom, and sanctity."[23] In what follows then, I will base myself largely on what Reformation authors and Christians from

---

20 *Ibid.*
21 Donne, *Annunciation*. Donne does not mean, of course, to confuse the Persons of the Trinity, or to imply, any more than Christians down the centuries have, the blasphemous notion that she is the source of Godhead. Rather, he is asserting, by the rhetorical use of paradox, that she gave birth to him who was the source of her own existence. The fact that he can do so, just like the title "Mother of God" shows how far away any thought of paganism, or exalting Mary above God, was from his mind.
22 As one Cardinal Ratzinger noted, all too often one finds the more "Catholic" position taken by people hailing from the reformed traditions. Joseph Ratzinger, *Church, Ecumenism, and Politics: New Endeavours in Ecclesiology*, NY: Crossroad Pub. Co, 1988, p. 106.
23 Luther, *Sermon on the Feast of the Visitation*, 1537.

the first few centuries have said about Mary.[24]

Mary the Mother of God

Luther and Zwingli, as Karl Barth notes with approval, use the title "Mother of God", against the Calvinist tradition. Here is Luther, for instance, on Mary as the Mother of God:

> God did not derive his divinity from Mary; but it does not follow that it is therefore wrong to say that God was born of Mary, that God is Mary's Son, and that Mary is God's mother ... She is the true mother of God and bearer of God ... Mary suckled God, rocked God to sleep, prepared broth and soup for God, etc. For God and man are one person, one Christ, one Son, one Jesus, not two Christs ... just as your son is not two sons ... even though he has two natures, body and soul, the body from you, the soul from God alone.[25]

Indeed, Barth himself sees it as a test of orthodoxy, as demonstrating an understanding of Christology, and what happened to humanity in Christ. For him, indeed, this title, Theotokos is necessary to affirm unequivocally that,

> [firstly] Jesus Christ really belongs to the unity of the human race ... [and secondly that] he whom Mary bore is not something else, some second thing, in addition to being God's Son. He who was here born is the very same who in eternity is born of the Father ... revelation and therefore the Word of God, and therefore God himself is not to be sought anywhere else save in him who was born of the Virgin Mary, and again, in him who was born of the Virgin Mary, nothing

---

24 One of the best more recent Protestant appreciations of Mary is John de Satgé's *Mary and the Christian Gospel*, London: SPCK, 1976 and its companion *Down to Earth: The new Protestant vision of the Virgin Mary*, London: Consortium, 1976. Tim Perry's *Mary for Evangelicals: Toward an Understanding of the Mother of Our Lord*, Downers Grove: IVP, 2006, is likewise written from an Evangelical Protestant perspective as is Scott McKnight's *The Real Mary: Why Evangelical Christians Can Embrace the Mother of Jesus*, Massachusetts: Paraclete Press, 2006. Jaroslav Pelikan's *Mary through the Centuries* is a very good resource not just for Marian dogma, but also for its impartial historical record of the ways in which Mary has been viewed in Christian history. Eric Mascall's T*he Mother of God: A Symposium*, London: Dacre Press, 1959 and *The Blessed Virgin Mary* offer perspectives from a variety of different Anglican traditions. Mark Shea's three volume *Mary Mother of the Son*, Catholic Answers, 2009, is one of the best sustained explanations of Catholic belief on Mary for non-Catholics.
25 Luther, *On the Councils and the Church*, 1539.

else is to be sought than revelation, God's Word, and therefore God himself.[26]

Thus, Mary's title is necessary in order to defend the notion that Christ is truly God and truly man. Galea acknowledges that this is so, but says that this title is used (illegitimately he implies) as the basis for devotion to Mary (p.88). Here, and here alone, does he have any support from Protestant rhetoric to any significant extent, but that support is self-contradictory, either being contradicted by the words and practices of Luther and other Protestants, or indeed, by other doctrines they believe.

Let me start by laying to rest one fear, that somehow Mariology counts as something independent in "Roman Catholicism" from Christ. I have already said above that Mary points to Christ. One could perhaps treat this best by looking at the theology of Karl Barth. For Barth, our blessedness is not self-given, but always conferred on us by God. Barth makes the interesting, and correct, observation that no one in the New Testament calls him or herself blessed[27], not even Mary who only says "All generations will call me blessed" (Lk 1:48) because of God's special grace to her:

> A man can only experience the fact that he *is called blessed. The Gospel beatitudes ... do not refer to human endowments or the exercise of human virtues. They are the proclamation in human words of a divine judgement ... The New Testament beatitudes speak of the blessedness of the kingdom of God. And so what they say to those to whom they apply is something quite novel. It can be said only by the royal man who himself brings and is this new thing ... who is for them as the work of God's revelation; who in their own name can give them the authoritative information about themselves which they could never give: "Blessed are ye." It is he alone who can pronounce this human Word, for he is this Word.*[28]

Barth then goes on to consider what the New Testament usage of blessedness implies. The blessedness is brought about by God, and Mary, for example, is called blessed because she has heard the word of God and believed it, first by Elizabeth (Lk 1:45), and then in an echoing paradox, by Jesus (Lk 11:28). It is man's action *as determined by God* that makes

---

26 Barth, *Church Dogmatics*, "The Mystery of Revelation", I, 2, pp. 138-139.
27 The one exception, Acts 26:2, is a rhetorical usage.
28 Barth, *Church Dogmatics*, IV, 2, "The Exaltation of the Son of Man", p.188.

him blessed. "It is as *kecharitomine* that Mary believes,"[29] and thus it is only by the grace, freely given by God, that anyone at all is called blessed. But this blessedness, as Barth also points out, is not a nominal thing. God is not playing a cosmic game of Peek-a-boo. Or, as the Scriptures put it, "the word that goes forth from [God's] mouth does not return void, but it shall accomplish that which [he] please[s], and it shall prosper in the thing whereto [he] sent it" (Is. 55:11). So, what was the Word sent to do? We have seen the Scriptural answer to that above: He was sent so that we may "[behold] his glory, the glory as of the only-begotten of the Father, full of grace and truth" (Jn 1:14), so that we may be "born again" (Jn 3:3), that we may reap the everlasting life that he has sown (Jn 4:36-38). But is this beholding, so to speak, an external beholding, from a safe distance as it were? No, for that would negate what Jesus himself says: "He who believes in me, as the Scripture says, out of his belly shall flow rivers of living water"(Jn 7:38). The truth frees us (Jn 8:32) but does something more, for whoever believes in Jesus, the Truth, will do the works that he does, and indeed greater works (Jn 14:12). Ultimately, if any person keeps his commandments in love, God himself–the Father, the Son and the Holy Spirit–will "come to him, and make our home with him" (Jn 14:23-27).

But what about Mary? How does Jesus relate to Mary? Now when it comes to Mary, Barth shows a skittishness that is out of character with the rest of what he writes about the transforming nature of the glory revealed in Christ. He notes, rightly, that the first few centuries showed interest in Mary because she pointed to Christ, but suspects that "Roman Catholics" turned it into an *independent* Mariology, that Mary is shown to be "pious and righteous and holy *in [herself]*"[30] and thus having no need for God. I have made the point above that Mariology is not, for Catholics, independent of Christ. Such independence would not only go against Christianity, but it would also be a kind of self-denial. To separate Mary from Christ is to deny her significance. But who *is* it that is separating Mary from Christ? Catholics? Surely not, for the point of the title 'Mother of God' is precisely to acknowledge that Mary is important precisely because of the relationship she has with Jesus, and the point of calling her immaculately conceived, as I shall argue below, is to emphasise

---

29 *Ibid.*, p. 189.
30 *Ibid.*, p. 10.

her dependence on God's redemption of her. Barth is slightly more subtle than that, however, and sees the problem as being the Catholic emphasis on Mary's *willing co-operation* with God's grace. This, for Barth, raises the main issue that he has with Catholicism, what he once described as the only good reason not to become Catholic, all others being frivolous: the idea that creation, in and of itself, can somehow raise itself up to God.[31] As in many things, Barth is here expressing his suspicion that, really, Catholics see grace as a kind of sugar topping to the cake, an added extra. But this is simply not true. I have already quoted the Council of Trent as to man's utter dependence on the grace of God. What is at issue with Mary, however, is whether what she willingly bore and formed in her womb in any way transforms her. Mary herself gives the answer, unsurprisingly, without the use of "I." Rather, she says (Lk 1:46-49):

> My soul magnifies the Lord,
> And my spirit rejoices in God my Saviour.
> For he has looked with favour on the lowliness of his servant:
> Surely, from now on all generations will call me blessed;
> for the Mighty One has done great things for me, and holy is his name.

This, of course, is the *Magnificat*, which was and is prayed at Evening Prayers (or Evensong) by Catholics and Anglicans, and indeed many other Christians. I am not sure whether this is indeed commonly considered preaching material for Anglicans in the Sydney Archdiocese, but the traditional Reformation certainly did so consider it. Here is Luther, for instance on the *Magnificat*:

> One should honour Mary as she herself wished and as she expressed it in the Magnificat. She praised God for his deeds. How then can we praise her? The true honour of Mary is the honour of God, the praise of God's grace ... Mary is nothing for the sake of herself, but for the sake of Christ ... Mary does not wish that we come to her, but **through her to God.**"[32]

Ten years later Luther would assert:

> [She is the] highest woman and the noblest gem in Christianity after

---

31 Barth, *Church Dogmatics*, II,1, passim.
32 Luther, *Explanation of the Magnificat*, 1521.

Christ ... She is nobility, wisdom, and holiness personified. We can never honour her enough. Still honour and praise must be given to her in such a way as to injure neither Christ nor the Scriptures.[33]

So, what happens to Mary in the mystery of the Incarnation? Well, the Scriptures give us an answer over and over again. Mary is described repeatedly as "ponder[ing]" or "marvelling" at what she had heard, keeping everything in her heart (Lk 2:19, 33 & 51). Mary is blessed not just because of her physical relationship with Jesus, but because she was transformed by her relationship. Thus, as St Augustine argues:

> Didn't the Virgin Mary do the will of the Father? I mean, she believed by faith, she conceived by faith, she was chosen to be the one from whom salvation in the very midst of the human race would be born for us, she was created by Christ before Christ was created in her. She did, yes of course holy Mary did the will of the Father. And therefore it means more for Mary to have been a disciple of Christ than to have been the mother of Christ. It means more for her, an altogether greater blessing, to have been Christ's disciple, than to have been Christ's mother. That is why Mary was blessed, because even before she gave him birth, she bore her teacher in her womb ... So that's why Mary too is blessed, because she heard the word of God and kept it. She kept truth safe in her mind even better than she kept flesh safe in her womb. Christ is truth; Christ is flesh; Christ as truth was in Mary's mind, Christ as flesh in Mary's womb; that which is in the mind is greater than that which is in the womb."[34]

Thus far, I have been arguing that Mary, as Luther argued, is worthy of honour, not independently from Christ, but because of Christ. Mary was indeed not just the physical resting place of the Son, to be thrown aside like an empty eggshell once he was born.[35] Nor is she merely incidental to the mystery of Christ. Rather, as St Paul argues, God assumed humanity "of a woman ... under the law" (Gal. 4:4). He might have been able to do it some other way. But this is what he chose to do. This means that, in some sense, recognition of Christ itself calls for recognition of Mary. We meditate on

---
33 Luther, *Christmas Sermon*, 1531.
34 St Augustine, *op. cit.*, p. 118.
35 As some Protestants whom I have heard referring to her, as a simple "incubator" would prefer to think.

Mary, because Mary meditated on Christ. To ignore Mary's part in the events of our redemption is to ignore what God did, the most significant thing that God did among men.

What is all of this meant to show? It is meant to make the argument that God, in becoming man in Jesus Christ, intends to transform men into his "brothers and sisters and mothers" that we might lead others to him, and that we might ourselves "keep his commandments" and become like him. St Augustine indeed places the stress on mother, in this passage, arguing that we are not only called to be Christ's brothers and sisters in being his fellow heirs of the Kingdom, but also his mother, in keeping the purity of our minds, in keeping the integrity of our Faith, indeed in keeping the integrity of the whole Christ in our minds.[36] But there is yet another dimension to this transformation to which we are called. Again and again, we see Jesus in the Gospels transforming people, drawing them away, and turning them into emissaries. Jesus could have directly healed St Paul. Rather, he chose to lead Ananias to him, showing Ananias in the process that even enemies of the faith are to be loved, so that St Paul could be healed through Ananias' loving embrace (Acts 9). Again, Jesus could simply have shown himself to Cornelius. Rather, he sends an angel to Cornelius, and three dreams to St Peter to show him that God is "no respecter of persons." God takes the risk that St Peter would be regarded as a god by Cornelius (which Cornelius does, and St Peter corrects him). And finally, through Peter, Cornelius is baptised (Acts 10). Again, Jesus could and did appear to the Apostles himself. Yet, he told St Mary Magdalene, whom he had saved, to tell the Apostles of his approaching ascension (Jn 20:17). Another aspect of this imitating of the Mother of Christ is to do what Mary did. Again, I cannot improve on St Augustine:

> And so, just as Mary gave birth in her womb as a virgin to Christ, so let the members of Christ give birth in their minds, and in this way you will be mothers of Christ. It is not something out of your reach … You became children, become mothers too. You were the mother's children when you were baptised, then you were born as members of Christ. Bring whomever you can along to the bath of baptism, so that just as you became children when you were born, you may likewise be able, by bringing others along to be born,

---

36 St Augustine, *op. cit.*, pp. 118-119.

to become mothers of Christ as well.[37]

Thus, we are called to preserve what Christ has given us, to be Christians, to bring forth Christ in what we do, and doing this, to bring others to Christ as well. In particular, Mary shows us that evangelisation is not a fringe, or optional activity, but essential to what we are called to become. Further, she shows us that this evangelisation must proceed from what we are, from our own bringing forth of Christ. In ignoring his mother, we are ignoring the fullness of what God has done in Christ, denying what God is offering to do in Christ in our own lives, and vitally misreading how God means people to relate to each other.

The Perpetual Virginity of Mary

Martin Luther repeatedly returned to the perpetual virginity of Mary, which he accepted as a valid Apostolic Tradition, throughout the entirety of his life. For example, in the late 1530s, he says:

> Christ ... was the only Son of Mary, and the Virgin Mary bore no children besides him ... "brothers" really means "cousins" here, for Holy Writ and the Jews always call cousins brothers.[38]

But hang on, was not this the same exegesis that Galea says is "exceedingly weak" (p. 88)? Luther repeats this in 1541:

> She was, without doubt, a pure, chaste virgin before the birth, in birth, and after the birth, and she was neither sick nor weakened from the birth, and certainly could have gone out of the house after giving birth, not only because of her exemption under the Law, but also because of the uninterrupted soundness of her body. For her Son did not detract from her virginity but actually strengthened it; but, in spite of this, not only the mother, but also the Son, both allowed themselves to be considered unclean according to the Law.[39]

And in 1543 in even stronger terms:

> Helvidius, that fool, was also willing to credit Mary with more sons

---

37 St Augustine, *op. cit.*, p. 119.
38 Luther, *Sermons on John*, chapters 1-4, 1537-39.
39 Luther, "The Day of the Holy Innocents" (Sermon on Matthew 2:13-23) [1541], *The Complete Sermons of Martin Luther* (Grand Rapids, Michigan: Baker Books, 2000), Vol. 7, pp. 255-256.

after Christ's birth because of the words of the Evangelist: "And he knew her not till she had brought forth her first-born Son." This had to be understood, so he thought, as though she had more sons after the first-born Son. How stupid he was! He received a fitting answer from Jerome.[40]

Luther's basic position remained the same as in his 1523 exegesis on this passage[41], namely that the "until" of Matthew 1:25 is an "until" used in analogy with Isaiah 42:4: "He shall not fail nor be discouraged, till he have set judgment in the earth: and the isles shall wait for his law." This was also the position of Calvin, who said "Helvidius displayed excessive ignorance in concluding that Mary must have had many sons, because Christ's 'brothers' are sometimes mentioned"[42] noting that "Under the word 'brethren' the Hebrews include all cousins and other relations, whatever may be the degree of affinity."[43] Calvin translates *adelphoi*, the Greek word in this passage, as 'cousin' or 'relative.'[44] Calvin also considers the description of Jesus as Mary's "first-born":

> [On Matt 1:25] No just and well-grounded inference can be drawn from these words ... as to what took place after the birth of Christ. He is called 'first-born'; but it is for the sole purpose of informing us that he was born of a virgin ... What took place afterwards the historian does not inform us ... No man will obstinately keep up the argument, except from an extreme fondness for disputation.[45]

The Anglican Bishop Pearson likewise says "she continued for ever in the same virginity, according to the tradition of the Fathers and the constant doctrine of the Church."[46] He goes on to give several reasons for this: the honour due to the Son, the fact that God overshadowed her,

---

40 "Vom Schem Hamphoras und vom Geschlecht Christi", 1543, St. L. XX: 2098; quoted in F. Pieper, *Christian Dogmatics, Vol. II* [Saint Louis: Concordia Publishing House, 1951], p. 308. Notice the date of this. It is very late Luther.
41 Luther That Jesus Christ was born a Jew, quoted from http://www.angelfire.com/ny4/djw/lutherantheology.clausosemper.html
42 Calvin, *Harmony of Matthew, Mark & Luke*, sec. 39 (Geneva, 1562), vol. 2. From *Calvin's Commentaries*, tr. William Pringle, Grand Rapids, MI: Eerdmans, 1949, pp. 215.
43 Pringle, *ibid.*, vol. 1, p.283 / Commentary on John 7:3.
44 Max Thurian, "Mariology" in *Ways of Worship* (ed) Edwall, Hayman, and Maxwell, London: S.C.M. Press, 1951, as quoted in Bernard Leeming SJ "Protestants and our Lady" at http://itq.sagepub.com/cgi/reprint/27/2/91.pdf.
45 Pringle, *ibid.*, vol. I, p. 107.
46 John Pearson, *On the Creed*, III, Article 3, Chapter 3, "born of a virgin".

and hallowed her. Like Luther, he also gives several examples of the use of "until" to mean "never" such as "Michal the daughter of Saul had no child until the day of her death" (2 Sam. 6:23). Pearson further makes the point that "first-born" has a special significance in Jewish law. Every first-born had to be redeemed, and this had to be done at birth and involved no relation to a second child. He also considers in great detail the question of brethren and points out that Lot was considered Abraham's brother (Gen. 14:14 and 16), whereas he was his nephew, and that,

> Moses called Mishael and Elzaphan, the sons of Uzziel the uncle of Aaron, and said unto them, Come near, carry your brethren from before the sanctuary (Lev. 10:4) whereas those brethren were Nadab and Abihu, the sons, not of Uzziel, but of Aaron.[47]

He also notes that his brethren are named "James and Joses, and Simon and Judas", and that their mother is identified as Mary the wife of Cleophas. Lastly, Pearson, following the Fathers, applies to her the prophecy of Ezekiel 44:2: "And he said to me, 'This gate shall remain shut; it shall not be opened, and no one shall enter by it; for the Lord, the God of Israel, has entered by it; therefore it shall remain shut.'" What does he mean? As Mark Shea notes, Jesus refers to himself and his body as a temple (Jn 2:19-21), as well as the source of living water (Jn 4:10-14; Jn 7:37-38). Now, the exact quote in this passage is "He who believes in me, as the scripture says, 'Out of his heart shall flow rivers of living water.'" Indeed, St John insists that, after Jesus' side was pierced, water and blood flowed out, something he saw with his own eyes (Jn 19:34-35). All of this relates to the vision of Ezekiel, who sees water flowing, not out of a person's side[48], but out of the Temple. To paraphrase Mark Shea, St John relates Ezekiel's description of the Temple directly to Jesus' body, not to any earthly temple, out of which, after all, water does not really flow. All of this is meant to emphasise that Jesus represents the fulfilment of the presence of God in the Old Testament, in the ark, and in the Temple. But both of these presences were intimately hedged around with very careful safeguards. Consider for instance, what happened when Uzzah reached out to stop the ark from falling. He was struck down by the Lord (2 Sam. 6:6-7). Now, Mary, like the ark, is carrying God. So, what applies to the

---

47 *Ibid.*
48 Likewise Zechariah 14:8, which sees water flowing out of Jerusalem.

ark in the Old Testament applies even more to Mary in the New. Lest we be tempted to see things as having changed, Ezekiel 44:2 underlines the point that the gate through which the Lord enters will be shut, and no man shall enter through it.[49]

I could cite numerous others, Zwingli, Bullinger, and even Wesley. All of these Protestant exegetes echo a very ancient belief of Christians that Mary was indeed a perpetual Virgin. Thus, the second century *Protoevangelium of James*[50] speaks of Mary as one originally vowed to virginity, who was taken by St Joseph for guarding and that St Joseph being an old man, he had other sons.[51] This tradition was handed down until in the 4th century, Helvidius, "that fool" as Luther calls him, challenged this. To this, St Jerome, the greatest biblical scholar of early Christianity, wrote a response[52] making many of the same points that Luther, Calvin and Pearson repeated after him, not out of an empty piety, but because they believed it to be true and fitting. Other evidence might be produced. For instance, why when he has his own mother, and she presumably had other sons, does Our Lord hand Mary over to the care of St John? (Jn 19:26-27). It is particularly fitting too, for the same reason that Pearson gives: that Mary was someone overshadowed by the Holy Spirit, and thus it was inappropriate for St Joseph to have marital relations with her.

For some reason, it is asserted that this reflects a view of sex as dirty. On the contrary, Catholics view marriage as a sacrament, something that leads people to God.[53] Sex, as a part of marriage, is indeed itself, a good, and God's good gift. This is explicit, for instance, in the late Pope John Paul II's *Theology of the Body*.[54] Thus, he speaks of how man and woman find themselves by giving themselves to each other in marital love. Again, it was the Church Father who did most to establish the beauty of marriage as a Christian calling, namely St Augustine, who also insisted on

---

49 For this entire discussion, see Mark Shea's discussion in *Mary, Mother of the Son*: vol. II, pp. 67-72.
50 *Protoevangelium of James*, c. AD 170 http://www.newadvent.org/fathers/0847.htm.
51 *Ibid.*, 17-18.
52 St Jerome, *Against Helvidius* 17 & 18, c. AD 383.
53 *Catechism of the Catholic Church* #1601.
54 For the Papal documents, for instance *Man and Woman: A Mutual Gift for Each Other, or Language of the Body Strengthens the Marriage Covenant*, or *The Language of the Body: Actions and Duties Forming the Spirituality of Marriage*: http://www.ewtn.com/library/PAPALDOC/jp2tb112.htm

the importance of consecrated virginity in the homily I have already cited above. Thus, St Augustine on the one hand says that "the first natural bond of human society is man and wife", that further even had there not been a fall, there would have been sexual intercourse and reproduction, and goes on to detail the many goods of marriage.[55] On the other hand, St Augustine also sings the praise of virginity, and urges people to embrace it as a greater good than marriage. He also points out that Mary's words to the angel asking "How shall this be, seeing I know not a man?" (Lk 1:34) signifies an intention to dedicate herself to virginity even before the annunciation. St Augustine's point is that she could have "married with purpose of sexual intercourse"[56] and thus conceived, but her question shows that such a thought was not in her mind.

How then this paradox, that virginity and marriage are both praised? It has its origins in 1 Corinthians 7, St Paul's discourse on marriage and virginity, and before that, in Jesus himself. Jesus, talking about marriage and divorce with the Pharisees, states that there are people who have "made themselves eunuchs for the sake of the kingdom." Now, he is clearly speaking here of celibacy. He speaks of this as a gift (Mt 19:11). In the same chapter, Jesus speaks of people forsaking "houses, or brothers or sisters or father or mother or children or fields, for my name's sake" (Mt 19:29). This is a difficult teaching and Jesus recognises it as such. He says, "Let anyone accept this who can" (Mt 19:12). Jesus is introducing here something qualitatively superior to what was seen in the Old Testament, but not entirely unknown prior to Jesus. The prophet Elijah, for instance, is not recorded as being married, and he is succeeded by Elisha, who takes what is rightfully a first son's heritage, the "double portion" (2 Kgs 2:9). Elisha himself is likewise not recorded as having been married or had a son. St John the Baptist evidently had neither wife nor son. Most importantly of all, Jesus himself never married. Indeed, this was the motivating factor behind the early Christian (and subsequent) treatment of marriage as a good, but of virginity as a higher good, in the first place as an imitation of Christ, and in the second, as a way of devoting oneself undividedly to God's service (1 Cor. 7).

What about Galea's claim, quoting St Paul, that it is "wrong for

---

55 St Augustine, *On the Good of Marriage* 24, AD 401.
56 St Augustine, *On Holy Virginity* 4, AD 401, http://www.newadvent.org/fathers/1310.htm

husbands and wives to deny each other sexually" (1 Cor. 7:5). What St Paul says is qualified by what he says at the beginning and at the end of that passage: "It is well for a man not to touch a woman" (1 Cor. 7:1). and "I say this by way of concession, not of command. I wish that all were as I myself am. But each has his own special gift from God, one of one kind and one of another" (1 Cor. 7:6). Within the limits then of those who are not given the gift of virginity but are given the gift of marriage, he advises that their bodies belong to each other, and that they must only abstain for a time by consent. This does not obviously apply to Mary and St Joseph, or indeed any exceptional cases, but to ordinary married couples. For those who are given the gift of celibacy, however, it is better not to be married, because "The unmarried man is anxious about the affairs of the Lord, how to please the Lord; but the married man is anxious about worldly affairs, how to please his wife" (1 Cor. 7:32-33).

Thus, St Paul argues that, in a sense, those who are not married can dedicate themselves to the things of the Lord better than one who is married. It is not I, or the Catholic Church, or St Augustine, who invented this. It is St Paul himself, developing what Jesus said. If Galea wants to know, "in what sense virginity [is a] sign of devotion or consecration to God" (p. 89) let him ask St Paul.

As for the instances Galea mentions, of Moses and St Peter, it would seem that these examples are much less clear than what he supposes them to be. In the first place, as we have seen it is Jesus who raises virginity as a higher vocation. But the answer does not stop there. So far as we are told, Moses only had two children, Gershom and Eliezer (Ex. 18:2), a rarity indeed among Old Testament Patriarchs. One explanation for this is that Moses, on receiving the revelation on Mt Sinai, kept himself from his wife for the rest of his life.[57] Likewise, we have no record of St Peter's children, nor those of any of the other Apostles. This is again odd. After all, it would be expected that we would know the sons of the Apostles if they had existed, at least by name. Other details about the Apostles indeed have come down to us via tradition, for example, where and how they met their deaths. We have record, for instance, of the disciples of Sts John, Peter and Paul. But we hear no tell of their children, unlike for

---

57 Midrash Exodus Rabbah 19:3 and 46:3 as quoted in Br. Anthony Opisso, M.D., O. Cist. http://www.ewtn.com/library/ANSWERS/TALMUD.htm

example of the daughters of Philip. Neither of these two are conclusive arguments, but it does tend to suggest that the case is far from closed about Moses and St Peter. Moreover, in one significant way, what happens with Moses at Sinai indeed does answer one problem that Galea raises. In Exodus, Moses is told to sanctify his people, and he is told, "Go to the people and consecrate them today and tomorrow, and let them wash their garments" (Ex. 19:10). And so Moses does. But when he goes away he does not just get them to wash their clothes, but something more for as we hear "And he said to the people, 'Be ready by the third day; do not go near a woman'" (Ex. 19:15). Now, there is obviously some connection here between encountering God and not having sexual relations. Moses makes this connection. Likewise, in Leviticus any emission of seed is considered unclean and prevents a man from entering the Tabernacle (Lev. 15:16ff.). Now none of the above, the Levitical law, Moses' injunction, and the Catholic Church is saying that sex is dirty, only that virginity and consecration to God go together.

Thus, what the Church asserts of virginity is sufficiently attested by Moses, the Levitical law, Sts Paul, Augustine and Jerome, and ultimately by Jesus Christ himself. As for what the Church holds on the perpetual virginity of Mary, it was held not only by virtually every single prominent Christian witness in the first few centuries of the Church, but also by every major Protestant Reformer. It is related to her dignity, and the significance of Christ. It is also related to the fullness of following Christ and our eschatological end. To deny the worth of virginity is again to deny something significant of God's plan for humanity in Christ.

The Immaculate Conception

Before providing any defence of the Catholic dogma of the Immaculate Conception, it is necessary to understand what Catholics really mean by it. Essentially, Catholics believe that God created Mary in grace, that Mary was from the moment of her conception kept free from all stain of Original Sin. Or, as I once heard it said[58]: "It is not that there is something negative called Original Sin, which we have and Mary did not. It is that Mary, from the first moment of her existence, had something positive called grace, which we do not have."

---

58 By that prolific author "anonymous."

The first clarification that needs to be made about this dogma is that it does not mean that Mary was exempt from redemption, exempt from a redeemer. Like all children of Adam, Mary needed redemption, needed grace. Only a redeemer could supply both of these. In other words, just like the rest of us, Mary is not justified by her own works, but through the life, death and resurrection of Jesus Christ, and the Holy Spirit given to her. That said, unless we are to believe that someone can do good without the grace won for us by Christ on the Cross, then the "walking with God" (Gen. 6:9) of Noah, the faith of Abraham, the works of Moses, the repentance of David, the lives of Job and Jeremiah, the faithfulness of Daniel, all of these, and many more, took place in response to grace given in advance, in lieu of something special that would happen in the future. This is not (yet) to say, of course, that the Immaculate Conception did happen, but that it could have, in the same sense that anything pleasing to God could have occurred before Christ. But notice another fact about these things. In all of these, through all the ins and outs of the history of the Chosen People of God, God himself is at work, moving them slowly, by degrees, to the point at which he will reveal himself. The grace given is given with that in view, as what is sometimes called "remote preparation" for the Gospel. Now, as we have seen above, God in revealing himself to humanity makes it possible for us to behold his glory. Nor is this beholding of his glory without its consequences for "man to whom revelation happens."[59] It transforms him.

What then of Mary, and her role in bringing Christ into the world? First, we need to note a certain thing concealed by the phrase "her role in bringing Christ into the world." It was not that Christ entered Mary's womb fully formed, and passed through her: she was not accidental to the whole process. This is what St Paul means when he speaks of God sending his only Son to be "made of a woman, made under the law" (Gal. 4:4). Christ derived his humanity from Mary. Lancelot Andrewes, the great Anglican Bishop, especially emphasises this, that Adam is not called Son of the earth, from which he is formed, nor Eve Adam's daughter. Yet, Jesus is called the Son of Mary. Andrewes goes on to say:

> This we are to hold; to conceive is more than to receive. It is so to receive as we yield somewhat of our own also. A vessel is not said to conceive the liquor that is put into it. Why? because it yieldeth

---

59 Barth, *op. cit.*

nothing from itself. The blessed Virgin is, and therefore is because she did. She did both give and take. Give of her own substance whereof his body was framed; and take or receive power from the Holy Spirit, whereby was supplied the office and efficacy of the masculine seed.[60]

Therefore, according to the will of God, if not for Mary he would have no part in us, no part in our humanity. This is not to deny, of course, either the omnipotence of God, or the free will of Mary. Yet, granting both, it is through Mary that God chose to act, and Mary freely assented to God. As I have outlined above, through this assent, as the Fathers (going back to the second century) read it, Adam and Eve's fault is reversed. From here one can follow two lines of thought.

The first is along Barthian lines. Barth speaks of Israel's election in the concrete:

> ... form of Mary, who concludes the history of this people. It was not however, Israel or Mary who acted, but God—acting toward Israel, and finally (in fulfilment of the promise given with its election) towards Mary. In all these forms, man was and is only admitted and adopted into unity with the Son of God ... Even the *fiat mihi* of Mary is preceded by the resolve and promise of God. It confirmed his work, but it did not add anything at all to it. It confirmed the election of Israel and Mary, but it did not give it either its truth or power. In what could and can all the participation of man in this work of God, the becoming and being of the Son of God as the Son of Man, consist, but in the fact that in good or evil (and more in evil than in good) he is its object and is willing to be this?[61]

God always precedes human response to his work. God works in us. God moves us. God prepares Mary for the response she will give, though in no way impairing her freedom of will. So far, Barth's basic position stands, that it is God who acts in the Incarnation. However, the same cannot be said for Barth's assertion that the recipient of the revelation is not transformed by it, or his tendency to under-emphasise the role of humanity in the process, which ultimately tends towards a denial that Mary did not just receive, but conceived. This also fits better with what

---

60 Lancelot Andrewes, *Sermon on Isaiah. 4, The Works of Lancelot Andrewes,* (ed.) J. Bliss and J. P. Watson, Oxford, 1841-54, vol. 1, p. 140.
61 Barth, *Church Dogmatics,* IV, 45, "The Homecoming of the Son of Man".

Scripture tells us about how God views Israel and the Church. Again and again, God makes it clear that he views the covenant with Israel as a marital covenant (Is. 50:1; Jer. 3:20; Jer. 31:32; Hos. 1:1). It is also clear that when God took Israel to wife, he washed her with water, cleansing away the blood with which she was covered, and anointed her with oil (Ezek. 16:9). This same image is repeated again in the Song of Songs (6:9): "My dove, my perfect one, is only one, the darling of her mother, flawless to her that bore her." Now, this unblemished and faithful bride is evidently not Israel, which from its very inception kept falling away. So, to what does it refer? Well, in Christ, God offers a New Covenant, which is characterised by holiness, because it is a covenant whereby humanity, sinful as it is, is cleansed and taken up into the life of the Godhead. Thus, the undefiled bride of the passage in Song of Songs is the Church, which is pure because its head is pure. Yet, the purity of the bride is the purity not just of the head but of the body as well. Nor is it only a future purity, but also a present one. So, it is appropriate then that some part of the body also is wholly pure and undefiled. Catholics believe that this part is Mary, who was especially prepared for her role in the Incarnation by being given the singular grace of being created redeemed and never under the dominion of Satan. This is not because man, in and of himself, is capable of attaining God, but because God is capable of transforming men in his interactions with them, and God did choose to be conceived of Mary, and thus reverse the "no" of a sinless virgin, with the "yes" of a sinless virgin.

Keeping this in mind, we should consider now what it is that Mary's Son reverses: Adam and Eve, being in the grace of God, freely chose to deny God's will. The second Adam, being also completely free, in no way constrained by concupiscence or tendency to sin, undid the sin of Adam. How about Eve? Is it not fitting then that God, who was denied by a sinless creature, should also be able to create again a sinless creature, who will be obedient to him? Indeed, in Christ, God "makes all things new" (Rev. 21:5). Further, as I pointed out above, Jesus is conceived in Mary's womb: he assumes his humanity from her. But it is not a sinful humanity that he assumes but one without sin. As John Donne expresses it, Christ...

> So, faithful Virgin, yields himself to lie
> In prison, in thy womb; and *though he there*
> *Can take no sin, nor thou give, yet he'll wear*

Taken from thence, flesh, which death's force may try.[62]

There is a fittingness then that Mary should have been conceived without sin. It is a fittingness appropriate not to Mary's glory, but to God's who created her. Indeed, nowhere as in the consideration of the Immaculate Conception does the bizarre central assumption of extreme[63] Protestantism become clearer: its tendency to see human beings as defined by sin, rather than their relationship with God. Thus, Galea thinks that for Mary to be sinless is for her to be "put on a sinless, virginal, and maternal pedestal *apart from other believers*" (pp. 91-92; my italics). The difference between the Virgin who bore God in flesh and in her mind, and in whose womb God was enfleshed, and the rest of humanity, who are called to carry God in their lives and in their minds and bring him to other people, is perceived here as a division, making her more than human. The basis of this division is the view that we have a characteristic called sin, which defines us as human beings, which Mary does not have. What defines man, as man, however, is not his sin but his descent from Adam and Eve, who were created free from sin. What defines him as a creature, of course, is his relationship of dependence on God. This is not changed by the fact of being redeemed. Rather, it is deepened. This means that Mary's being free from sin does not set her apart from other believers, any more than our being redeemed in Christ means that we are no longer creatures depending on God. Rather, it means that we have a deeper relationship of dependence on God. Likewise, sin in man is contrary to the will of God. Man without sin does not become less, but more human, closer to what God intended him to be. Thus, the redemption of Mary is a witness to God's power of re-creation, the fullest such witness. To put it in John Donne's words, Mary is "at once receiver and the legacy" of God's revelation to humanity.[64]

The early Luther agreed with this, always specifying, as does the Church, that this freedom from sin is due to God's protection of her, when he said:

> She is full of grace, proclaimed to be entirely without sin—something exceedingly great. For God's grace fills her with everything good and makes her devoid of all evil ... God is with her, meaning that all she

---

62 *La Corona, 2,* Annunciation.
63 I use the word "extreme" here, just as I use the word "pagan" above, not as a pejorative, but as a descriptive, and as a comparative with what has been self-called the "Conservative Reformation."
64 Donne, *The Annunciation and Passion.*

did or left undone is divine and the action of God in her. Moreover, God guarded and protected her from all that might be hurtful to her.[65]

It is a sweet and pious belief that the infusion of Mary's soul was effected without original sin; so that in the very infusion of her soul she was also purified from original sin and adorned with God's gifts, receiving a pure soul infused by God; thus from the first moment of her existence she was free from all sin.[66]

The historical Anglican Church, which always retained a feast of the Conception of the Blessed Virgin Mary, also believed in this.[67] This is interesting because feasts usually celebrate a holy person, to celebrate God's work in that person. The usual place of celebrating a person is the day they met their death. It is exceedingly odd to celebrate a conception, because at the moment of conception, they are still under the bondage of sin. This is also reflected in their teaching. Thus, Jeremy Taylor in *Holy Living*, speaking of the preservation of chastity, urges us to consider the Blessed Virgin in her purity, but speaks of her as being *unspotted and holy*:

> Therefore, hither bring in succor from consideration of the Divine presence and of his holy angels, mediation of death, and the passions of Christ upon the cross, imitation of his purities, and of the Virgin Mary, his unspotted and holy mother, and of such eminent saints, who, in their generations, were burning and shining lights, unmingled with such uncleannesses, which defile the soul, and who now follow the Lamb, withersoever he goes.[68]

Now, 'immaculate' literally means unspotted. Elsewhere, Taylor calls her a "rare repository of divine graces."[69] He spoke of her devotion, her care for the child and so on. But front, square and centre, he places the reason for the honour given to her. Indeed, he parallels the two, the spotless

---

65 Luther, *Little Prayer Book*, 1522.
66 Sermon: *On the Day of the Conception of the Mother of God*, 1527.
67 See *The Immaculate Conception of Saint Mary The Virgin: An Eirenic Essay* by F. Hastings Smyth, http://www.anglocatholicsocialism.org/conception.html
68 Taylor, *Holy Living*, "Of Chastity", http://www.anglicanlibrary.org/taylor/holyliving/09chap2sect3.htm
69 Jeremy Taylor, *The Life of Our Blessed Lord and Saviour Jesus Christ*, in *The Whole Works of the Right Reverend Jeremy Taylor D.D. Lord Bishop of Down, Connor, and Drowmore*, ed. C.P. Eden, 10 volumes, London, 1847-1853, vol. 2, p. 49.

womb, and the immaculateness of the Son of God:

> ... she was full of joy, yet she was carried like a full vessel, without the violent tossings of a tempestuous passion, or the wrecks of a stormy imagination: and, as the power of the Holy Ghost did descend upon her like rain into a fleece of wool, without any obstreperous noises or violences to nature, but only the extraordinariness of an exaltation; so her spirit received it with the gentleness and tranquillity fitted for the entertainment of the spirit of love, and a quietness symbolical to the holy guest of her spotless womb, the Lamb of God; for she meekly replied, "Behold the handmaid of the Lord; be it unto me according unto thy word. And the angel departed from her," having done his message. And at the same time the Holy Spirit of God did make her to conceive in her womb the immaculate Son of God, the Saviour of the world.

The reformers from Luther to Taylor were following on a great medieval tradition, which itself derived from the early Fathers. St Augustine, for instance, when speaking of Original Sin, explicitly excludes Mary from consideration. What is even more surprising in St Augustine is that this exclusion happens in his argument with Pelagius, who had asserted that several of the Old Testament Prophets had remained free from sin. St Augustine, responding that this was not the case, citing 1 John 1:8, argues of the rest that they would be lying, had they declared that they were free of sin. But he says:

> We must except the holy Virgin Mary, concerning whom I wish to raise no question when it touches the subject of sins, out of honour to the Lord; for from him we know what abundance of grace for overcoming sin in every particular was conferred upon her who had the merit to conceive and bear him who undoubtedly had no sin.[70]

Now, this is fascinating. St Augustine in his argument with Pelagius typically (and rightly) took no prisoners. Pelagianism was a terrible heresy, and it threatened to destroy the Church, and turn Christianity into a kind of spiritual elitism. It is instructive that in the heat of this argument, in AD 415, towards the end of his life, St Augustine should explicitly exclude the Blessed Virgin from his consideration. This established then, let us consider whether Mary could have sinned. First, granting the Immaculate

---

70 St Augustine, *On Nature and Grace*, 44, AD 415.

Conception, let us consider what it would have meant for Mary to sin. Of course, the answer to that question is obvious. It would be precisely the same as the sin of Adam and Eve of turning away from God, but a greater sin since she received a much greater gift than they did–the carrying of Jesus in her womb, and the beholding of the glory of God. This in mind, I think that had she sinned we would have received a written record of it. Even St Peter's grave sins are retold in the Scriptures. I have already dealt with two cases of this: the supposed demand for a miracle at Cana, and the supposed repudiation in Mark 3:31-35. But what about her question to Our Lord, "Son, why have you treated us like this? Look, your father and I have been searching for you in great anxiety" (Lk 2:48). Here, Jesus, as God, is teaching a lesson to Mary, anticipating his passion, and gently letting her know that she must suffer in its course. But it is not at all obvious how a mother seeking a Son who is lost, and then asking him why he went away, is sinful. Indeed, Mary knew very well that the child of her womb was God. She asked him why something happened. What is sinful in respectfully asking of God why he let something that causes sorrow to others to happen? The gloss on the passage is "but his mother treasured all these things in her heart" suggesting that she meekly accepted the will of God, just as he "went down with them and came to Nazareth, and was obedient to them" (Lk 2:48-52).

Galea cites Jesus saying, "No one is good but God alone" (Mk 10:18). Jesus is not trying to make a point so much about creatures, but pointing out that goodness is properly only an attribute of God: no creature is absolute goodness in the sense that God is Good, with the exception of Jesus, who is both Creator and creature. This statement in its fullness applies, of course, to *all* creatures. There is no limitation here to earthly creatures. No creature is good in the same sense as God, not even the angels. In other words, all creatures are good by sharing in the goodness of the Creator, who creates them, but none of them approach the goodness of the Creator. What is Our Lord's point? Of course, it is to point out to the young man that he was God.

Secondly, Galea cites Romans 3:23, that "For all have sinned, and come short of the glory of God." To say that this verse is a proof-text for the universal sinfulness of mankind is taking the verse out of context. St Paul is quoting from Psalm 14, which draws a distinction between the wicked, and the "generation of the righteous" (v. 5). The wicked are those who say in their hearts "There is no God." They are the corrupt that do abominable deeds, who seek not after God and have gone astray. The words quoted by St Paul refer exclusively to them. On the other hand, God is with the righteous and is their refuge (v. 6).

In the context of his letter to the Romans, St Paul is quoting Psalm 14 to make the point that the Jews are no better off simply because they received the knowledge of the truth before the Gentiles. In saying that "None is righteous, no, not one" St Paul is telling his readers that the Jews as well as the Gentiles labour under the power of sin (v. 9). He is not speaking of all *individuals* being in sin but of all *races* and gives the specific example of Greeks as well (*ibid.*). Though collectively races may be estranged from God that does not preclude the possibility of individuals within those races being exceptions. Thus, neither of the texts Galea uses, read in context, disproves the Immaculate Conception of the Mary.

As with the other Marian dogmas, this is again not incidental. Recognising Mary as totally free from sin shows us the fullness of what God promises us in Christ: that sin will not have the last word, that God's revelation happens to us so that we may be totally caught up in his vision, ultimately, that people are not defined by sin as some Protestants have tended to assume, but by their relationship to God.

The Assumption

The theological reasoning for belief in the Assumption of Mary is as follows: The first Adam and the first Eve both shared the same fate due to their sin, namely death and decomposition into dust. It follows that the New Adam and the New Eve should also share the same reward for their fidelity. Jesus Christ, by his death, resurrection and ascension, gained a perfect victory over the devil, Hell, sin and death. The Virgin Mary, as the immaculately conceived Mother of God, is most intimately associated with Christ's perfect victory. But where is *that* in the Bible, you might ask. In Genesis 3:15, God tells the serpent that he is going to "put enmity between thee and the woman, and between thy seed and her seed." It is already a little odd that God should make this statement not of the seed of Adam, but the "seed" of the woman. Of course, in the context of the Messiah being "born of a woman" (Gal. 4:4) this does make sense.

But there is something more. Jesus is not merely Son of Mary, but also "Son of David."[71] But this sonship of David, just like the sonship of Mary earlier, is not to be understood in a purely physical sense. Jesus fulfils David's Kingship. By extension then, Jesus brings to its fulfilment every single individual aspect of the Davidic Kingship. But throughout the Old Testament (as indeed in modern Jewish practice, and implicitly in Gal. 4:4), the kingship of the son is always set side-by-side with the role of the Queen Mother, or Gebirah.[72] The Gebirah was highly influential, often (as in the case of Solomon himself), played a part in his ascending the throne (1 Kgs 1:11ff.). Now, if indeed, Jesus was Son of David, fulfilling all that was of David's Kingdom, we can expect that the queen mother would also play a role in his Kingdom. Indeed, where, from 1 Kings to Jeremiah 13, we see a record of failure, we can expect to see Jesus triumph, because he was God. This is part of what is being alluded to by St John in Revelation 12:1-5, when he describes "A great portent [appearing] in heaven: a woman clothed with the sun, with the moon under her feet, and on her head a crown of twelve stars ... And she gave birth to a son, a male child, who is to rule all the nations with a rod of iron." Thus, Jesus the perfect Son of David, like all the other Kings in the Davidic line has a Gebirah. But God brings the position of Gebirah to its fulfilment in Mary, and gives her a share in his victory. But what is the victory that Jesus has won for us? As we have seen, this is twofold. Firstly and most importantly, Christ has won for us, the contemplation of God's glory. But as part of this, Christ has also won for us a victory over death, a victory that is completed in his own resurrection from the dead. But then, if Mary is Gebirah, she has a share in both of these privileges. Thus, on the one hand, she too would have a share in the fulfilment of contemplation, and on the other, she too has a share in the defeat of death. But both of these point to one conclusion. The fulfilment of contemplation is a bodily contemplation of God, since human beings are bodily creatures. Thus, Job speaks of seeing in his *flesh*, his God (Job 19:12). On the other hand, to share perfectly in Christ's defeat of death is also to share in his bodily resurrection. If indeed Mary, like a Gebirah, is to humbly share in the victory of her Son, then, she has

---

71 The Biblical references range from 2 Chronicles 31:5 to Matthew 21:9.
72 The full list can be found here http://www.agapebiblestudy.com/charts/Institution%20of%20the%20Gebirah.htm.

to share in the bodily assumption. If there was no assumption of Mary, she would have been vanquished by death and that sharing in Christ's victory, which is really Christ's fulfilment of the Davidic Kingdom, would, therefore, be destroyed. Further, in Psalm 45:9ff., which like the rest of the Psalms is understood to be speaking of Jesus, it is specifically stated that the victory of the King is shared with the queen "in gold of Ophir", glorious, and whose name is "remembered in all generations." Note here the echo of the line of Mary herself: "All generations will call me blessed."

Scripture tells us further that God has taken, in the past, other individuals both body and soul from the world and translated them into paradise. Such was the privilege granted to Enoch (Gen. 5:24; Heb. 11:5) and the Prophet Elijah (2 Kgs 2:1-13). St Jude may have believed that the same privilege was given to Moses by referring to the apocryphal work *Assumption of Moses* in his short epistle (v.9). Indeed at the transfiguration, both Moses and Elijah appear beside the glorified Jesus, the completion of the Law and the Prophets. There is no sign whatsoever that these are ghosts. Further, in Matthew's account of the Passion, when Jesus dies, "the graves were opened; and many bodies of the saints which slept arose, and came out of the graves after his resurrection, and went into the holy city, and appeared unto many" (Mt 27:52-53). Again, it is bodies that arise from their graves, and this rising is linked to the rending of the veil of the Temple. There is a hint here that Jesus' kingdom is already being anticipated in the resurrection of the "saints." Considering such precedents, it is not unreasonable to believe that God would bestow upon Mary an even more sublime privilege, namely a glorious assumption into heaven, in view of her being the Mother of God. Such an opinion was certainly held by the 16th century Protestant Reformer, Bullinger:

> Elijah was transported, body and soul, in a chariot of fire; he was not buried ... but mounted up to Heaven, so that ... we might know what immortality and recompense God prepares for his faithful prophets and for his most outstanding and incomparable creatures ... It is for this reason, we believe, that the pure and immaculate embodiment of the Mother of God, the Virgin Mary, the Temple of the Holy Spirit, that is to say, her saintly body, was carried up to heaven by the angels.[73]

---

73 Bullinger, *On Original Sin*, 16, 1568.

The non-juring Anglican Bishop Thomas Ken describes in a poem Mary's assumption:

> Heaven with transcendent joys her entrance graced,
> Next to his throne her Son his Mother placed;
> And here below, now she's of heaven possest,
> All generations are to call her blest.[74]

Likewise, Pearson, writing on the Creed, says:

> If Elisabeth cried out with so loud a voice Blessed art thou among women, when Christ was but newly conceived in her womb, what expressions of honour and admiration can we think sufficient now that Christ is in heaven, and that mother with him.[75]

Again, the Reformers and the Anglican divines were basing themselves on the primitive tradition, dating explicitly from the fourth century when Galea believes he could have been a Catholic, though implicitly older. The "falling asleep of the Blessed Virgin Mary" was celebrated in Palestine, including a place where her tomb was. However, this tomb was known to be empty. At Chalcedon, as related by the 8th century Father, St John Damascene, Juvenal the Bishop of Jerusalem had to explain that there were no relics of Mary, because when the Apostles opened her tomb, they found it empty. Before that, various accounts of the Assumption of Mary were in circulation in the 4th century.[76]

What about Galea's claim that belief in the assumption of Mary contradicts the teaching of Scripture that the resurrection will occur "at the last day"(p. 93)? This does not pose a problem, any more than the assumption of Moses, or Elijah, or Enoch, or the resurrection that occurs in Matthew's gospel of the saints poses such a problem. The resurrection on the 'Last Day' is the *General Resurrection* of all people who have ever lived. This does not prevent God making an exception and resurrecting and assuming Mary beforehand for a special reason: to complete the Heavenly Temple, as he promised to his people in the Old Testament. On earth during the days of the Tabernacle and Temple in Ancient Israel, God dwelt over the Ark of the Covenant in the form of the *Shekinah*

---

74 Thomas Ken, *Christian Year*, http://www.oremus.org/hymnal/h/h203.html
75 Pearson, *op cit*.
76 Fr William Saunders, *The Assumption of Mary*, http://www.ewtn.com/Faith/teachings/maryc3c.htm

Kabod in the Holy of Holies. The Ark was a vessel that both enclosed ancient relics (which were symbols of Christ) and upon which God was enthroned (Heb. 9). Once a year on the Day of Atonement, the High Priest would enter the Holy of Holies and make the required sacrifices in the presence of the Shekinah. All this was a shadow of a greater reality, namely the Heavenly Temple where God is enthroned in all his glory. Christ entered the Heavenly Temple on the day of his ascension and now sits at the right-hand of the Father as the eternal High Priest presenting his "sprinkled blood" (Heb. 12:24). But where is the Ark of the Covenant in the Heavenly Temple? Without an ark that both contained Christ and enthroned God the Heavenly Temple would be incomplete vis á vis the earthly Temple. St John sees the Heavenly Ark as recorded in Revelation 11, a vision juxtaposed next to the "woman clothed with the sun" in chapter 12. What is happening in these two chapters is that the ark in chapter 11 becomes more clearly revealed as the woman in chapter 12. That woman 'arrived' in heaven after God assumed her into heavenly glory in order to complete the Heavenly Temple with all its necessary 'furnishings.' Mary is that ark because she both contained Christ in her womb before delivery and enthroned God in her arms on the day she presented the baby Jesus in the Temple (Lk 2). That the Ark would be in heaven and share in the victory of the Lord is also expressed in Psalm 132:6: "Arise, O Lord, into thy rest; thou, and the ark of thy strength."

The bodies of the Apostles, the martyrs who shed their blood for Christ, men and women noted for their holiness, have been carefully preserved and venerated in the Church from the beginning of Christianity. While the remains of Sts Peter and Paul are jealously possessed in Rome, no Christian city or centre has ever claimed to possess the bodily remains of Mary. No doubt her relics would have been regarded of greater value than those of other Apostles or Saints, so close was she to Christ.

Of Mary no relics were to remain. The Immaculate Conception, formed by the Holy Spirit, and which formed the body of Christ, would not be allowed to see corruption. In her assumption Mary shows forth the fullness of redemption and is an example of what will happen to all one day. In an age which is all too prone to deny even the bodily resurrection of Jesus, what it establishes is that our own final bodily destiny is heaven, that our bodies are good, and meant for heaven. After all, as God took her glorified body into heaven, so will he take the glorified bodies of all the just on the Last Day. But should not Jesus' resurrection be the focus of our hope of resurrection? Indeed, so it should. But keeping that as such, knowing that this promise of Jesus is already fulfilled in one who was no more than human[77] is entirely within keeping. It is not deflecting the focus of our hope, but recognising what God has done for us.

Mary, Mother, Co-Redemptrix, Mediatrix?

Some of the language used by Catholics (and the Orthodox) today about Mary might strike Protestants as scandalous, tending to suggest that Mary is what she obviously is not, something more than a creature. But it is no Catholic, but the semi-Calvinist John Donne, who has spoken of Mary as being "God's partner" and furnishing "Half of that sacrifice which ransom'd us."[78] Donne indeed goes further, combining the asking of Mary's prayers, her role in the redemption, and her "one claim for innocence" for the generation of men:

> For that fair blessed mother-maid,
> Whose flesh redeem'd us, that she-cherubin,
> Which unlock'd paradise, and made
> One claim for innocence, and disseizèd sin,
> Whose womb was a strange heaven, for there
> God clothed himself, and grew,
> Our zealous thanks we pour. As her deeds were
> Our helps, so are her prayers; nor can she sue
> In vain, who hath such titles unto you.[79]

Jeremy Taylor speaks of the efficacy of Mary's prayers in his preaching: "And possibly her prayers obtained energy and force to my sermon, and made the ground fruitful, and the seed spring up to life eternal."[80]

Taylor even speaks of imitating Mary:

> The pure virgin pious soul is this she who brings forth Christ; the nourishing and cherishing of him and all his gifts and graces, is this wrapping him in swaddling clothes, the laying up his word,

---

77 To echo Pelikan's phrase cited earlier.
78 Donne, *Good Friday 1613: Riding Westward.*
79 Donne, *The Litanie*, 1608.
80 Jeremy Taylor, "The Life of our Blessed Lord and Saviour Jesus Christ", in Taylor, *Whole Works*, vol. 2, p. 90.

his promises and precepts in our hearts, is the laying him in the manger.[81]

So, what is being got at by calling her Mediatrix and Co-redemptrix, neither of which it may be noted are dogmatic claims? Well, as outlined above, Mary's 'yes' mediates to us God's will for us. Had she not said 'yes,' as I have said above, we can speculate about what would have happened, but it would be idle speculation. Thus, Mary plays a role in the unique mediation of Christ, and in our redemption, by her 'yes.'

How about her being called mother? As I have outlined above, Mary is the mother of Christ, the mother of the members of Christ, as St. Augustine puts it in the homily I quoted. But we are the members of Christ. Thus, Mary is our mother. So, Luther can say:

> Mary is the Mother of Jesus and the Mother of all of us even though it was Christ alone who reposed on her knees ... If he is ours, we ought to be in his situation; there where he is, we ought also to be and all that he has ought to be ours, and his mother is also our mother.[82]

Mary a goddess?

Galea, to his credit, does not assert that Catholics see Mary as a goddess. Barth, going further, sees the problem not so much in Mary as goddess, but as exultation of the creature. However, many Protestants charge that, even though Catholic doctrine officially regards Mary as a creature, Catholic practice renders the charge moot—whatever their theology says, Catholics treat Mary like a goddess. To this, I am in a position to bring a certain point of view, which not many Westerners, even in these benighted days, can lay claim to: that of having grown up a pagan. I have already defined above what I see paganism to be: the idea that somehow creatures are themselves gods or themselves worthy of worship (*latria*), or the contrasting idea that we should be aiming at self-annihilation. The problem is amplified by the fact that the English language in its sinuousness can and has changed, so that, for instance, "worship" could be used in the sense of honour, as when a judge is addressed as "your worship" or venerate, as when Donne speaks

---

81 *Ibid.*, p. 90.
82 Luther, *Christmas Sermon*, 1529.

of Angels being "worshipped"[83], and the worship due to God alone. I hope that what has been said above serves to show the extent to which Catholics emphasise Mary's dependence on the Holy Trinity for her creation, redemption and sanctification. I hope it is clear that in honouring Mary, we hope to honour her Son, just as two friends might honour one another's parents out of love for each other. But there is still another matter to be addressed: the old ghost of the "taking away from God" theory. In prayers of petition (including the Hail Mary) why not ask God directly? Why ask Mary? Is it because we have the view of God as an angry Father, so that we need to rush to our human mother? Is it because God is too busy, or too remote, or too fearful?

In praying the Hail Mary, we are doing no more than we do normally with each other: we are noting God's great grace to humanity in Jesus that was won for us by his life, death and resurrection. We have difficulties and we ask for one another's prayers, either because Christ himself tells us that "when two or three are gathered in my name" there he will be (Mt 18:20), or because he tells us to ask insistently and repeatedly (Lk 11:5-8 and 18:1-8), or because we ourselves find it difficult to pray. But there is another element here: most of us will ask someone else to pray for us who we feel—rightly or wrongly—is closer to God than us. Partly it is because we trust them; trust that where we fail, they, walking closer with God, will actually pray for us. But there is another reason, which is quite present in both Old and New Testaments: because God especially favours certain people (Heb. 11). This favour is not earned in any of the cases. Indeed, in some of those cases (Jacob, David) people fell away and returned to God. Nonetheless, there is a connection between walking closer with God and God hearing our prayers. This does not mean, of course, that only these especially favoured by God may pray. Nevertheless, God does hear the prayers of the just in a special way. This is not repugnant to the Reformed tradition. Thus, to take one example of many, in Russell Conwell's life of Charles Spurgeon, in reference to Spurgeon himself, James 5:16 is quoted[84]: "The prayers of a righteous man avails much." Now, in line with what I have drawn out above, Mary was indeed both highly favoured by

---

83 Donne, *Air and Angels.*
84 *Life of Charles Haddon Spurgeon, the world's great preacher*, by Russell H. Conwell http://www.reformedreader.org/rbb/spurgeon/conwell/bosch12.htm

God, and was righteous, righteous in that she heard and believed God (Lk 1:45), that she stood at the side of the Cross after his Apostles had run away (Jn 19:25-27), and that she prayed with the Apostles at Pentecost (Acts 1:14). Indeed, as outlined above, Mary is close to Jesus in another very significant way. Jesus derives his humanity from Mary. For all of these reasons, Catholics and other Christians frequently call on and honour Mary as the highest of all creatures, apart from the Creator who became a creature in her womb. But never for an instant is it forgotten that Mary is a creature, and she is exalted not for her own sake, but because of the role she was chosen to play by God in our redemption. This is light years away from the paganism that Protestants fear so viscerally when confronted with Marian devotion. She is no goddess such as the pagans worship. I should know. I was one.

Conclusion: Mary and Manners—How to Speak to other Christians

I have tried to be comprehensive in answering Ray Galea's claims, because most of them are based on genuine worries that Protestants do have. Nonetheless, at the end of the chapter I feel a word is in order about Mary and what she (reflecting Our Lord) can teach us about how to approach other Christians, even if we believe they are wrong. St Augustine sees Mary as a model to be imitated, as I outlined above. We become Christ's mothers, says he, if we bear the members of Christ in our body. Lastly, we saw that he related this to bringing others to baptism. Now, these two parts are not accidentally related to each other. We cannot preach a Christ whom we do not have, and we cannot show something about Christ, if we do not see it ourselves. Indeed, we cannot show Christ to others, if he is not at work within us. Mary heard the Word, assented to him, kept him in her heart, pondered on him, and finally brought him forth into the world, heard him, and pondered on him again. All too often, we tend not to take the Marian path to which St Augustine rightly calls us, but end up preaching "with wisdom of words" which are all too human, tending to "make the Cross of Christ of no effect" (1 Cor. 1:17). So also, the Scriptures are too many times read not so to encounter the living Christ, but to disprove other Christians, to throw proof texts at them. The New Testament figure of Mary suggests another way, a way in which not only all Christian prayer, but all Christian conversation, ought to happen: in a living encounter with the living Christ, the living Word, pondered upon, and brought forth in our lives and in our words.

8
It Is Finished

Thomas Kwok[1]

Introduction

Ray Galea's eighth chapter, entitled 'It is finished', can be divided into three parts, aimed respectively at providing: (i) a review of key topics addressed in preceding chapters; (ii) an attack against the Catholic practice of invoking the Saints; and (iii) an emotive plea to his Catholic readers to do what he once did, namely, renounce the Catholic Faith in favour of the "surpassing worth of knowing Christ Jesus" (p. 104). While Galea remains mostly dispassionate and polite throughout, like his other chapters there are unfortunately many inaccurate representations of Catholicism that underlie his critiques.

In this chapter I will respond to Galea in two parts, providing: (i) a point-by-point rebuttal of Galea's review of previous topics; and (ii) a reasoned and biblical defence of the practice of invoking the Saints. Robert Haddad will provide a response to Galea's plea to renounce the Catholic Faith in a separate Postscript.

Galea's Recapitulation

Galea's general thesis is that every distinctive Catholic teaching undermines the person and work of Jesus Christ (p. 98). In the process, Galea cites the following as examples of this alleged "undermining" of Christ:

(a) The Mass shifts the focus from Christ to "human priests re-offering Christ on the altar."

Is this really the case? Rather, when looking at Scripture we find:

(i) That Christ himself commanded us to engage in the continuous repetition of what he did in the Last Supper: "And he took

---
[1] Thomas Kwok is a graduate in Law after having studied in Beijing and Canberra (ANU). He currently lives in Sydney with his wife and young family and practises law.

bread, and when he had given thanks he broke it and gave it to them, saying, 'This is my body which is given for you. *Do this in remembrance of me*'" (Lk 22:19).

(ii) That Christians in St Paul's time had "*an altar* (θυσιαστήριον) from which those who serve the tent have no right to eat" (Heb. 13:10).

(iii) That the Mass and the Eucharist for Christians in the Acts of the Apostles was as central as preaching and prayer: "And they devoted themselves to the Apostles' teaching and fellowship, to the *breaking of bread* and the prayers" (Acts 2:42).

(iv) That St Paul himself recognised the Eucharistic bread and wine to be actually the Body and Blood of Christ: "The cup of blessing which we bless, is it not *a participation in the blood of Christ*? The bread which we break, is it not *a participation in the body of Christ*?" (cf. 1 Cor. 10:14-22).

(v) That St Paul warned that unworthy reception of the Eucharist amounted to profaning the Body and Blood of the Lord Jesus: "Whoever, therefore, eats the bread or drinks the cup of the Lord in an unworthy manner will be guilty of *profaning the body and blood of the Lord*" (cf. 1 Cor. 11:23-31).

Undoubtedly, Galea has read the Bible many times, yet his critique of the Mass and Real Presence strangely mentions none of the above quotes from St Luke and St Paul. It is also significant to note that Galea is willing to attend a Catholic wedding or funeral but feels it necessary in conscience to abstain from further participating when "the 'liturgy of the Eucharist' begins" (p. 103). Does such behaviour sound familiar? It would to readers of the Church Fathers. The Gnostics in the early Church behaved in precisely the same way. According to St Ignatius of Antioch (a disciple of St John the Apostle), the Docetae ... "*abstain from the Eucharist and from prayer, because they do not confess that the Eucharist is the flesh of our Saviour Jesus Christ, flesh which suffered for our sins and which the Father, in his goodness, raised up again. They who deny the gift of God are perishing in their disputes*" (*Letter to the Smyrnaeans* 7).

(b) The Catholic Church places itself "between the believer and God, as the mediator of revelation."

Is it the Catholic Church that places itself between the believer and

God, or rather Christ who establishes and commissions the Catholic Church to continue his work? Consider the following:

(i) Christ himself establishes his Church on the rock of St Peter: "You are Peter, and on this rock *I will build my church*" (Mt 16:18).

(ii) Christ grants his Church the power and authority to make and unmake laws on earth: "I will give you the keys of the kingdom of heaven, *and whatever you bind on earth will be bound in heaven, and whatever you loose on earth will be loosed in heaven*" (Mt 16:18-19).

(iii) As head of the Church on earth, Christ prays for St Peter in particular, so that through St Peter the Church will be strengthened *"I have prayed for thee, that thy faith fail not: and thou, being once converted, confirm thy brethren"* (Lk 22:32) and "Feed my lambs ... Feed my sheep" (Jn 21:15-17).

(iv) St Peter and the Apostles, as rulers of the Church on earth, are to be obeyed: *"Obey your leaders and submit to them,* for they are keeping watch over your souls, as men who will have to give account" (Heb. 13:17).

(v) To obey St Peter and the Apostles, and logically their successors, is to obey Christ: *"He who hears you hears me, and he who rejects you rejects me"* (Lk 10:16); "Truly, truly, I say to you, *he who receives any one whom I send receives me; and he who receives me receives him who sent me"* (Jn 13:20); "... *if he refuses to listen even to the church,* let him be to you as a Gentile and a tax collector" (Mt 18:17).

(vi) Christ invested his Church with his own mission (Jn 20:21); the power to forgive sins (Jn 20:23); the power to sanctify the faithful (Jn 15:16); the authority to baptise (Mt 28:19), and the authority to teach (Mt 28:20).

(vii) The Church of the living God is *"...the pillar and bulwark of the truth"* (1 Tim. 3:15).

(viii) Where is this authority today? The Scriptures themselves show that the Apostles handed on their office through the laying of hands to subsequent generations as their successors (Acts 13:2; 1 Tim. 4:14; Tit. 5-10).

(ix) Finally, Christ promised that his Church would continue until the end of the world: "... the gates of hades will not prevail against it" (Mt 16:18); "And remember, I am with you always, to the end of the age" (Mt 28:20).

(c) The Catholic Church views grace as "a kind of power or aid, which is channelled to believers through the sacraments of the church", rather than God's freely given generosity to sinners.

The grace of God is certainly a free gift that takes a variety of forms and comes to us in a variety of ways, including the sacraments as testified by Scripture:

(i) The sacrament of Baptism: *"Go therefore and make disciples of all nations, baptising them in the name of the Father and of the Son and of the Holy Spirit"* (Mt 28:19).

(ii) The sacrament of Confirmation: *"Now when the apostles at Jerusalem heard that Samaria had received the word of God, they sent to them Peter and John, who came down and prayed for them that they might receive the Holy Spirit; for it had not yet fallen on any of them, but they had only been baptised in the name of the Lord Jesus. Then they laid their hands on them and they received the Holy Spirit"* (Acts 8:14-17).

(iii) The sacrament of Eucharist: *"I am the living bread which came down from heaven; if any one eats of this bread, he will live for ever; and the bread which I shall give for the life of the world is my flesh"* (Jn 6:51).

(iv) The sacrament of Penance: *"'Peace be with you. As the Father has sent me, so I send you.' When he had said this, he breathed on them and said to them, 'Receive the Holy Spirit. If you forgive the sins of any, they are forgiven them; if you retain the sins of any, they are retained'"* (Jn 20:21-23).

(v) The sacrament of Anointing of the Sick: *"Is any among you sick? Let him call for the elders of the church, and let them pray over him, anointing him with oil in the name of the Lord; and the prayer of faith will save the sick man, and the Lord will raise him up; and if he has committed sins, he will be forgiven"* (Js 5:14-15).

(vi) The sacrament of Holy Matrimony: *"What therefore God has joined together, let not man put asunder"* (Mt 19:6).

(vii) The sacrament of Holy Orders: *"I remind you to rekindle the gift of God that is within you through the laying on of my hands ..."* (2 Tim. 1:6).

To believe that the Sacraments are some sort of innovation is itself an innovation. In fact, the concept of Sacraments, that is, a physical action or sign (e.g., baptism by water or laying on of hands) that conveys the grace of God in a special manner, is not only a continuation of immemorial Christian tradition, but also clearly biblical.

(d) Catholicism is unrelenting in its determination "to insert the Church and its rituals and works into God's plan of salvation", rendering Christ's death, the Bible, and the Gospel promises "insufficient."

Against this line of argument, the Catholic Church can immediately respond that it was Christ himself who willed to institute rituals (e.g., the words of consecration for the Eucharist [1 Cor. 11:24-25], the formula for Baptism [Mt 28:19], the laying of hands for ordination [2 Tim. 1:6]); and that while the Bible is the Word of God, the Church of the living God is "... the pillar and bulwark of the truth" (1 Tim. 3:15). Furthermore, the following are examples of how in actual fact it was Christ who inserted the "human" and the Church into "God's plan of salvation":

(i) Requiring Mary's free consent to the offer delivered by the Angel Gabriel (Lk 1:38);

(ii) Giving the twelve disciples authority to cast out demons and heal all kinds of disease (Mt 10:1);

(iii) Authorising the disciples to distribute the multiplied bread and fishes to the hungry (Mt 14:16);

(iv) Bestowing upon St Peter the keys of the kingdom of heaven to bind and loose (Mt 16:19); a similar power to bind and loose is given to the other disciples as well (Mt 18:18);

(v) Making clear that those who do not listen to the Church are to be counted on par with the heathen and the publican (Mt 18:17);

(vi) Commissioning the disciples to anoint the sick with oil (Mk 6:13);

(vii) Allotting to the disciples twelve thrones from which they will judge the twelve tribes of Israel (Lk 22:30);

(viii) Investing in St Peter the responsibility to strengthen his brethren (Lk 22:32) and feed Christ's lambs and sheep (Jn 21:15-18);

(ix) Reminding believers that welcoming those he sends is akin to welcoming him (Jn 13:20);

(x) Commanding the disciples to teach the whole world to observe all the commandments of the New Law (Mt 28:20);

(xi) Breathing the Holy Spirit upon his disciples to empower them to continue his mission and forgive/retain the sins of others (Jn 20:21-23).

From the above, it is patently clear that Catholicism's "unrelenting need" to insert the human/Church/rituals into the plan of salvation is in actual fact nothing more than Catholicism's unrelenting need to imitate the Lord Jesus.

(e) The Catholic Church continually exalts Mary in the plan of salvation through "biblically unfounded conclusions ..."

Is it true that the Marian dogmas have no foundation in the Bible? The following would indicate otherwise:

(i) Mother of God: "And why is this granted me, *that the Mother of my Lord should come to me?*" (Lk 1:43);

(ii) The Immaculate Conception: "Hail, *full of grace*, the Lord is with thee"; "Blessed art thou among women" (Lk 1:28, 42); "For behold, henceforth all generations will call me blessed" (Lk 1:48);

(iii) Perpetual Virginity: the brothers and sisters of Jesus are actually his cousins, children of Mary married to Cleophas. This conclusion is reached when examining the implications of Mt 10:2, Mk 3:16, Lk 6:14, Acts 1:13, Jn 19:25, Mk 15:40, Gal. 1:19. According to the second century Christian chronicler, Hegesippus, Cleophas was the "Lord's uncle", or St Joseph's brother.

(iv) The Assumption into heaven: *"A great portent appeared in heaven: a woman clothed with the sun, with the moon under her feet, and on her head a crown of twelve stars ... And she gave birth to a son, a male child, who is to rule all the nations with a rod of iron"* (Rev. 12:1 & 5).

(v) Mother of the Church: *"the dragon was angry with the woman, and went off to make war on the rest of her children, those who keep the commandments of God and hold the testimony of Jesus"* (Rev. 12:17).

Kiran Newman has treated the Catholic teachings on Mary in much more detail in Chapter 7 of this book.

Intercession of the Saints

Rather than allowing the Catholic Church's teaching on the topic of the intercession of the saints to speak for itself, Galea concludes that the practice of praying to the Saints is "just another example" of unbiblical Catholic belief (p. 101). Furthermore, he goes on to charge—in emotive language—that the practice of praying to the saints is a "slap in the face of Christ", for it implies that his intercession is imperfect and requires additional human mediation "to get us there" (p. 101).

As a remedy to Galea's line of argument it is necessary to start from 'first principles' and outline what the Catholic Church actually teaches about the intercession of the saints. A good first port of call in this examination is 1 Timothy 2:1-4, where St Paul writes:

> *I desire therefore, first of all, that supplications, prayers, intercessions, and thanksgivings be made for all men ... For this is good and acceptable in the sight of God our Saviour, Who will have all men to be saved, and to come to the knowledge of the truth. For there is one God, and one mediator of God and men, the man Christ Jesus.*

Here, St Paul specifically asks the Church of God to make supplication, pray and intercede for all men. This human participation in God's providence is *"good and acceptable in the sight of God."* St Paul does not see any contradiction between this human participation and the fact that *"there is one God, and one mediator of God and men, the man Christ Jesus."* Nor does it appear to St Paul that such human participation renders Christ's sacrifice "imperfect or inadequate." On the contrary, Scripture is replete with examples of prayers offered up by humans on behalf of others; St Paul himself even asks others to pray for him, for example, in Romans 15:30: *"I appeal to you, brethren, by our Lord Jesus Christ and by the love of the Spirit, to strive together with me in your prayers to God on my behalf."* We can conclude from this that it is good and acceptable to pray for others. This first principle is a point of agreement between Catholics and Protestants.

The second fundamental principle is that the faithful departed who are in heaven can continue to pray and intercede for us before the throne of God. Note Revelation 6:9-10 and 11:16-18, in which, St. John recounts the following visions:

> *When he opened the fifth seal, I saw under the altar the souls of those who had been slain for the word of God and for the witness they had borne; they cried out with a loud voice, 'O Sovereign Lord, holy and true, how long before thou wilt judge and avenge our blood on those who dwell upon the earth?'*
>
> *And the twenty-four elders who sit on their thrones before God fell on their faces and worshiped God, saying, 'We give thanks to thee, Lord God Almighty, who art and who wast, that thou hast taken thy great power and begun to reign. The nations raged, but thy wrath came, and the time for the dead to be judged, for rewarding thy servants, the prophets and saints, and those who fear thy name, both small and great, and for destroying the destroyers of the earth.'*

For Catholics, these visions are not a fantasy or a mere dream. They are visions of heaven granted by God to St John in which the latter clearly beheld those who had been martyred for Christ in heaven, communicating and talking to God. We can conclude from this that the saints and angels in heaven are not 'dead' or 'silent.' They are living, worshipping God and communicating with him through supplication, prayer and intercession.

Also of significance is Revelation 8:3-4, where St John records the following:

> *And another angel came and stood at the altar with a golden censer; and he was given much incense to mingle with the prayers of all the saints upon the golden altar before the throne; and the smoke of the incense rose with the prayers of the saints from the hand of the angel before God.*

We see here a clear example of a creature in heaven (in this case an angel rather than a martyr) bringing the prayers of the saints (understood here as the Church on earth) before God. It is *"from the hand of the angel"* that the *"prayers of the saints"* are brought to God. This ought not to be happening, and God would have been wrong to grant this vision to St John, if, as Galea asserts, the Catholic belief in the intercession of saints and angels is false.

Detractors from Catholic doctrine often argue that dead saints cannot hear our invocations since Psalm 115 [113]:17 says, "The dead do not praise the Lord ..." It should be noted that this psalm was written at a time when Jewish understanding of the after-life was not yet fully developed.

By the second century BC the Jews would have a better understanding of both the after-life and the intercessory role of the dead. So it was that Onias saw the deceased prophet Jeremiah praying for Israel:

What he saw was this: Onias, who had been high priest, a noble and good man, of modest bearing and gentle manner, one who spoke fittingly and had been trained from childhood in all that belongs to excellence, was praying with outstretched hands for the whole body of the Jews. Then in the same fashion another appeared, distinguished by his gray hair and dignity, and of marvellous majesty and authority. And Onias spoke, saying, This is a man who loves the family of Israel and prays much for the people and the holy city—Jeremiah, the prophet of God. Jeremiah stretched out his right hand and gave to Judas a golden sword, and as he gave it he addressed him thus: Take this holy sword, a gift from God, with which you will strike down your adversaries (2 Macc. 15:12-16).

At the Transfiguration on Mount Tabor, Moses and Elijah appeared talking with Christ (Mt 17:3). In Hebrews 12:1 the Old Testament saints are called "a great cloud of witnesses" that surrounds the believers in Christ. Furthermore, in relating to the Pharisees the parable of the Lost Sheep, Christ stated "there is joy in the presence of the angels of God over one sinner who repents" (Lk 15:10), while St Paul relates that the Apostles were "a spectacle to the world, *to angels* and to men" (1 Cor. 4:9). Hence, it follows that both angels and humans in heaven are aware of what is happening on earth. This is because they possess the Beatific Vision, which enables them to see in God whatever knowledge is relevant to them. That is, they become "multi-scient": "Now I know in part; then I shall understand fully" (1 Cor. 13:12). In their glorified state the saints are capable of unimaginable things, including hearing multiple prayers in various languages.

Having established these two fundamental principles—i.e., that it is good to pray for others, and that this prayer continues in heaven—it is easy, and logical, to understand the Catholic teaching on the intercession of the Saints. Contrary to Galea's assertions, the Catholic Church's teaching on the intercession of Saints is not about "making up" for some supposed "insufficiency" of Christ. Rather, the doctrine of the intercession of the saints is recognition, first, of the biblical fact that we can and should pray for each other and, second, that this prayer continues on in heaven. Based on these facts, we then conclude logically by saying, *"Well, if you as my friend in faith can pray for me while you are here on earth, what is stopping you from praying for me once you get to heaven?"*

It is important to let the official teaching of the Church speak for itself on this topic. The *Catechism of the Catholic Church* states the following in #956, quoting from the Second Vatican Council document *Lumen Gentium*:

> Being more closely united to Christ, those who dwell in heaven fix the whole Church more firmly in holiness ... They do not cease to intercede with the Father for us, as they proffer the merits which they acquired on earth through the one mediator between God and men, Christ Jesus ... So by their fraternal concern is our weakness greatly helped.

Explained simply, the Catholic teaching on the intercession of the Saints holds that those members of the Church who are in heaven—i.e., those who have died and gone to heaven or the angels who already dwell with God—can and do continue to pray for the Church here on earth. When Catholics say that we "pray to the saints" we do not mean that we 'worship' saints but, rather, that we are simply asking those in heaven to continue interceding for us here on earth.

It is no small wonder, therefore, that many ancient Christian monuments and stones, especially tombs, record inscriptions of prayers to saints which are in substance no different from those said by Catholics today. For example, in the Catacomb of St Priscilla, which was used as a Christian burial ground in Rome from the second century, a burial inscription can be found stating:

> Anatolius erected this for his well-deserving son who lived seven years, seven months and twenty days. May thy soul find rest in God. *Pray for thy sister.*

In the catacomb of Sts Gordian and Epimachus, another inscription can be found stating:

> O Sabbatius, sweet soul, ask and *pray for your brothers and companions.*

In the Capitol Museum, Rome, a stone plaque on display contains the following invocation:

> O Atticus, sleep in peace and in the security of thy salvation and *pray earnestly for our sins.*

Likewise, in the Lateran Museum, Rome, another stone plaque reads:

> Gentianus, faithful, in peace who lived twelve years, eight months and sixteen days. *You will intercede for us in your prayers* because we know that you are in Christ.

In continuing our response to Galea, it is helpful to emphasise specifically what the intercession of the saints is *not*. It is not about...

- "worshipping" saints and angels. While Catholics honour (i.e., venerate) saints and angels, only God can receive the worship of adoration. Rather, it is about asking saints and angels in heaven to offer up supplication, prayers and intercession for the Church here on earth, or to be secondary instruments in the dispensing and application of Christ's graces (cf. Rev. 1:4).

- "making up" for some perceived 'imperfection' or 'inadequacy' in Jesus' salvific work. Catholics believe that Jesus Christ's sacrifice was perfect, whole, complete and infinitely meritorious. Rather, it is about co-operating with heavenly members of Christ's Body to ask them to do what the book of Revelation shows them already doing—praying before the throne of God.

- needing "some human component" to mediate our salvation before the Father. Catholics believe that Jesus Christ is the one mediator of salvation between God and man, but that this does not prevent humans from 'mediating' for others in the form of supplications, prayers and intercession, as asked for by St Paul.

- requiring "some other form of mediation" of salvation to get us to heaven. Once again, Catholics believe that Jesus Christ is the one mediator of salvation between God and man. Catholics certainly agree that one can (and indeed, should) turn to Jesus directly in prayer. In any case, all the prayers of the saints and angels go to the Father through Christ our Lord.

What about the allegation that speaking to the dead is forbidden in the Old Testament?" The relevant passage in the Old Testament is Deuteronomy 18:10-12:

> *There shall not be found among you any one who burns his son or his daughter as an offering, any one who practices divination, a soothsayer, or an augur, or a sorcerer, or a charmer, or a medium, or a wizard, or*

> *a necromancer. For whoever does these things is an abomination to the Lord; and because of these abominable practices the Lord your God is driving them out before you.*

Any critic of the Catholic Church would have to admit that clearly what Deuteronomy forbids is the *conjuring* of the dead through trances, mediums or séances in order to obtain supernatural or prophetic information.

Practises used to conjure up the dead are essentially diabolical. The power employed is that of the Devil. The persons contacted are either demons impersonating dead people or the souls of the damned. The information obtained is mixed with lies and deceptions. This is why the Catholic Church from earliest times down to the present has condemned necromancy.[2] It has no resemblance to the pious practice of calling upon those in heaven to pray to God in order to obtain his spiritual favours and blessings. In fact, talking to those in heaven (in this case the angels) is practised in the Psalms:

> *Bless the Lord, O you his angels, you mighty ones who do his word, hearkening to the voice of his word! Bless the Lord, all his hosts, his ministers that do his will!* (Ps. 103:20-21).

Again, when Christ talked about his death to Moses and Elijah on Tabor was he guilty of necromancy? (Lk 9:30). Some may argue that Elijah was not one of the dead as he was taken from the world by a fiery chariot; however, Moses did die (Deut. 34:5).

It is also noteworthy that while Christ was dying on the Cross he cried out *"Eli, Eli, lema sabachthani?"* (Mt 27:46). The Chief Priests and Scribes failed to discern that Christ was in fact quoting the first verse of Psalm 21 (22), thinking instead that he was calling upon the Prophet Elijah. Their response was not to condemn Christ for necromancy or idolatry, but rather to declare, "let us see whether Elijah will come to save him" (v. 49). The belief in the intercessory power of Elijah is still held by the Jews today, as Elijah is said to be invisibly present at all Brit Millah, or circumcision ceremonies.

---

2 CCC #1852, 2110-2117.

Conclusion

It is clear, given the above, that the intercession of Saints is both historical and Scriptural, and that the standard Protestant attempts to discredit Catholic teaching on this topic miss the mark. However, the question remains as to what value there is in asking the saints in heaven to pray to God on our behalf? Galea's view—as shown in the conversation he repeats on pp. 100 and 101—is that the intercession of saints, besides being an insult to Christ, is vain and useless and contrary to God's love and omnipotent power. The Catholic Church does not disagree that Christian believers can and should approach the omnipotent God directly. In fact, the Catholic Church's formal spiritual and liturgical tradition both practises and insists on this. However, while Catholics believe that one can and should turn to God directly, the Bible in James 5:16 states that "the prayer of a righteous man has great power in its effects." Based on this, the Catholic spiritual tradition has always encouraged intercessory prayer for one another. The intercession of saints merely means that this intercessory prayer does not end when we get to heaven. If the prayer of a "righteous man" has great power in this world, how much more powerful is the prayer of the righteous man in heaven? In light of this, the question really becomes: if the intercession of saints is in accordance with the Bible, is evidenced in early Christian belief and potentially avails much for our salvation, why would one *not* seek the intercession of the Saints in heaven?

Postscript

Robert M. Haddad

As noted in the Preface, it was my decision to join a team of writers to respond to Galea's book principally because it was time that a rebuttal to standard arguments against the teachings of the Church founded by Christ be put forward by Australian Catholics.

All contributors to this book would agree with Galea on one point—we must be prepared to leave everything in order to be faithful to Christ. This a number of our writers chose to do when they left Protestantism to join the Catholic family. Some reading this might be shocked and bewildered at how they could make such a decision. Hopefully others, perhaps some, after reading this book, can now understand why even if they do not ultimately agree with the decision.

They could no longer remain in a tradition that had the following deficiencies:

- Was not founded by Christ in the first century AD.
- Has no central teaching authority as the source of doctrinal and disciplinary unity.
- Ignores or minimalises the contradictions between Luther, Calvin and Zwingli.
- Esteems Luther and Calvin while not agreeing with everything they themselves taught.
- Cannot agree on whether four or five points of the TULIP formula should be adhered to.
- Speaks of Protestantism as a monolithic unity while pretending to ignore its continued fragmentation.
- Adheres to the doctrine of *Sola Scriptura*, which has no support in Scripture or Tradition.
- Adheres to *Sola Fide*, which is contradicted by numerous passages in Scripture.
- Adheres to TULIP, which exaggerates the consequences of

Original Sin, limits the atoning merits of Christ's Cross, denies the role of human cooperation with grace, and substitutes hope with a presumptuous sense of eternal security.
- Advocates false dichotomies that place Jesus and Mary, Scripture and Tradition, faith and works, and nature and grace at enmity with each other.
- Denies the necessity of Baptism and its efficacy to forgive sins.
- Rejects the sacrament of Penance.
- Ignores those passages in the New Testament, especially St Paul's first letter to the Corinthians, which support belief in the Real Presence of Christ in the Eucharist.
- Denies the sacrament of Holy Matrimony, thereby reducing marriage to a natural contract.
- Maintains a silence on the issue of contraception.
- Gives scant regard to the charism of celibacy.
- Advocates a relationship with Christ the Head but ignores having a relationship with Christ the Body (the Church).
- Has no communion with the friends of Christ in heaven; rather, considers them as impediments to a relationship with Christ.
- Does not pray for the souls of the deceased.
- Claims to be Catholic but has no universality in jurisdiction or races.

Scripture is very clear that Jesus founded a Church of his own, on the Rock of St Peter, promised to send the Holy Spirit to guide it in all truth, and guaranteed that it would endure until the end of the world. Jesus also prayed that his followers "may all be one." The Church founded by Christ must not only still exist today, but must be able to show that it has existed "all days" since Jesus ascended into heaven. Only one Church can satisfy these demands—the one, holy, Catholic and apostolic Church.

By joining the Catholic Church converts also know that they are joining a Church that has problems of its own. I believe there is much we can learn from our separated brethren in many practical areas including the urgent need to present the Gospel of Jesus Christ to all non-Christians. However, though the gates of hell will not prevail, they will always be very mischievous. In many ways the Catholic Church is a troubled family, but it is still Christ's family. Converts will hopefully play a significant part to help re-strengthen the Church and regain its evangelical fervour.

In many ways I empathise with Galea and his journey out of Catholicism. I have met many Catholics who no longer adhere to the Catholic Faith who were denied the fullness of their Catholic heritage in all its truth, goodness and beauty and experienced a watered down and dispassionate version. He like so many others was right to reject such a version of Christianity. Yet, I believe that Galea needs to revisit Catholicism—the Catholicism of the Saints, Martyrs, Fathers, and Doctors the Church. The Catholicism that began in Jerusalem and converted the Roman Empire. The Catholicism that canonised and interpreted the Scriptures under the guidance of the Holy Spirit. The Catholicism of the Councils and Papal teachings. The Catholicism that has witnessed every empire and heresy of the last 2,000 years come and go and which will endure until the end of the world.

When I reflect on Protestantism I cannot help but conclude that the Reformation was a tragedy that only weakened further, rather than strengthened, Christendom. The true reformation was the Catholic Reformation. It is an exciting time to be Catholic with the strengthening of the Church under Pope Benedict XVI. It is my prayer that many more converts will join the Catholic Church and bring with them their love of Christ, love of his inspired Word, fervent prayer life and recognition of the urgent need to share the Gospel with so many who have not yet heard God's gracious offer of reconciliation. It is my hope and prayer that all may know Catholicism free of ignorance and prejudice and fulfill Christ's will to be united under "one Lord and one shepherd."

Appendix:
The New Catholicism
David Schutz[1]

Reading Ray Galea's *Nothing in my hand I bring* was a strange experience for me. Like him, I too had paid a "cost I would pay a thousand times over" in order to fully know Jesus and "to submit to his Lordship." Like him, I paid the cost of "leaving the church of my family and my people" (p. 104). Only, for me, it was leaving a Protestant church to enter into full communion with the Catholic Church.

Like Galea, I had strong cultural attachments to the church in which I was raised. I was a Lutheran pastor, born into an old South Australian "Barossa-Deutsch" family. For me, the Bible was not a discovery I made later in life. It was my mother's milk and my bread-and-butter—for which I still thank God every day. I knew the Bible, but I did not know the Church that gave us the Bible in the first place.

As a Lutheran pastor, I spent time every day studying the Word of God but I eventually came to realise that my own particular Protestant tradition was lacking the authenticity and continuity that gives the Church the authority to teach in the name of Jesus. Protestants claim that the Scriptures alone are both sufficient and clear in every way for Christian life and teaching. Yet, there are so many different Protestant denominations—all appealing to the authority of Scripture, but divided from one another over the interpretation of that same Scripture. Even within my own denomination the pastors were divided evenly between supporters and opponents of the ordination of women, although both sides appealed to "Scripture alone" as the basis for their teaching.

This is not the place for my conversion story (which you can read

---

[1] David Schutz is a former Lutheran Pastor and convert to Catholicism (confirmed 16 June, 2003). He currently lives in Melbourne with his wife and children and works for the Catholic Archdiocese of Melbourne as the Executive Officer for the Ecumenical and Interfaith Commission. His passions include liturgical music, adult faith formation, and blogging. www.scecclesia.wordpress.com).

elsewhere), but there is another curious similarity between my own journey and Galea's. He ends his book with an appendix entitled *The New Catholicism*, in which he addresses the presence of "universalism" in modern Catholic theology. Long after I had come to understand and accept what the Catholic Church teaches about the sacrifice of the Mass, Purgatory, Mary, the intercession of the Saints, the infallibility of the Pope, etc.—issues which Galea treats in the main part of his book—this last issue remained for me a sticking point.

I have always believed, and still do, that Christ alone is my Saviour, that he is the only Saviour, and that his salvation is for all people. The two so-called 'exclusive' texts of the New Testament are very dear to me: "No-one comes to the Father but by me" (Jn 14:6) and "There is no other name under heaven by which we are saved" (Acts 4:12). I believe that the 'good news' that Jesus died and rose again for our salvation urgently needs to be taken to the whole world. Today, I am still a 'Great Commission' Christian. I am an 'evangelical' Christian who believes that for the sake of the obedience to the Gospel it is necessary to belong to the Church that is in communion with the Bishop of Rome!

So the last great sticking point for me was that Catholicism seemed to be a universalist religion. It did not appear to defend Jesus as the exclusive and universal Saviour. I knew of particular Catholic priests and theologians who taught that other religions were valid paths to salvation alongside Christianity. Moreover, the Church itself appeared to teach this officially in the documents of the Second Vatican Council:

> Those also can attain to salvation who through no fault of their own do not know the Gospel of Christ or his Church, yet sincerely seek God and moved by grace strive by their deeds to do his will as it is known to them through the dictates of conscience.[2]

To my Protestant ears this sounded like heresy. How could anyone be saved without knowing the Gospel of Christ? Was not "striving by one's deeds" the epitome of 'works righteousness'? At the time, back in the year 2000, I had no answer to this.

Yet I had reason to hope. Over the years, I had investigated all those other doctrines which Galea points out in the rest of his book; doctrines which appear to prove that the Catholic Church "undermine[s] the work

---

2 Vatican Council II, *Lumen Gentium* 16.

of the Christ I had come to love" (p. 20). In every case I came to realise that my objections were based on misunderstandings and misrepresentations of the Catholic Faith. In every case, I discovered what the Church really taught, that is, what the Church's official and public teaching was, rather than what some Catholic theologian, or school child, or neighbour *thinks* is "Catholic". And I found it was indeed in full agreement with the faith of the Apostles as it was received by the first Christians in the New Testament and handed on down through the centuries.

For instance, as a Lutheran, the doctrine of justification by faith alone through Christ alone by grace alone was central for me. How could I be Catholic while the Council of Trent condemned this belief? The answer came in 1999 with the *Joint Declaration on the Doctrine of Justification*, a document signed jointly between the Catholic Church and the Lutheran World Federation (and recently the World Methodist Council). This document set out the *authentic* faith of the Catholic Church in regard to this old controversy, stating that:

> ... the subscribing Lutheran churches and the Roman Catholic Church are now able to articulate a common understanding of our justification by God's grace through faith in Christ ... Together we confess: By grace alone, in faith in Christ's saving work and not because of any merit on our part, we are accepted by God and receive the Holy Spirit, who renews our hearts while equipping and calling us to good works.[3]

This is the *authentic* teaching of the Catholic Church, not a mere private opinion. It is in this light that all other previous statements (including Trent) must be understood.

The question now was: could I hope for such a clarification with regard to the apparent universalism in modern Catholic theology?

Coincidences are funny things, like nudges from God trying to tell you something. Well, in this case the coincidence was that in the midst of my doubts and questions about the universalism of modern Catholic theology the Vatican's Congregation for the Doctrine of the Faith released an authoritative 'declaration' called *Dominus Iesus: On the Unicity*[4] *and*

---

3 *Joint Declaration* §§5, 15.
4 "Unicity" is a rare word the Church uses to translate the Latin *unicitate*, which could also be rendered "uniqueness" or (in ordinary English) "only-ness."

Salvific Universality of Jesus Christ and the Church. If anyone wishes to search this Declaration on the internet they will see that it explicitly rejects the following ideas:

- that the revelation of God in Jesus is somehow limited, or incomplete, or imperfect, and that other religions might give us "complementary" or parallel revelation (§6);
- that Jesus is one of many "divine" figures in history who are "saviours", and that other religious figures might also be regarded as having saving power (§§11, 13-15, 20-22);
- that the Person of the Word of God is somehow communicated to people in a way apart from the Word who became flesh in Jesus of Nazareth (§5, 6, 10, 11, 15);
- that the effect of the Holy Spirit reaches more broadly and more universally than the effect of the crucified and risen Incarnate Word (§12, 19, 20).

In short, quoting the two "exclusive" texts of the New Testament (Jn 14:6 and Acts 4:12) and many other passages of Scripture, the Declaration condemns any denial of the fact that Jesus is the only and universal Saviour, or that the will of the One and Triune God is offered and accomplished once for all in the mystery of his incarnation, death, and resurrection. In its concluding comments, the document declares that:

> the Church, guided by charity and respect for freedom, must be primarily committed to proclaiming to all people the truth definitively revealed by the Lord, and to announcing the necessity of conversion to Jesus Christ and of adherence to the Church through Baptism and the other sacraments, in order to participate fully in communion with God, the Father, Son and Holy Spirit. Thus, the certainty of the universal salvific [i.e. saving] will of God does not diminish, but rather increases the duty and urgency of the proclamation of salvation and of conversion to the Lord Jesus Christ.[5]

As I read it, this document cleared away the final misunderstanding that prevented me from full-hearted acceptance of the Catholic Faith. Given that *Dominus Iesus* was so widely reported in the media at the time

---

5 *Dominus Iesus* §22.

of its release, it surprises me that no mention is made of it in Galea's book. Since the release of this document, the Holy See has again and again reaffirmed its commitment to the teaching of Jesus as the only and universal Saviour in a number of documents, most recently in a *Doctrinal Note on some aspects of Evangelisation* (2007). This document re-emphasised the fact that every Catholic is called to be a living witness of Jesus Christ to others, and *rejects* a number of false ideas that some Catholics have adopted about evangelisation. Among the ideas rejected include:

- that any attempt to convince others of the truth of the Christian faith would be disrespectful of their religious freedom (§3-8);
- that the aim of evangelisation is simply to make people better human beings (i.e., that Muslims become better Muslims, Hindus better Hindus, etc.) (§3, 10);
- that since God in his freedom can offer salvation even to those who do not have explicit knowledge of Christ and who have not been formally incorporated into the Church, we should not proclaim Christ to those who do not know him nor should we encourage others to join the Church (§3, 7).

There have also been a number of disciplinary statements released against theologians teaching relativist or pluralistic doctrines that suggest there is some other path of salvation apart from the grace of God revealed and made available to all in Jesus Christ.[6] Again, it surprises me that Galea does not refer to these statements. These condemnations are at least as significant as the disciplinary action meted out against Fr Leonard Feeney fifty years ago for asserting the diametrically opposite opinion that salvation was totally restricted to baptised Catholics.

I hope the reader is, by this stage, quite clear about the fact that the Catholic Church is able to read the Bible just as well as anyone else, and that when we read John 14 we know that Jesus is *"the"* Way and not *"a"* Way to the Father. Certainly, it is clear that for the Catholic Church, there is "no other name under heaven by which we are saved" (Acts 4).

I have so far focused on the issue of interfaith relations, because I think the most serious accusation Galea makes in his book is that the Catholic Church obscures the person and work of Christ. Unfortunately, I do not

---

6 E.g., against the relativist and pluralist elements in the teachings of Jon Sobrino, Roger Haight, Peter Phan, and Jaques Dupuis.

have the space to deal with Galea's concerns about the Catholic Church's relationship with Christians who do not formally belong to it. I suggest that the reader search out and read two major documents in this regard. The first is from the Second Vatican Council, and is called, in Latin, *Unitatis Redintegratio*. The second is an encyclical by Pope John Paul II in 1995, entitled *Ut Unum Sint* ("That they may be one"). Both documents address the fact that baptised Catholics are in a real but not yet full communion with other baptised believers—such that we regard one another as brothers and sisters in Christ. Nevertheless, it is patently obvious that we are still not visibly united in the way Christ prayed for. The work of seeking this full, visible unity of all Christians is called "ecumenism" and is fundamentally different from interfaith dialogue.

The Church understands interfaith dialogue to be a part of her *evangelising* mission.[7] As demonstrated, Catholics believe that Jesus Christ is the Saviour of the World. In earlier chapters, Galea has addressed the "doctrine of Justification" (p. 61 ff.). He has also spoken of the importance for all Christians to have "a personal relationship with Jesus" (pp. 19 & 21, etc.). Catholics believe that to be "saved" is more than just to be declared "righteous" by God, as if we were standing in the dock of some court of law. Salvation really has to do with coming into a full relationship (into "communion") with the Father through Jesus his Son in the power of his Holy Spirit. Both the Scriptures and the faith of the Church point to baptism into Christ as the way in which one concretely enters this relationship and the way in which one is known to be in this saving relationship (Mk 16:16). Every human being is somewhere on the journey in regards to this relationship—whether they are lost and wandering away from God, or whether, by God's grace and Spirit through Christ, they are being drawn towards him. Even St Paul recognised that salvation in this sense is a "process", saying that we must "work out our salvation with fear and trembling" (Phil. 2:12). We may reject language that focuses on the 'degree' of salvation that we have attained, nevertheless, it cannot be

---

7 Here I would refer Galea and the reader to two other Vatican documents that should be better known than they are (both available on the internet): *The Attitude of the Church toward Followers of Other Religions: Reflections and Orientations on Dialogue and Mission* (1984) and *Dialogue and Proclamation: Reflection and Orientations on Interreligious Dialogue and the Proclamation of the Gospel of Jesus Christ* (1991). At the time of this writing, the Pontifical Council for Interreligious Dialogue is meeting in Rome to work on a new document on interfaith dialogue, addressing the very new contexts arising in the 21st century.

denied that we are all still travelling at one point or another along the spiritual journey.

This has some bearing on the question of ecumenism and the unity of the Church. It is not primarily about being converted to this or that denomination, but about being converted to Christ and living under his Lordship. This conversion is an ongoing, daily process (as even the Reformers taught). Paradoxically, therefore, Galea and I are actually much closer in unity with one another now than we were before our respective "conversions." Personally, I cannot imagine how one can submit to the Lordship of Jesus without submitting to his Church. We cannot have one without the other. As St Paul states, "Christ is the head of the church, his body" (Eph. 5:23). Therefore, it is not Christ alone but Christ and his body that together form the centre of unity. Nor is the Church simply a collection of individual groups of "two or three" Christians gathered in his name, for there must be "one Lord, one faith, one baptism" (Eph. 4:5) and a "unity of the faith" (Eph. 4:13) among all believers. Galea, on the other hand, felt that his discovery of and growth in a personal relationship with Jesus made it necessary for him to leave the Catholic Church (p. 20) (something I deeply regret). Nevertheless, I have no doubt that he is closer to Jesus now than he was in the past and that by this token he—like me—is nearer to salvation now than he was before. Galea's journey, like mine, has not yet ended.

What about salvation for non-Christians? What does the Catholic Church really teach? Since God is the creator of every human being, and since he loves all that he has created, we must affirm that he seeks the salvation of every human being. The Scriptures teach that God "desires all men to be saved and to come to the knowledge of the truth" through the "one mediator between God and men, the man Christ Jesus" (1 Tim. 2:4-5). In other words, he wants every human being to come into a relationship with him, into communion with God the Father, Son and Holy Spirit.

Now we—Catholics and Protestants—both know that this can only happen through Jesus, since, as we have established, there is no other Way or Name by which we will be saved. The problem is: how is this possible for those who have not heard the Good News of Jesus Christ? Do the Scriptures require us to believe that all who do not explicitly confess faith in Jesus Christ will be condemned to Hell? Catholics believe Hell is the final end for those who in their hearts deliberately reject God's grace in Jesus Christ. However, do the Scriptures give us reason to hope that since Christ died for all people ("the righteous for the unrighteous": 1 Pet. 3:18) that somehow, in a way known only to him, God's grace would be made available to all people?

St Paul, in Romans 1, indicates that God does make himself known in ways outside the Scriptures—including through the created world and the individual conscience. Could it be that some have responded—in shadows and darkness and uncertainty—to this (rather dim) revelation? St Peter himself said, "God shows no partiality, but in every nation any one who fears him and does what is right is acceptable to him" (Acts 10:35). Is it possible that people who are honestly searching for the true God, responding to the limited revelation they have of God in creation and in their conscience, may be saved, even if they have not yet found the clarity of the one who called himself "The Light" and "The Way"? The Catholic Church believes the answer to this question is yes—*with the proviso* that such open-hearted response, where it exists, can only be the work of God's grace and the merits of Jesus Christ, for there is no other Saviour and we cannot save ourselves.

It is not that the other religions become "alternative paths" to salvation. Nor is it that God has revealed himself in other religions in the same way that he has through Christ in his Church. Nor do we consider members of other religions "latent Christians" or say, "devout followers of all religions will be rewarded with heaven." Rather, we recognise that God judges each individual according to the law that they know (Rom. 2:12) and requires everyone to live in sincere agreement with their conscience, however erroneous it may objectively be (Rom. 14:23). God only condemns where he finds fault, where a person wilfully rejects what truth he/she does know (Rom. 1:21). Where there are people who are in error through no fault of their own (invincible ignorance) and who try their best to do the will of God as they know it (following their conscience) we find God present and continually bestowing grace to draw them into the full truth that is in Christ Jesus.

Here is perhaps the moment for us to also understand the relationship between the old maxim *extra ecclesia nulla salus* and the teaching of the Second Vatican Council. There is no contradiction between the two;

rather, they are complementary. Understood positively, the old maxim means that Christ, the Church, faith and baptism are all necessary for salvation (*Catechism of the Catholic Church* #846). It is only those who realise that Christ founded the Catholic Church as necessary for salvation but wilfully refuse either to enter in or remain in it who cannot be saved. Again, however, those "who through no fault of their own do not know the Gospel of Christ or his Church" may and can "attain to salvation."

To complete my personal story, today I work full time for the Catholic Archdiocese of Melbourne as the Executive Officer for the Ecumenical and Interfaith Commission. In this work, I have discovered that the questions surrounding the relationships of the Catholic Church with other Christian communities and with people of other religions are far more complex than I could ever have dreamed. But I have come to a simple understanding of what is always at stake for Catholics in these matters. The real issue is not "Who can be saved?", but always the biblical question of "Who is the Saviour?" And to this question both Ray and myself can reply with one voice: Jesus Christ, the eternal Son of God who took flesh as the Son of Mary and died and rose again for my salvation and the salvation of all the world.

Further Reading

Aquilina, Mike, *The Fathers of the Church* (Our Sunday Visitor, 1999).

Aquilina, Mike, *The Mass of the Early Christians* (Our Sunday Visitor, 2001).

Armstrong, Dave, *The Church Fathers Were Catholic* (Privately published, 2007).

Armstrong, Dave, *A Biblical Defense of Catholicism* (Sophia Institute Press, 2003).

Armstrong, Dave, *The Catholic Verses* (Sophia Institute Press, 2004).

Beckwith, Francis J., *Return to Rome* (Brazos Press, 2009).

Bennett, Rod, *Four Witnesses—The Early Church in Her Own Words* (Ignatius Press, 2002).

Bettenson, Henry, *Documents of the Christian Church* (Oxford University Press, 1967).

Bettenson, Henry, *The Later Christian Fathers* (Oxford University Press, 1970).

Brookby, Peter, *Virgin Wholly Marvellous* (The Ravengate Press, 1981).

Butler, Scott; Dahlgren, Norman and Hess, David, *Jesus, Peter & the Keys* (Queenship Publishing, 1996).

Catechism of the Catholic Church (Society of St. Paul, 1994).

Chacon, Father Frank and Burnham, Jim, *Beginning Apologetics—How to Explain and Defend the Catholic Faith* (San Juan Catholic Seminars 1996).

Coffey, John Francis, *The Gospel According to Jehovah's Witnesses* (The Polding Press, Melbourne, 1979).

Congar OP, Yves M.-J., *Tradition and Traditions* (Burns & Oats, 1966).

Flader, Father John, *Question Time: 150 Questions and Answers on the Catholic Faith* (Connor Court, 2008).

Gambero, Father Luigi, *Mary and the Fathers of the Church* (Ignatius Press, 1999).

Glenn, Mgr. Paul, *Apologetics* (Herder Book Co., 1931).

Graham, Rev. Henry G., *Where We Got the Bible* (TAN Books and Publishers Inc.

1977).

Haddad, Robert M., *Defend the Faith!* (Parousia Media, 2011).

Henry VIII, *Defence of the Seven Sacraments* (Raymond de Souza ed., St Gabriel Communications Int., 2007).

Jurgens, William A., *The Faith of the Early Fathers* (Liturgical Press, 1970).

Keating, Karl, *Catholicism and Fundamentalism* (Ignatius Press, 1988).

Keating, Karl, *What Catholics Really Believe* (Ignatius Press, 1995).

Laux, Father John, *Church History* (TAN Books and Publishers Inc., 1989).

Madrid, Patrick, *Any Friend of God is a Friend of Mine* (Basilica Press, 1996).

Madrid, Patrick, *Pope Fiction* (Basilica Press, 1999).

Madrid, Patrick, *Surprised by Truth* (Basilica Press, 1994).

Madrid, Patrick, *Surprised by Truth 2* (Basilica Press, 2000).

Madrid, Patrick, *Where is that in the Bible?* (Our Sunday Visitor, 2001).

O'Brien, Father John, *The Faith of Millions* (W. H. Allen, 1952).

Olson, Carl E., *Will Catholics be "Left Behind"* (Ignatius Press, 2003).

Ray, Stephen K., *Crossing the Tiber* (Ignatius Press, 1997).

Rumble and Carty, *Radio Replies* (TAN Books & Publishers Inc., 1979).

Saadeh and Madros, Fathers, *Faith and Scripture, Challenges and Responses* (St Sophronius Editions, 1986).

Shea, Mark, *Making Senses Out of Scripture* (Basilica Press, 1999).

Shea, Mark, *Mother of the Son Vols. 1-2-3* (Catholic Answers, 2009).

Sheehan, Archbishop Michael, *Apologetics and Catholic Doctrine* (Baronius Press, London, revised by Father Peter Joseph, 2009).

Stenhouse MSC, Fr Paul, *Catholic Answers to Bible Christians* (Chevalier Press, 1988).

Sungenis, Robert, *Not by Bread Alone* (Queenship Publishing, 2000).

Sungenis, Robert, *Not by Faith Alone* (Queenship Publishing, 1998).

Sungenis, Robert, *Not by Scripture Alone* (Queenship Publishing, 1997).

Walsh, William Thomas, *Characters of the Inquisition* (TAN Books & Publisher Inc, 1987).

Ward, Maisie, *Catholic Evidence Guidelines* (Sheed and Ward, 1925).

www.ingramcontent.com/pod-product-compliance
Ingram Content Group UK Ltd.
Pitfield, Milton Keynes, MK11 3LW, UK
UKHW021300180426
11947UKWH00015B/940